Business Process Reengineering

Prof. K. Shridhara Bhat
Asst. Professor,
Department of Management Studies,
B.M.S. College of Engineering,
Bengaluru – 560 019,
Karnataka – India.

Himalaya Publishing House
ISO 9001:2015 CERTIFIED

First Edition : 2007
Second Edition : 2010
Edition : 2019

Published by : Mrs. Meena Pandey for **Himalaya Publishing House Pvt. Ltd.,**
"Ramdoot", Dr. Bhalerao Marg, Girgaon, Mumbai - 400 004.
Phone: 022-23860170, 23863863; **Fax:** 022-23877178
E-mail: himpub@bharatmail.co.in; **Website:** www.himpub.com

Branch Offices :

New Delhi : "Pooja Apartments", 4-B, Murari Lal Street, Ansari Road, Darya Ganj, New Delhi - 110 002. Phone: 011-23270392, 23278631; Fax: 011-23256286

Nagpur : Kundanlal Chandak Industrial Estate, Ghat Road, Nagpur - 440 018. Phone: 0712-2721215, 3296733; Telefax: 0712-2721216

Bengaluru : Plot No. 91-33, 2nd Main Road, Seshadripuram, Behind Nataraja Theatre, Bengaluru - 560 020. Phone: 080-41138821; Mobile: 09379847017, 09379847005

Hyderabad : No. 3-4-184, Lingampally, Besides Raghavendra Swamy Matham, Kachiguda, Hyderabad - 500 027. Phone: 040-27560041, 27550139

Chennai : New No. 48/2, Old No. 28/2, Ground Floor, Sarangapani Street, T. Nagar, Chennai - 600 012. Mobile: 09380460419

Pune : "Laksha" Apartment, First Floor, No. 527, Mehunpura, Shaniwarpeth (Near Prabhat Theatre), Pune - 411 030. Phone: 020-24496323, 24496333; Mobile: 09370579333

Lucknow : House No. 731, Shekhupura Colony, Near B.D. Convent School, Aliganj, Lucknow - 226 022. Phone: 0522-4012353; Mobile: 09307501549

Ahmedabad : 114, "SHAIL", 1st Floor, Opp. Madhu Sudan House, C.G. Road, Navrang Pura, Ahmedabad - 380 009. Phone: 079-26560126; Mobile: 09377088847

Ernakulam : 39/176 (New No. 60/251), 1st Floor, Karikkamuri Road, Ernakulam, Kochi - 682 011. Phone: 0484-2378012, 2378016; Mobile: 09387122121

Bhubaneswar : New LIC Colony, Behind Kamala Mandap, Badambadi, Cuttack - 753 012, Odisha. Mobile: 09338746007

Kolkata : 108/4, Beliaghata Main Road, Near ID Hospital, Opp. SBI Bank, Kolkata - 700 010. Phone: 033-32449649; Mobile: 07439040301

DTP by : M/S. Page Designer. Bengaluru.

Printed at : Trinity Academy. On behalf of HPH.

PREFACE

In an environment of rapid change, the ability to learn faster, reconfigure process faster and execute process faster is a competitive advantage. Reengineering projects are taken up in response to a break through goal for rapid, dramatic improvement in process performance. Radical redesign of business processes enable firms to achieve dramatic improvements in critical, contemporary measures of performance, such as cost, quality, service and speed. Manufacturing firms have undertaken reengineering by implementing concurrent engineering, lean production, cellular manufacturing, group technology and pull-type production systems. Rapid advances in information technology and its applications have enabled service firms to implement business process reengineering in their services.

Reengineering is most successful in organizations that have a clear vision and strategic motivation for change, have genuine interest in listening to their customers, view their system as a set of processes overlapping functional areas and rethink and simplify how value is provided to their customers.

In view of the importance of reengineering for firms to meet the ever-growing challenges in the highly competitive market, global interest in business process reengineering has grown rapidly.

Running through 9 chapters, this book presents a concise view of the various topics which are relevant to understand the concepts and techniques of business process reengineering.

As there are not many textbooks written on this subject, a humble attempt is made by me to present this book for the benefit of the readers. This book consists of exhibits, box illustrations, chapter summary, review question, process reengineering in action and case illustrations to augment the contents.

I sincerely thank Sri Niraj Pandey of Himalaya Publishing House Pvt. Ltd., who are the main initiators and motivators for the publication of this book.

I also thank Shri B. S. Madhu of M/s. Page Designers for the excellent DTP work and cover page design, which were completed in time.

Last, but not the least, I owe my gratitude to my wife and daughters who appreciated my effort and extended their whole-hearted support even through at the cost of their quality time with me.

I invite readers, faculty members and students to offer their valuable suggestions to me as a feed-back for improving this book.

K. Shridhara Bhat
No.680, 'Akshaya', 1st Main,
Kempegowda Layout, 3rd Block,
3rd Phase, Banashankari III Stage
Bengaluru - 560 085. Ph : (080) 26694761
Email: sbhat 680@yahoo.com.

CONTENTS

1 Chapter
BUSINESS PROCESS REENGINEERING – AN OVERVIEW

Objectives

After going through this chapter, you would be able to :

- Understand the meaning of term 'BPRE' (BUSINESS PROCESS REENGINEERING) and the logic behind various organisations trying to introduce the concept of BPRE.
- Know how the concept of BPRE is evolved.
- Know main principles of BPRE.
- Relation of BPRE with quality as well as process improvement.
- Advantages and limitations of BPRE.

Structure

1.1 INTRODUCTION

Customer satisfaction has increasingly become the cardinal principle governing any successful business. In some cases, marketing campaigns have been reformulated and new slogans invented to take advantage of the impact of advertising on customers. Despite the new emphasis on customer satisfaction by companies, there has been a high incidence of complaints, anger, rage and acute disappointment over products. One of the reasons for this lies in the fact that the old ways and processes have become severely inadequate and that the mere realignment of old values (old wine in a new bottle!) is no longer acceptable. In many cases, the present system can no longer be fixed and incremental improvements are not sufficient. What is needed is the reengineering of the entire system which is referred to as Business Process Reengineering (BPRE).

1.2 WHAT IS BUSINESS PROCESS REENGINEERING OR REENGINEERING?

According to Michael Hammer of the US who coined the term **"reengineering"**, the definition of reengineering is as follows : Reengineering has been defined as ***"the fundamental rethinking and radical design of business processes to achieve dramatic improvements in critical contemporary measures of performance such as cost, quality, service and speed"***. The term is also known as "Process reengineering" or "Business process reengineering".

Reengineering does not strive to revamp an existing process. It involves asking basic questions about business processes: why do we do it? Why is it done this way? Such questioning often uncovers obsolete, erroneous or inappropriate assumptions. Radical redesigning involves tossing out existing procedures and reinventing the process, not just incrementally improving it. The goal is to achieve quantum leaps in performance.

Reengineering seeks to enhance the celerity of the delivery of a product without compromising its quality by improving the utilisation of materials, labour and equipment. According to Janson, a proponent of reengineering, by focussing on making improvements in all dimensions of the service organisation – human dimension, work process dimension and the technological dimension – reengineering helps companies overcome systematic work barriers that interfere with efforts to achieve higher levels of customer satisfaction. According to Lawrence, another proponent of reengineering, "reengineering involves redesigning business processes to take advantage of the enormous potential of the computer and information technology". In order for companies to embrace the concept of reengineering, they must be able to break away from previously followed conventional rules and policies and be open to changes that would make their businesses more productive.

Hammer states that "Reengineering strives to break away from the old rules about how we organise and conduct business. It involves recognising and rejecting some of them and finding imaginative new ways to accomplish work".

Box 1.1 : Reengineering at IBM Credit Corporation

IBM Credit Corporation cut the process of financing IBM Computers, software and services from *seven days* to *four hours* by rethinking the process. Originally, the process was designed to handle difficult applications and required four highly trained specialists and a series of hand offs. The actual work took only 1 to 5 hours, the rest of the time was spent in transit or delay. By questioning the assumption that every application was unique and difficult to process, IBM Credit Corporation was able to replace the specialists by a single individual supported by a user friendly, computer system that provided access to all the data and tools that the specialists would use.

Source : James R. Evans and William M. Lindsay; *"The Management And Control of Quality"*, 4th Edition, South-Western College Publishing, p. 374.

1.3 WHY REENGINEERING?

"Business Process Reengineering" or ***"process reengineering"*** (or process redesign) or simply ***"reengineering"*** is focussed on *"break through"* improvement to dramatically improve the quality and speed of work and to reduce its cost by fundamentally changing the processes by which work gets done.

For organisations that want to survive and grow, improvement is not an option but a compulsion. For organisations that seek to thrive, dramatic improvement is often the only key to success. Small improvements are always necessary, but sometimes quantum leaps are needed if an organisation is to forge ahead. (Ten percent improvement can be created by tinkering, but 50 percent improvements call for process redesign).

Whether an organisation realises that the old ways of doing things needs changing or its customers are demanding a change or competitors are taking over its market share, or not, many processes in the organisation may need reengineering, not a minor tweak, but a major overhaul. Some of the symptoms that signal that it is time to start reengineering are:

(i) it takes too long for an organisation to move its products from conception to the market place as compared to its competitors.

(ii) the budgeting process may be too complex and

(iii) the services provided by the organisation are not compatible with its customers' needs.

Business process reengineering is a refreshing new approach to do business. There is plenty of evidence that it works well – perhaps with performance gains of 100 to 300 percent for some recognised processes.

Success in reengineering requires fundamental understanding of processes, creative thinking to break away from old tradition and assumptions and effective use of information technology. Pepsi-Cola, *for example,* had embarked on a program to reengineer all of its key business processes such as selling and delivery, equipment service and repair, procurement and financial reporting. In the selling and delivery of its product, *for example,* customer representatives typically experience stock-outs of as much as 25 percent of the products by the end of the day. Many other routes would return with overstock of other products, increasing handling costs. By redesigning the system to include hand held computers, the customer representatives could confirm and deliver that day's order and also take a future order for the next delivery to that customer.

1.4 HISTORY AND DEVELOPMENT OF BUSINESS PROCESS REENGINEERING

The concept of reengineering has been around for nearly two decades and was implemented in a piecemeal fashion in organisations. Production organisations have been in the vanguard without knowing it. They have undertaken reengineering by implementing ***concurrent engineering, lean production, cellular manufacturing, group-technology*** **and** ***pull – type production systems***. These represent fundamental rethinking of the manufacturing process. Manufacturers generally made significant improvements in their internal operations during the 1980s. But excellence in manufacturing has not always translated to superior sustainable results in the market place. More recently, the focus appears to have shifted out of the manufacturing process to other inter-functional and inter-organisational and customer-based processes. Rapid advances in information technology and its applications have been a major enabler of business process reengineering in services.

In 1990, two Americans, James Champy and Michael Hammer presented the idea of business process reengineering. They coined the word "Business Process Reengineering", (BPR in short form) in their famous book, ***"Reengineering the Corporation"***, published in 1993. Their argument was that most business processes had been antiquated and needed to be completely redesigned. Hammer and Champy advocated radical redesign as compared to the more incremental approach associated with total quality management.

Box 1.2 : Reengineering in a major insurance company

Consider this problem in a major insurance company: When the customer called the home office about an insurance problem, the call was taken by the incoming calls department. The problem was entered into the computer and passed electronically to one of the several departments: underwriting, policy service and accounting. The problem was waited in line, often for several days until a clerk had time to check it out. In some cases, the customer's problem had been routed to the wrong department and had to be routed to another department again taking several days in the queue. If the problem required more than one department to answer the question, the process of waiting was repeated. Finally, some one in customer service would get back to the customer after several weeks. In many cases, the original question was not completely answered or answered wrongly.

This process was reengineered by completely reorganising the entire insurance operation around customer services representatives who would attempt to handle the customer's request on the phone, if possible, using detailed computer protocols and standard scripts. If more detailed work was required, the customer service representative checked with other specialists and got back to the customer in one week or less with an answer. This greatly improved the speed and accuracy of the service while saving many millions of dollars. It also provided a single point of contact and less hassle for the customer.

Source : Roger G. Schroeder, *"Operations Management"*, International Edition, Irwin-McGraw Hill Publications, p. 121.

1.5 PRINCIPLES OR RULES OF REENGINEERING

Reengineering is about achieving a significant improvement in process so that contemporary customer requirements of quality, speed, innovations, customisation and service are met. This entails *seven new* rules of doing work proposed by Hammer, relating to *who does the work, where and when it is done* and information gathering and integration. These seven rules are :

Rule 1 : Organise around outcomes, Not tasks

Several specialised tasks previously performed by different people should be combined into a single job. The new job created should involve all the steps in a process that creates a well-defined outcome. Organising around outcomes eliminates the need for hand-offs, resulting in greater speed, productivity and customer responsiveness.

- **Activity A**

Identify any one process or operation in your organisation, where you can merge a few operations performed by different people or at different locations into a single activity.

....

....

....

....

....

....

....

Rule 2 : Have those who use the output of the process perform the process

In other words, "work should be carried out where it is", makes the most sense to do it. This results in people closest to the process actually performing the work, which shifts work across traditional intra and inter-organisational boundaries. For instance, employees can make some of their purchases without going through the purchasing department. Customers can perform simple repairs themselves and suppliers can be asked to manage parts inventory.

Rule 3 : Merge information processing work into the real work that produces the information

This means that people who collect information should also be responsible for processing it which greatly reduces errors by cutting the numbers of external contact points for a process.

Rule 4 : Treat geographically dispersed resources as though they work centralised

Centralised databases and telecommunication networks allow companies to link separate units or individual field personnel, providing them with economies of scale while maintaining their individual flexibility and responsiveness to customers.

Rule 5 : Link parallel activities instead of integrating their results

The concept of only integrating the outcome of parallel activities that must eventually come together is the primary cause of rework, high costs and delays in the outcome of the overall process. Such parallel activities should be linked continuously and coordinated during the process.

Rule 6 : Put the decision point where the work is performed and build control into the process

Decision-making should be made part of the work performed. This is possible today with a more educated and knowledgeable workforce plus decision–aiding technology. Controls are now made part of the process.

Rule 7 : Capture information once – at the source

Information should be collected and captured in the company's on-line information system only once at the source where it is created. This approach avoids erroneous data entries and costly re-entries.

Exhibit 1.1 : Five Key Principles of Business Process Reengineering

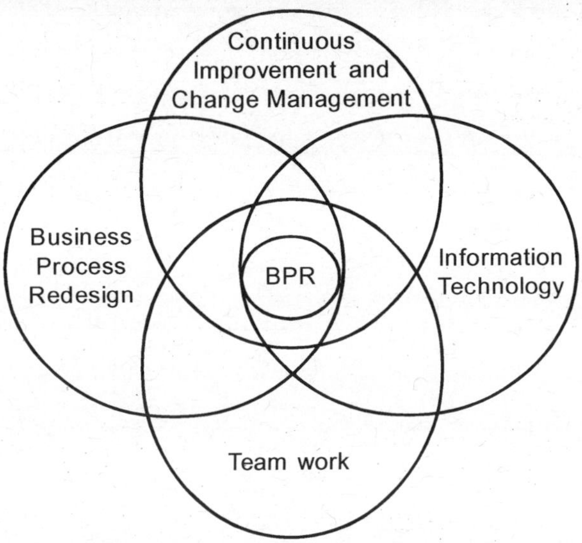

BPR focusses on strategic business processes such as order processing, logistics, manufacturing systems, procurement and supplies, cash flow management etc. Five key principles of BPR are :

(i) Strategic redesign of process.

(ii) Involvement of right teams of people

(iii) Wise use of information technology

(iv) Changed management style

(v) Continuous improvement of processes.

1.6 APPLICATION OF REENGINEERING

Reengineering as applied to any business process

Hammer states that business process may be defined as a set of logically related tasks to achieve a defined business outcome. A set of processes forms a business system – the way in which a business unit or a collection of units carries out its business.

Assuming that a company has decided that its processes are ineffective and inefficient, the following are the major steps the company should embark on to redesign its process, according to Hammer :

(i) **Develop business vision and process objectives :** This step involves prioritising objectives and setting targets for the future. A BPR vision statement describes the ideal state of a process.

(ii) **Identify processes to be redesigned :** This involves identifying critical or bottleneck processes and envisioning the steps to avert shortcomings in them.

(iii) **Understand and measure existing processes :** This involves identifying current problems and setting a base line.

(iv) **Identify information technology levels :** This involves bringing those involved in the process to a brain-storming session to identify new approaches.

(v) **Design and build a prototype of the process :** This includes implementing organisational and technical aspects.

Process reengineering in a manufacturing organisation

A process is a group of activities that takes an input, adds value to it and provides an output to an internal or external customer. Processes enable the organisation to focus on the customer. Viewing the material transformation process in terms of those activities tied to transforming material into something of value to the customer is a process view. Such a view examines inventory in terms of customer value, not internal economies. Such a view can be the basis of reengineering processes. *Exhibit 1.2* presents one view of process reengineering.

Exhibit 1.2 : Process Reengineering

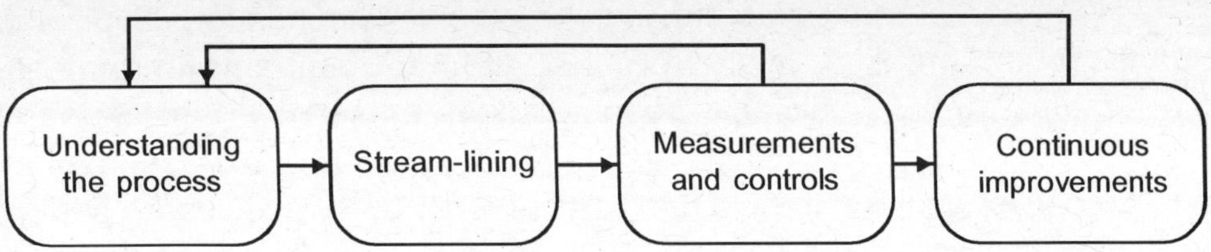

Source : Michael J. Stahl, *"Total Quality Management in the Global Environment"*, First Indian Edition 2000, Infinity Books, p. 503.

Box 1.3 : BPRE Project at Ford Motor Company

The accounts department of Ford employed 500 people before reengineering and represented an opportunity for major improvement. Ford had formed a joint venture with Mazda and decided to benchmark their accounts payable department only to learn that Mazda had only five employees in accounts payable department. Even after accounting for the difference in sizes of the two companies, this could only be attributed to a much different process.

The process that was being used by Ford before reengineering started with the purchasing department issuing a purchase order to the supplier with a copy to accounts payable. When the merchandise was received from the supplier, a receiving document was sent to accounts payable. Later, the supplier sent an invoice to Ford accounts payable for the merchandise. If account payable could match the three documents, they would authorise payment to the supplier. Most of the time in accounts payable, however, was spent in mismatches among documents. A clerk would hold up payment until the source of the mismatch could be identified and the problem resolved.

Under the reengineered system, the purchasing department entered the purchase order into a database and did not send a copy to anyone. When the merchandise arrived, the receiving clerk would enter the database and determine whether the shipment agreed with the electronic purchase order. If it did, payment was authorised to be made at the appropriate time. If it didn't match, the merchandise would be returned or the Ford purchasing department would be notified to give the okay nod to receive the material. Ford also instituted *"invoiceless purchasing"* where the supplier did not need to send an invoice to be paid. This generally simplified the process for all concerned. As a result, Ford was able to reduce the work of its accounts payable department and the headcount by 75 percent.

Source : Roger G. Schroeder, *op. cit,* p. 121 & 122.

1.7 THE ESSENCE OF REENGINEERING

At the heart of reengineering, is the notion of discontinuous thinking of organising and breaking away from the outdated rules and fundamental assumptions that underlie operations. Unless these rules are changed, *break-throughs* in performance are extremely difficult. Old assumptions must be challenged and the old rules that made the business under perform must be discarded. Most contemporary businesses are run on the basis of decade old policies. These assumptions about technologies, people and organisational goals probably are outdated and no longer valid.

Quality and *customer service* are increasingly becoming the primary focus of any company. A large portion of the population is educated and capable of assuming responsibility and workers cherish their autonomy, expect to have a say in how the business is run and demand quality. Consequently, the present business process and structures are outmoded and obsolete. Work structure and processes have not kept pace with changes in technology, demographics and business objectives. Conventional process structures are fragmented, piecemeal and myopic. Consequently, employees substitute the narrow goals of their particular department for the larger goals of the process as a whole. Reengineering seeks to provide a new perspective to business operations and processes. According to Hammer and Champy, "Reengineering requires looking at the fundamental processes of the business from a cross-functional perspective."

One way to ensure that reengineering has a cross functional perspective is to assemble a team that represents the functional units involved in the process being reengineered and all the units that depend on it. Rather than looking for opportunities to improve the current process, the team should determine which of its processes really add value and search for new ways to achieve the end results.

In short, reengineering efforts strive for dramatic levels of improvement. They break away from conventional wisdom and the constraints of organisational boundaries and are broad and cross-functional in scope. They use information technology not to automate an existing process but to create a new one.

1.8 THE THREE 'R'S OF REENGINEERING

Janson states that every reengineering effort involves three basic phases :

1. **Rethink :** This phase requires examining the organisation's current objectives and underlying assumptions to determine how well they incorporate the renewed commitment to customer satisfaction. Another valuable exercise in this phase is to examine the critical success factors – those areas in which the organisation clearly stands apart from the competition and to check whether they contribute to the new customer satisfaction goals.
2. **Redesign :** This phase requires an analysis of the way the organisation produces the products or services it sells – how jobs are structured, who accomplishes what tasks and the results of each procedure. Then, a determination must be made as to which elements should be redesigned to make jobs more satisfying and more customer focussed.
3. **Retool :** This phase requires a thorough evaluation of the current use of advanced technologies, especially electronic data processing systems, to identify opportunities for change that can improve quality of services and customer satisfaction.

- **Activity B**

Identify any one operation or function in your organisation, where you feel that intelligent use of technology like automation or software support will help to boost the productivity.

....

....

....

....

....

....

....

....

1.9 REQUIREMENT OF REENGINEERING PROCESS

A process selected for reengineering should be a core process, which has great scope for 'breakthrough' improvements rather than incremental improvement. Reengineering is accompanied by massive change involving lay-offs and large cash outflows for investments in information technology and automation. However, reengineering processes can result in big pay-offs. Bell Atlantic, *for example,* reengineered its telephone business. After five years of sustained effort, it cut the time to connect new customers from 16 days to just few hours. The changes caused Bell Atlantic to lay off 20,000 employees, but the company has become decidedly more competitive.

Reengineering requires focussing on *critical processes,* often using cross-functional teams, information technology, leadership and process analysis. These are explained in the following paragraphs.

(i) **Critical processes :** The emphasis of reengineering should be on core business processes, rather than functional departments such as purchasing or marketing. By focussing on core processes, managers may spot opportunities to eliminate unnecessary work and supervisory activities. Reengineering should be reassured for essential processes, such as new product development or customer services because of the time and energy involved.

(ii) **Strong leadership :** Senior executives must provide strong leadership for reengineering to be successful. Otherwise cynicism, resistance ("we tried that before") and boundaries between functional areas can block radical changes. Managers can help overcome resistance by providing the clout necessary to ensure that the project proceeds within a strategic context. Executives should set and monitor key performance objectives for the process. Top management should also create a sense of urgency, making a case for change that is compelling and constantly refreshed.

(iii) **Cross-functional teams :** A team consisting of members from each functional area affected by the process is charged with carrying out a reengineering project. Reengineering works best at high-involvement work places, where self-managing teams and employee empowerment are the rule rather than exception. Top-down and bottom-up initiatives can be combined – the top down for performance targets and the bottom-up for deciding how to achieve the targets.

(iv) **Information technology :** Information technology is a primary enabler of process reengineering. Most reengineering projects design processes around information flows such as customer order fulfilment. The "process owners" who will actually be responding to events in the market place need information network and computer technology to be more effective in their jobs. The reengineering team must think

through and find answers to questions : who needs the information, when they need it and where.

(v) **"Clean slate philosophy" :** Reengineering requires a "clean slate philosophy", that is starting with the way the customer wants to deal with the company. To ensure a customer orientation, teams begin with internal and external customer objectives for the process. Teams often first establish a price target for the product or service, deduct profits desired and then find a process that provides what the customer wants at the price the customer will pay. Reengineers start from the future and work backward, unconstrained by current approaches.

(vi) **Process analysis :** Despite the clean slate philosophy, a reengineering team must understand things about the current process : what it does, how well it performs and what factors affect it. Such an understanding can reveal areas in which new thinking will provide the biggest pay-off. The team must work at every procedure involved in the process throughout the organisation, recording each step, questioning why it is done and then eliminating it if it isn't really necessary. Information on standing relative to competition process by process is also valuable.

1.10 REENGINEERING IN THE SERVICE INDUSTRY

In the service sector, despite speed and courtesy in addressing customers, customer's hostility persists due to the inability of the service provider to maintain consistency in delivery and service. Another frequent problem is delay, due to the inability of the service employee to make pertinent and satisfying decisions when confronted by an impatient customer. Sufficient evidence of this is found in banks and fast food restaurants. Even though some companies which start anew seem to better satisfy their customers in the beginning, after some years, they become sluggish due to growth in size and becoming increasingly intense and complex. Work habits evolve into unacceptable levels of performance which further complicate their problems. To remain competitive today, service organisations need to focus on customer satisfaction and on real customer needs and expectations. They need to operate according to the standards of the customers.

According to Janson, the concept of reengineering holds a significant promise for the service sector. The following are some of the salient features:

(i) **Make the customer the starting point for change :** This means identifying what the customers really want and then creating the kinds

of jobs and organisational structures that can satisfy those expectations.

(ii) **Design work processes in light of organisational goals :** Companies that design work processes according to organisational goals become more focussed towards the customer. Organisations that reengineer often make drastic changes in existing jobs by integrating work procedures or tasks and empowering workers with more authority and responsibility.

(iii) **Restructure to support front-line performance :** In a customer focussed environment, every aspect of the organisation strives to promote the highest level of service to its customers, especially those who come in direct contact with customers. Consequently, organisations that undertake reengineering build work teams to support their customer service representatives or create "work-station professionals" who can perform both front and back office functions.

The impact of reengineering on the service industry

According to Janson, reengineering represents a major advance over conventional management strategies for improvement. As an integral approach, it involves three dimensions of a service organisation :

(i) **The human dimension :** To achieve a stronger customer focus, employees at all levels must readjust their thinking and recognise that customer satisfaction is the overriding goal. Some companies achieve this by rewriting their mission statement to reflect the primacy of the customer or by promoting a new vision to reinforce the central role that customer satisfaction now plays. Some other companies engage in training to help employees become better listeners, probe for customer concerns more effectively or satisfy customer needs more creatively. The motive in reengineering is to become more motivated to provide superior service and be skilled at doing it.

(ii) **The work process dimension :** Work systems must be designed not according to their internal logic or any external definition of efficiency, but according to how well they satisfy customer needs. This sometimes requires substantial structural changes in an organisation – changes that do more than just revamp job descriptions. It may mean setting up work teams to perform all the functions once divided among several departments or combining several individual jobs to create, one *"multi-skilled customer service professional."* In every case, total reevaluation of the management's role in the organisation comes into play and lower level workers typically assume far greater responsibility for service quality.

(iii) **The technology dimension :** New technologies should be introduced not only because they are more advanced, but because they truly support the organisation in its drive to achieve higher levels of customer satisfaction. Most importantly, technology should be used to automate secondary work functions, leaving service workers free to concentrate on more critical matters such as satisfying customer needs and solving problems.

1.11 QUALITY AND REENGINEERING

Reengineering is not completely different from total quality principles. The issue is not ***Kaizen*** versus ***break-through*** improvement. Infact, Juran talked about breakthrough improvement long before Hammer and Champy popularised the term ***reengineering***. Incremental and break-through improvement are complementary approaches that fall under the total quality umbrella, both are necessary to remain competitive. Infact, some suggest that reengineering requires support of total quality management in order to be successful. If reengineering alone is driven by top management without the support and understanding of the rest of the organisation, the radical innovations may end up as failures. The total quality philosophy encourages participation and systematic study, measurement and verification of results that support reengineering efforts.

Continuous Process Improvement versus Process Reengineering

Some organisations shy away from process reengineering because they feel it is too costly and too time consuming. The questions asked by them are : "Why scrap a process when we can try to fix it instead?" The answer is to investigate and appreciate the problem. We need to determine whether a certain process within the organisation requires minor healing (continuous process improvement) or major surgery (process reengineering).

Both continuous process improvement (referred to as CPI) and process reengineering are necessary to drive "break-throughs" (significant advances) in organisational performance but they differ in a number of ways. The differences are :

(i) **Management Involvement :** CPI typically involves employees at all levels and emphasise continuous incremental improvement of work processes. Process reengineering typically involves managers in a more *"hands-on"* role, since it often leads to changing organisational structure and redesigning jobs.

(ii) **Intensity of Team Member Involvement :** CPI involves team members on an "as needed" part-time basis over an extended time

frame. Process reengineering requires much more intensive involvement of team members, often on a regular full time basis over a condensed time frame.

(iii) **Improvement Goals :** CPI results in the achievement of successive incremental improvements over a period of time, starting from how a work process currently operates and improving upon it. Process reengineering is periodic and focusses on the achievement of dramatic improvement, radically redesigning how a process operates without being constrained by how things were previously being done.

(iv) **Implementation Approach :** CPI builds on making incremental improvements that add up to significant improvement overall for an organisation. Process reengineering focusses on outcomes and on making break-through improvement at one time instead of adding up the sum of multiple gains.

(v) **Magnitude of organisational change :** With CPI, organisational changes happen over an extended period of time, often with limited disruption of existing jobs, management systems and organisational structures. With process reengineering, radical process changes go hand in hand with changes in job design, management systems, training and retraining, organisational structure and information technology.

(vi) **Extent of focus :** CPI focusses on narrowly defined processes, which often involve frontline employees who are working to improve a sub-process which is part of a higher level process. Process reengineering focusses on broad-based, cross-functional processes that span the larger part of an organisational system.

(vii) **Dependence upon information systems :** Organisations using CPI occasionally reinvent a process whereas those using process reengineering use information technology to pave the way for radical improvements in reduction of cycle time and information access.

Both CPI and process reengineering have a place in today's organisation. While CPI is the mainstay, process reengineering is necessary at certain times in certain situations, when CPI is not adequate for the job.

1.12 REENGINEERING AND TOTAL QUALITY MANAGEMENT

Some people have said that both TQM and Reengineering are the same, while others have argued that they are incompatible. Michael Hammer argues that the two concepts are compatible and actually complement each other. Both concepts have the same focus – customer satisfaction.

TQM has contributed the concept of ***teamwork, worker participation and empowerment, cross-functionality, process analysis and measurement, supplier involvement and benchmarking***. Also, TQM has emphasised the need for a "total" view of the organisations in its approach to problem solving. TQM has also influenced company culture and values by exposing organisations to the need for change.

TQM has advocated continuous and incremental improvement of processes (Kaizen) whereas reengineering is about radical discontinuous change (breakthrough improvement) through *process innovation. Exhibit 1.3* illustrates how TQM and reengineering fit together over time in the life of a process.

First, the process is ***enhanced*** until its useful life time is over, at which point it is ***reengineered***. Then enhancement is resumed and the entire cycle repeats again. Hammer points out that this is not a once-in-a-life time endeavour. As business circumstances change in major ways, so must process design.

Exhibit 1.3 : How TQM and Reengineering fit together over the life of a process

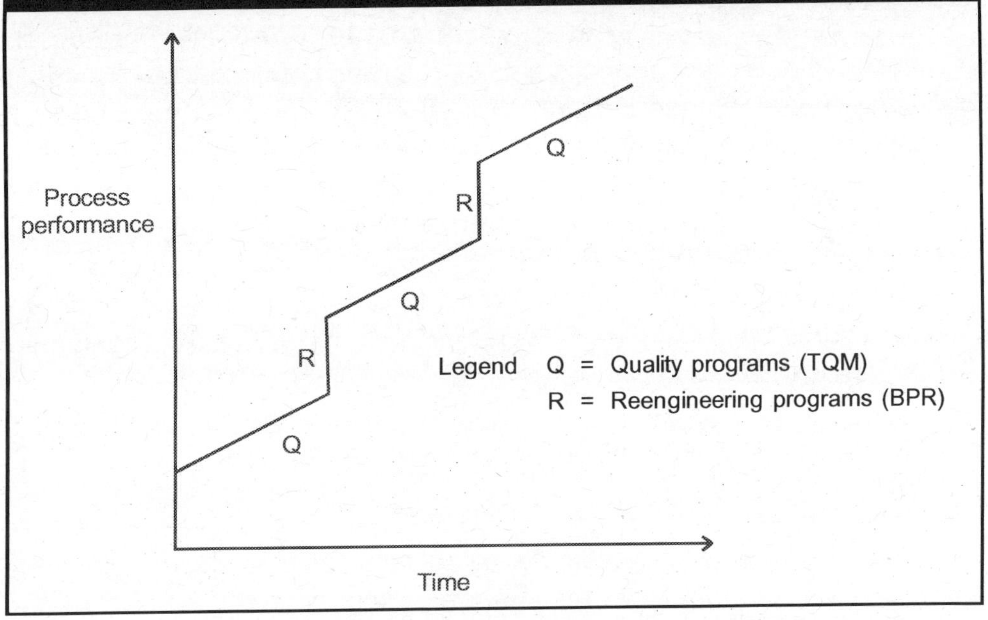

Source : Richard B. Chase, *et. al, op. cit,* p. 779.

Box 1.4 contains a list of some similarities between TQM/Continuous Improvement CPI and Reengineering (BPRE).

Box 1.4 : Reengineering versus TQM (CPI)

Similarities	**Reengineering (BPRE)**	**TQM (CPI)**
Basis of analysis	Processes	Processes
Performance measurement	Rigorous	Rigorous
Organisational change	Significant	Significant
Behavioural change	Significant	Significant
Time investment	Substantial	Substantial
Differences		
Level of change	Radical	Incremental
Starting point	Clean slate	Existing process
Participation	Top-down	Bottom-up
Typical scope	Broad, cross-functional	Narrow, within functions
Risk	High	Moderate
Primary enabler	Information technology	Statistical control
Type of change	Cultural and structural	Cultural

Source : Richard B. Chase, *et. al, op. cit,* p. 780.

The dissimilarities that have been identified may create an impression that reengineering is outside the realm of quality management. Hammer, the reengineering guru, together with quality gurus such as Deming and Juran, all agree that ***innovation*** and ***break-throughs*** in processes are essential parts of quality management. TQM assumes that the design of the process is sound and that all it needs is some improvement or enhancement. But if the world has changed dramatically since the process was first (or most recently) designed, the current design may be incapable of delivering the required performance. Reengineering is then necessary.

1.13 INTEGRATING REENGINEERING AND PROCESS IMPROVEMENT

Organisations must develop a framework for placing reengineering activity in the context of other change activities they may undertake. Integrating will help keep the different change initiatives, expectations, methods and results distinct from each other, thereby minimising the confusion and cynicism that usually result from undertaking an assortment of management initiatives. Four approaches to integrating process improvement and reengineering activities in organisations are :

(i) **Sequencing change initiatives :** This approach suggests cycling through ***process stabilisation, process reengineering*** and ***continuous improvement***. The drawback of this approach is that it may take at least *five years* to go through one cycle of change which would be longer than many ***organisational learning cycles*** or ***product life cycles***.

(ii) **Creating a portfolio of process change programs :** This method involves the categorisation of all processes and sub-processes in an organisation on the basis of the type of change necessary. The criteria for selecting processes for reengineering could include ***relevance to strategy, current performance levels, capability of sponsors, available investment*** **and** ***history of change***.

(iii) **Limiting the scope of work design :** In this approach, high level processes are designed by the responsible reengineering teams. But employees who perform the jobs design the detail work processes involved within the specifications decided by the reengineering team. This attempts to combine the participative nature of continuous improvement with the top down approach common to process reengineering.

(iv) **Undertaking improvement through innovation :** This approach combines short term improvement methods and long-term reengineering in the same process change effort. Improvement methods such as ***value analysis*** can be used to obtain quick benefits, which are then invested in the long-term reengineering effort. The improvement projects may also be a means to move the current process forward to a stage where radical process change is possible.

The different approaches to process change discussed above are complementary. Oganisations need to determine how and when they need to apply the appropriate methods to their different processes. While it is important to have an integrated approach to operational change, it is far more important to effect that change.

1.14 BENEFITS OF REENGINEERING

The following are the benefits of reengineering :

(i) By reengineering, an organisation can achieve radical changes in performance (as measured by cost, cycle time, service and quality).

(ii) It boosts competitiveness in the operations network through simpler, leaner and more productive processes.

(iii) Reengineering encourages organisations to abandon conventional approaches to problem solving and to “think big” (revolutionary thinking).

(iv) The slow, cautious process of incremental improvements leaves many organisations unprepared to compete in today's rapidly changing market place. Reengineering helps organisations make noticeable changes in the pace and quality of their response to customer needs (*i.e.* break-through improvements).

(v) Through reengineering, an organisation can be transformed from a rule driven and job centred organisation structure to a marketing organisation structure that focusses directly on the customer.

(vi) Reengineering often results in radically new organisational designs that can help companies respond better to competitive pressures, increase market share and profitability and improve cycle times, cost ratios and quality (organisational renewal).

(vii) The major accomplishment of the reengineering effort is the change that occurs in the corporate culture and the basic principles by which departments operate. Workers at all levels are encouraged to make suggestions for improvement and to believe that management will listen to what they have to say. Reengineering will eventually help the culture in the organisation to evolve from an insular one to one that accepts change and knows how to deal with it.

(viii) Reengineering has helped create more challenging and more rewarding jobs with broader responsibilities for employees (job redesign).

1.15 LIMITATIONS OF REENGINEERING

(i) Although business process reengineering is presented as a recipe for instant competitive advantage, it is not a panacea. Like any other management approach, how you apply it makes a difference.

(ii) It is not simple or easily done, nor is it appropriate for all processes for all organisations. Many firms can't invest the time and resources to implement a radical, clean slate approach.

(iii) Moderate gains that better fit corporate strategy and culture might give greater cumulative results than the pursuit of break-through.

(iv) Significant process improvements cannot be realised without use of information technology.

(v) It is not enough if a firm improves its cross-functional processes but also processes within each functional areas must be improved.

(vi) The best understanding of a process and how to improve it, often lies with all people who perform the work each day, not cross-functional teams or top management.

1.16 HOW DO YOU REENGINEER FOR SUCCESS?

There are many tools, but what is important is to get the sequence right. Few corporates have the expertise in house, but the technology varies, with total productive maintenance, manufacturing engineering or policy redeployment – all being used as synonyms for BPRE. In Sundaram Clayton, braking system manufacturer, reengineering is carried into shop floor under the guise of the Japanese quality management tool of policy management. Its manufacturing process undergoes **Deming's Cycle – Plan, Do, Check, Act** – but only after it was reengineered from scratch. Reengineering can and does have different tools and techniques. Every consultancy will have its own methodology.

Whatever is the approach to reengineering, there are certain steps to be followed:

1. Create a vision: Before corporates reengineer, they dream a vision of what they want to achieve. Precision is critical, for it is the vision that will energise everyone for reengineering. An articulate, well-defined and customer oriented vision is essential. Companies can reengineer any process. For example Elgi Equipments drew up a clear vision: become No. 1 company in its business in 10 years. And the enterprise-wide reengineering that it has embarked on was driven by this vision.

2. Pick the process: Choose the process to be reengineered. The first step for the choice is mapping the company's business not in terms of organisational structure, but as an outcome of its processes. Only then will the processes where the most value is added – and where dramatic improvement will deliver the smallest benefits to the bottom line – be identified.

Picking processes for reengineering is critical because it is fatal to reengineer every one of the firm's operations simultaneously. If the entire organisation starts reinventing itself, business gets disrupted. Focusing on a few processes also helps yield results quickly, which reengineering must do.

3. Find the facilitator: Who should lead reengineering in a company? Successful reengineers recommend picking people who are not only proven leaders, but are also well-liked and accepted by employees. The employees should feel that they trust the person ushering in the changes.

Box 1.5 : The Profile of a Reengineer

Process-orientation	Optimism
Holistic perspective	Persistence
Creativity	Tact
Restlessness	Team player
Enthusiasm	Communication skills

4. Manage change: Smart corporations ensure that their processes – reengineered or not – are owned by the people manning the processes. The traditional top-down controls is disappearing. Instead of expecting the employees to fall in line with the reengineering programme without demur, it is advisable to convince them that change is necessary to survive. According to James Champy, "Reengineering is a particular way of using our minds."

Eicher consultancy, starts off its reengineering facilitation programmes with a concept called the ***"appreciative enquiry process"***. Employees are made to concentrate on what is good within the company instead of just focusing on the negatives. In the process, a positive mindset, receptive to change begins to be built up. "Too many firms get started on the change without trying to build the energy within themselves to change" observes the managing director, Elgi Consultancy. "If one starts without the attitudinal change, the quality of the rest of the change will be poor".

In Indfos Industries, the management empowered workers for change before taking any step toward reengineering. The result was that workers began to volunteer to redesign process themselves.

1.17 WHY REENGINEERING FAILS?

There are top ten ways for an organisation to fail at reengineering. These are:

(i) Do not reengineer but say that you are
(ii) Do not focus on processes
(iii) Spend a lot of time analysing the current situation
(iv) Proceed without strong executive leadership
(v) Be timid in redesign
(vi) Go directly from conceptual design to implementation
(vii) Reengineer slowly
(viii) Place some aspects of the business off-limits
(ix) Adopt a conventional implementation style
(x) Ignore the concerns of your people

1.18 SUMMARY

"Business Process Reengineering" (BPR in short) is also known as "Process Reengineering" or simply "Reengineering". According to Michael Hammer Reengineering has been defined as *"the fundamental rethinking and radical design of business processes to achieve dramatic or break-through improvement in critical contemporary measures of performance such as cost, quality, service and speed".*

Reengineering does not strive to *revamp* the existing process but it involves *reinventing* the process to achieve quantum leaps in performance and to achieve higher levels of customer satisfaction.

Reengineering entails the following seven rules or principles :

(i) Organise around outcomes, not tasks.
(ii) Have those who use the output of the process perform the process.
(iii) Merge information processing work into the real work that produces the information.
(iv) Treat geographically dispersed resource as though they work centralised.
(v) Link parallel activities instead of integrating their results.
(vi) Put the decision point where the work is performed and build control into the process.
(vii) Capture information once – at the source.

According to Hammer the major steps the company should embark on to redesign its process are

(i) Develop business vision and process objectives
(ii) Identify processes to be redesigned
(iii) Understand and measure existing processes
(iv) Identify information technology levels and
(v) Design and build a prototype of the process.

Janson states that every reengineering effort involves three basic phases. They are : *(i)* Rethink, *(ii)* Redesign and *(iii)* Retool.

The reengineering process requires : *(i)* focusing on critical processes, *(ii)* strong leadership, *(iii)* cross-functional teams, *(iv)* information technology, *(v)* clean-slate philosophy and *(vi)* process analysis.

Reengineering is necessary not only in manufacturing industry, but in service industry as well. Three salient features of reengineering in the service sector are: *(i)* Make the customer the starting point for change, *(ii)* Design work-processes in light of organisational goals and *(iii)* Restructure to support front-line performance. Three dimensions of a service organisation on which reengineering has an impact are :

(i) The human dimension (focus on customers and employees)

(ii) The work process dimension (multiskilled service profession) and

(iii) The technology dimension (new technology and automation).

Reengineering is not opposed to total quality management even though the former focuses on breakthrough improvement as opposed to the continuous improvement (Kaizen) approach of the latter. Infact incremental and breakthrough improvements are complementary approaches that fall under TQM umbrella. Reengineering requires the support of TQM to be successful. The six steps involved in the reengineering process are :

(i) state a case for action

(ii) identify the process for reengineering

(iii) evaluate enablers for reengineering

(iv) understand the current process

(v) create a new process design

(vi) implement the reengineered process.

The various tools and techniques used in reengineering are : *(i)* Inductive thinking, *(ii)* Flow charting, *(iii)* Creative process redesign, *(iv)* Process benchmarking, *(v)* Simulation and *(vi)* Reengineering software.

The four approaches to integrating process improvement and reengineering activities in an organisation are : *(i)* Sequencing change initiatives, *(ii)* Creating a portfolio of process change programs, *(iii)* Limiting the scope for work design and *(iv)* Understanding improvement through innovation.

Some of the major benefits of reengineering are :

(i) Achievement of radical changes in performance measured by cost, cycle time, service and quality.

(ii) Boosting competitiveness in the operational network.

(iii) Helps to think big (revolutionary thinking)

(iv) Helps to make noticeable changes in the pace and quality of response to customers needs.

(v) Results in new organisational designs that help firms respond better to competitive pressures, increase market shares and profitability and improve cycle times, cost ratio and quality (organisational renewal).

(vi) Brings change in the corporate culture and the basic principles by which departments operate, encourages workers at all levels to make suggestions for improvements and eventually helps the culture in the organisation to evolve from an insular one to the one that accepts and knows how to deal with it.

However, reengineering has some limitations. They are :

(i) Not a panacea for all problems.

(ii) Not simple or easily done, nor is it appropriate for all processes for all organisations.

(iii) Use of information technology is a must to gain significant process improvement.

(iv) Improvement of processes require active participation of people who actually perform the work.

1.19 Self Assessment Questions

1. What is meant by "Business Process Reengineering"?
2. Why an organisation needs reengineering?
3. Discuss the seven rules or principles of reengineering.
4. Describe the reengineering process in a manufacturing organisation. How does it differ from that in a service organisation?
5. What do you understand by "the three 'R's" of reengineering?
6. Explain the requirements of reengineering process.
7. Discuss the impact of reengineering on the service industry.
8. Discuss the relationship between TQM and BPR.
9. Compare and contrast continuous process improvement and process reengineering.
10. "Some people have said that both TQM and Reengineering are the same, while others have argued that they are incompatible". Comment on this statement.
11. Explain how reengineering and process improvement are integrated.
12. State the benefits and limitations of reengineering.
13. Mention the similarities and differences between Reengineering and Continuous improvement.
14. Discuss the steps to be followed for reengineering for success.
15. What are the ten ways for an organisation to fail at reengineering?

◆ ◆ ◆ ◆ ◆

2

Chapter

BREAK-THROUGH IMPROVEMENT AND INNOVATION

Objectives

After going through this chapter, you would be able to :

- Learn why there is continuous need for improvement?
- Know of about two major approaches to improvement i.e. continuous improvement and breakthrough improvement
- Understand meaning of creativity as well as innovation and various types of innovation
- Learn about systematic approach to manage the process of innovation

Structure

2.1 INTRODUCTION

In any organisation, management is concerned about two things: *(i) Maintenance* function which is concerned with maintaining existing standard of technological, managerial and operational aspects of business and *(ii) Improvement* function which deals with improvement in the performance of current activities so as to improve products/service quality, achieve higher customer satisfaction, reduce costs, increase productivity, reduce absenteeism etc. Once improvement measures result in the achievement of new standards, these standards will become the revised standard of performance. Management is responsible to ensure that any employee adheres to certain rules and procedures called **"Standard Operating Procedures" (SOP)** for ensuring the smooth running of the organisation. Employees are trained and oriented to the standard operating procedures and they are liable for disciplinary action if they violate the same. During the course of improvement in the performance of current activities, the standard operating procedures are revised and the managers have the endeavour of not only ensuring the maintenance of SOP but also to evolve ways and measures of revising it for improved organisational performance on a continuous basis.

In Japanese organisations embracing total quality management philosophy, ***continuous improvement*** and ***innovations*** are two techniques of achieving improvement in quality, productivity and organisational performance. Every employee in the organisation is empowered to contribute to improvement. Employee participation in ***quality circles*** and ***suggestion schemes*** increase employee involvement in organisation's improvement. Employee involvement in the improvement task increases with the increase in the level of the employee in the organisational hierarchy, *for example,* workers, supervisors, middle managers and top managers.

Improvement may be achieved through continuous improvement (**Kaizen**) or innovation. While kaizen attempts to improve status-quo in small incremental steps, innovation involves drastic or dramatic improvements. Such radical, break through improvements may involve significant investments in new technology and/or machinery and equipment. Business process reengineering is a typical example of innovation or break-through improvement.

2.2 NEED FOR IMPROVEMENT

An organisation's ability to survive depends on how well the organisation adopts to demands imposed by the changing environment. The challenge of change in a business environment comes along many fronts : *(a)* competitors introduces new products, *(b)* industries develop new processes and technologies and *(c)* the scope of what constitute the business environment keeps expanding. Today, no firm could feel safe by capturing substantial market share in the domestic market alone. Firms should enter global markets and should be able to offer customers something different in terms of products and services that are more innovative, of higher quality, more focussed to satisfy customer needs and less costly.

Customer expectations are always expanding. A firm's ability to survive and succeed now depend on its ability to continuously improve products and services to meet and exceed customer expectations. To improve products and services, it is necessary to examine and improve materials and basic processes intrinsic to them. Thus ***continuous improvement*** is synonymous with ***continuous process improvement***.

2.3 FROM CONTINUOUS IMPROVEMENT TO INNOVATION IMPROVEMENT OR BREAK-THROUGH IMPROVEMENT

In Chapter 2, earlier we have discussed about the role of continuous improvement or kaizen in business process reengineering. Two kinds of improvement are : *(i)* ***incremental*** and *(ii)* ***innovation***.

Continuous improvement has a premise that process and products can be improved without limit. But we know that there is a limit to any improvement in products and processes because of the limitation on resources a firm can employ for improvement. Incremental improvement results from the process of making something better through the accumulation of small, piecemeal improvements, one at a time. Incremental improvement can, over time, lead to substantial improvement. But at some point of time, improvement will slow down and regardless of the magnitude of effort the gain in improvement will get smaller and smaller. At this stage, any improvement becomes economically not viable and improvement comes at great expense.

What happens when the improvement threshold is reached? The improvement for an existing technology, product or process will cease, for at least for the moment, because the cost of further gains becomes very high. Hence, there is a limit to the amount of incremental improvement at practical expense. But improvement can not be stopped because further improvement is necessary for the firm to survive. Then something new and perhaps radically different from incremental improvement becomes necessary. This kind of radical improvement is referred to as innovation improvement or break-through improvement.

Innovation improvement : Once the limit of incremental or continuous improvement is reached, a firm can improve its performance by adopting a new technology or a new process or methods – something fundamentally different and innovative. *For example,* vacuum tubes, propeller driven, aircraft engines and open-hearth method of producing steel were three technologies that were incrementally improved over decades Eventually when these technologies reached their threshold, additional improvement efforts were futile. Then big leap in performance came when these technologies were replaced by entirely new technologies : semi-conductors, jet engines for aircrafts and continuous steel casting respectively. These new technologies were far superior in performance than the old ones. Then new technologies were again subjected to incremental improvement till they were replaced by still better technologies. This kind of innovation improvement is facilitated by **process reengineering**.

However, it must be remembered that even after making the technological leap, it is essential to immediately begin incremental improvement to remain competitive. This is because, today many firms adopt a process called **"reverse engineering"** whereby one firm takes apart another firm's innovation, analyses it, copies it and improves it. Though inventions and intellectual property are protected through patents and laws, reverse engineering often gets around such protection. The point is that simply being the inventor of an idea or the first to introduce it does not guarantee that the inventing firm will retain the advantage. To retain leadership, the company should successfully improve and commercialise its invention. For this, **manufacturing process improvement** is equally important. In conclusion, it may be stated that, virtually everything about an organisation's operations can be improved through either incremental or innovative means.

2.4 INNOVATION AND CREATIVITY

Innovation is the process of creating and implementing a new idea. It is the process of taking **useful ideas** and converting them into useful products; services or processes or methods of operation. These useful ideas are the result of **creativity**, which is the prerequisite for innovation. **Creativity** in the ability to combine ideas in a unique way or to make useful association among ideas. ***Creativity provides new ideas for quality improvement in organisations and innovation puts these ideas into action***.

Change and innovation are closely related, even though they are not the same. Change often involves *new* and *better ideas.* The new idea may be the creation of a new product or process or it can be an idea about how to change completely the way business is carried out. Successful organisations understand that both innovation and change are required to satisfy their most important stake holders.

Strategic Importance of Innovation

For both established organisations as well as new organisations, innovation and change become important in a dynamic, changing environment. When a company fails to innovate and change as needed, its customers, employees and the community at large can all suffer. The ability to manage innovation and change is an essential part of a manager's competencies.

Types of Innovation : Three basic types of innovation are : ***(i) technical, (ii) process*** and ***(iii) administrative***.

Technical innovation involves creation of new goods and services. Many technical innovations occur through research and development efforts intended to satisfy demanding customers who are always seeking, new, better, faster and/or cheaper products.

Process innovation involves creating a new way of producing, selling or distributing an existing good or service.

Administrative innovation occurs when creation of a new organisation design better supports the creation, production and delivery of goods and services.

The various types of innovation often go hand in hand. *For example,* the rapid development of business to business e-commerce represents process innovation. But this new process requires many technical innovations in computer hardware and software. Also as firms began to use business to business e-commerce, administrative innovation soon followed. Further, implementation of process innovations necessitated organisational change. ***"Doing something new means doing something differently".*** Thus, innovation and organisational change go hand in hand.

Technology and Innovation : Technology is defined as the systematic application of scientific knowledge to a new product, process or service. It is also defined as the methods, processes, systems, and skills used to transform resources into products. Technology is embedded in every product, service, process and procedure used or produced.

"Innovation is a change in technology". When we find a better product, process or procedure to do our task, we have an innovation. ***Process innovations*** are changes which affect the methods of producing outputs. *For example,* manufacturing practices such as ***just-in-time, mass customerisation, simultaneous or concurrent engineering*** - are all innovations.

In contrast, ***product innovations*** are changes in the actual outputs themselves. Technological innovation is daunting in its complexity and pace of change. It is vital for a firm's ***competitive advantage*** because today's customers often demand products that are yet to be designed. As technologies develop, product obsolescence increases and innovative products will have to be introduced into the markets.

Managing technology requires that managers understand how technologies emerge, develop and affect the ways organisations compete and the way people work. Technology can greatly affect an organisation's competitiveness and managers have to integrate technology into their organisation's competitive strategy. Managers need to assess the technological needs of their organisations and the means by which these needs can be met.

Understanding the forces driving technological development and the patterns they follow can help a manager anticipate, monitor and manage technology more effectively.

- First, there must be a ***need*** or ***demand*** for the technology. The need acts as a driving force for technological innovation to occur.
- Second, it must be theoretically possible to meet the need using the ***knowledge*** available from basic science.
- Third, it must be possible to convert the scientific knowledge into practice in both engineering and economic terms.
- Fourth, the necessary resources such as ***finance, skilled labour, time, space*** and ***other resources*** must be available to develop the technology.
- Finally *entrepreneurial initiative* is needed to identify and put all the elements together.

The diffusion of technological innovations : for successful diffusion of a new technology over a period of time it should have the following attributes:

(i) Great advantage over its predecessor.

(ii) Compatible with existing systems, procedures, infrastructures and ways of thinking.

(iii) Has lesser complexity than its predecessor.

(iv) Can be easily tried and tested without significant cost or commitment.

(v) Can be easily observed and copied (or adopted).

Technological Innovation in a Competitive Environment

Technological change cannot occur naturally or automatically because any change is neither easy nor natural in organisations. Decisions about technology and innovation are very strategic and need to be approached systematically.

Two generic strategies a company can use to position itself in the market are *(i)* **low cost leader ship and** *(ii)* **differentiation strategy**:

With **low cost leadership** strategy, a firm can maintain competitive advantage because its products have a lower cost than its competitors. With a ***differentiation strategy*** a firm can gain advantage from having a unique product or service for which customers are willing to pay a premium price. Technological innovations can support either of these strategies by providing *(i)* ***cost advantage*** through low-cost product designs and creating low-cost processes or methods to perform the needed operations or *(ii)* ***differentiation*** by unique products or services which increase buyer value and thus command premium prices.

Technology leadership : Industry leaders are those companies which maintain their competitive positions through early development and application of new technologies. However technology leadership imposes costs and risks to the organisations which aspire for maintaining technological superiority or leadership. *Box. 31* lists the advantages and disadvantages of technological leadership.

Box. 2.1 : Advantages and disadvantages of technological leadership

Advantages	Disadvantages
• First-mover advantage • Little or no competition • Greater efficiency • Higher profit margins • Sustainable advantage • Reputation for innovation • Establishment of entry barriers for competitors • Occupying of best market niches • Opportunities to learn	• Greater risks • Cost of technology development • Costs of market development and customer education • Infrastructure costs • Costs of learning and eliminating defects • Possible cannibalisation of existing products

Technology followership : Not all firms are equally prepared to be technology leaders, nor would leadership benefit each firm equally. Whether a firm chooses to be a technology leader or a follower depends on how the firm positions itself to compete, the benefits gained through the use of a technology and the characteristics of the firm.

Technology followership also can be used to support both low-cost and differentiation strategies. The follower firm can learn from the experiences of the leader firm and can avoid the costs and risks associated with technological leadership, thereby helping to establish a low cost position. Followership can also support differentiation. The follower can learn from the leader and can adapt the products to more closely fit buyer's needs.

Assessing Technology needs

Assessing the technology needs of the organisation involves measuring current technologies as well as external trends affecting the industry. Before firms can divide strategies for developing and exploiting **technological innovation**, they must have a clear understanding of their current technology base. A **technology audit** helps to understand the key technologies upon which the firm depends. The most important dimension of a new technology is its **competitive value**. To measure competitive value, technologies are classified as:

(i) **emerging technologies** which are still under development and thus are unproved. These technologies have the potential to improve the competitiveness of a firm in the more distant future.

(ii) **Pacing technologies** which have to be proved yet their full value but have the potential to affect competition by providing significant advantage.

(iii) **Key technologies** which have proven to be effective, but also provide a strategic advantage because not every firm uses them. Since knowledge and dissemination of these technologies are limited, they provide some first-mover advantages.

(iv) **Base technologies** which are commonly used in the industry, every firm must have them to be able to operate and they provide little competition advantage.

Technologies can evolve rapidly through these categories. Decisions about technology must balance the strengths and weaknesses of the firm with external opportunities and threats. Firms can better understand how technology is changing within the industry by the following techniques.

(i) **Benchmarking :** Bench-marking is the process of comparing the organisation's practices with those of other firms. The ability to bench mark technologies against those of competitors can vary among industries. Also it is important to bench mark against potential competitors in other countries. A key or a pacing technology in use in another country can easily be imported and offer significant advantage to a firm. Also overseas firms may be more willing to share their technology with a firm if they are not direct competitors.

(ii) **Scanning :** Scanning focuses on what can be done and what is being developed whereas benchmarking focuses on what is being done currently. Bench marking examines key and more pacing technologies while scanning seeks out pacing and emerging technologies. Scanning emphasises on identifying and monitoring the sources of new technologies for an industry. It also involves executives of a firm reading more cutting edge research journals and attending research conferences and seminars.

Deciding about Technological Innovation

Once an organisation analyses thoroughly its current technological position, it can begin to make decisions about how to proceed into the future to either develop or exploit emerging technological innovations. The most effective approach to technology depends on the following:

(i) The potential of the technology to support the organisation's strategic needs and

(ii) The organisation's skills and capabilities to successfully exploit the technology.

Also, the organisation's competitive strategy, the technical abilities of its employees to deal with the new technology, the fit of the technology with the firm's operations, and the firm's ability to deal with the risks and ambiguities of adopting a new technology- all must be timed to coincide with the dynamic forces of a developing technology. A firm may have to change its capabilities and strategies to match the needs of the technology. This could involve hiring new employees, training existing employees, changing internal policies and procedures and changing strategies. The considerations which jointly influence decisions of a firm about technological innovations are:

(i) ***Market receptiveness :*** Assess external demand for the technology (short/long term).

(ii) ***Technological feasibility :*** Evaluate technical barriers to progress.

(iii) ***Economic viability :*** Examine any cost considerations and forecast profitability.

(iv) ***Competency development :*** Determine whether current competencies are sufficient.

(v) ***Organisational suitability :*** Assess the fit with culture and managerial systems.

- **Activity A**

Innovation is a process of taking useful ideas and converting them into useful products. Discuss any product / process you have come across as a result of this principle of innovation.

....

....

....

....

....

....

....

2.5 ORGANISING FOR INNOVATION

Organising for innovation requires a balance between unleashing people's creative energies and capabilities and controlling the results to market needs in a timely manner.

Managing creativity : The term ***creativity*** *and* ***innovation*** are often used interchangeably. ***Creativity has been described as the organisation of thoughts in a way that leads to different understandings of a situation.*** **Innovation** is more often associated with generating new products or services. Creativity is the process of generating new ideas, while innovation relates more to the process of implementing the new ideas for the benefit of the organisation.

Creativity in individuals : Every individual has creativity within himself or herself in the form of three components namely: *(i)* ***expertise,*** *(ii)* ***creative thinking skills*** and *(iii)* ***motivation***.

Exhibit 2.1 illustrates these three components and depicts how, when overlapping, they result in creativity.

Exhibit 2.1 : The three components of creativity

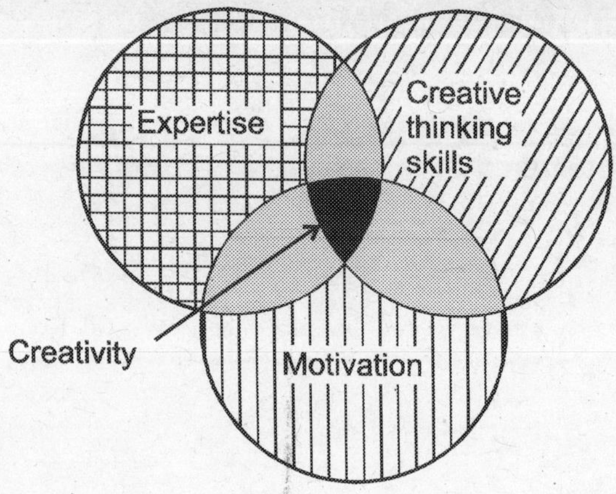

Expertise is everything an individual knows and can do in the broad domain of his or her work. This knowledge pertains to techniques and procedures related to work, as well as a thorough understanding of overall work circumstances.

Creative thinking is the capacity to put existing ideas together in new combinations. It determines how flexibly and imaginatively individuals approach problems. This capacity depends mainly on the individual's personality and work habits.

Motivation refers to an individual's need or passion to be creative. If an individual feels a need to be creative, that individual is more likely to do so.

Expertise and creative thinking are the individual's raw materials for being creative, but motivation determines whether or not an individual will actually be creative. Extrinsic motivators of creativity are organisational rewards and punishments whereas, intrinsic motivation could be the individual's interest and passion related to a situation. Normally people will be highly creative when motivated by personal interest, satisfaction and the challenge of the work.

To encourage individual creativity in organisations, managers should:

(i) Match individual expertise with work assignments.

(ii) Provide resources necessary for creativity and

(iii) Reward creativity.

Advantages of creativity : Every new product or service results initially from an idea which then follows an innovation cycle of testing, implementing and marketing. The key to competitiveness is generating and successfully exploiting new ideas. Generating new ideas is a must for an organisation. Generating new ideas that lead to successful innovation is at premium.

Obstacles to managing creativity : Any one managing creativity is likely to encounter the following obstacles:

(i) Free expression being stifled by a pervading culture of blame.

(ii) General resistance to change.

(iii) Reluctance to deviate from strict job descriptions.

(iv) Failure being regarded as a cause for penalties, not an opportunity to learn.

(v) A view that best ideas can only come from the top management.

(vi) Poor communication, or communication that only moves from the top down.

(vii) Rigid formalities and rules.

(viii) Inadequate or lack of incentives.

(ix) Slow decision making.

Do's and Don'ts for Managing Creativity

Do's

- Have a customer focus in order, to produce goods.
- Encourage trails and experiments and use failure to move on, not back.
- Weigh up the importance of creativity when recreating new staff.

Don'ts

- Don't accept that good ideas are the privilege of the few.
- Don't accept that all conflict is negative.
- Don't accept that creativity takes second place to order and routine.

2.6 ARCHITECTURE FOR INNOVATION

Because of the importance of innovation for success in a variety of industries, managers in all types of organisations are expected to help build infrastructures that encourage and support innovation and change. The management of a firm should ensure that the firm maintains a state of readiness so that it can move quickly and effectively when innovation is needed. Building an infrastructure and maintaining a state of readiness requires an architecture for innovation. *Box 2.2* lists several key features of that architecture.

Box 2.2 : Architecture for innovation

***(i)* Learning organisation**

- Managers allow employees to identity and solve major problems.
- Managers openly discuss organisational successes or failures with employees.
- Formal and informal systems keep employees informed of customers' preferences and their evaluations of the products and services offered by the organisation.
- Small scale experiments are used to resolve emerging problems before they become crisis.

***(ii)* Resilient workforce :**

- Hiring and promotion decisions are used to discard people who resist change.
- Employees are trained in the basics of organisational change and innovation.
- Successful efforts are celebrated to make employees gain confidence in the organisation's capacity for innovation and change.

***(iii)* Support for innovation :**

- Formal and informal systems facilitate the free flow of knowledge throughout the organisation.
- Reward and recognition systems encourage the development of competencies needed for innovation including technical knowledge, team work and communication.
- Key measures are monitored to assess the effectiveness of the process of innovation and the outcomes of innovation.

Managers should

(i) develop a learning orientation among employees

(ii) foster workforce resilience and

(iii) provide a support system for innovation.

2.7 LEARNING ORGANISATIONS

Organisations are redesigning themselves to become learning organisations capable of quickly adapting their practices to satisfy the needs of their customers. The basic feature of such organisations are: *(i)* shared leadership, *(ii)* a culture that supports innovation, *(iii)* a strategy focussed on customers, *(iv)* an organic organisation design and *(v)* an intensive use of information.

In a learning organisation, change is not a special event; it is a natural part of the organisational's continuous attempts to satisfy customers.

Unleashing creativity : Some reputed manufacturing firms such as 3M and Hewlett Packard company are strongly oriented toward ***intrapreneurship*** and they derive about one-third of their revenues from new products. These firms have established histories of producing many successful new technologies and products. They have an organisational culture that encourages innovation. *For example,* in innovating firms, even if a new product idea fails, the inventor is not punished. Strangely it may seem, ***celebrating failure*** can be vital to the innovation process. Failure is the essence of learning, growing and succeeding. **"Failure is the stepping stone to success"**.

Box 2.3 illustrates 3 M's rule for innovative culture.

Bureaucracy busting : Bureaucracy discourages innovation. While it can be useful to maintain orderliness and gain efficiencies, it also can work directly against innovativeness. Firms should have flexible (*i.e.,* organic) organisational structures to develop radically different technologies without any restrictions on thought and action. To facilitate this, firms create special temporary project organisation structures that are isolated from the rest of the organisation and allowed to function with greater freedom for action.

Box 2.3 : 3 M's rules for an innovative culture

- **Set goals for innovation :** 25 to 30 percent of annual sales must come from new products that are not more than 5 years old.
- **Commit to research and development :** 3 M invests in R&D at almost double the rate of the average US company. One R&D goal is to cut in half the time it takes to introduce new products.
- **Inspire intrapreneurship :** Innovative managers are encouraged to run with new ideas and they got a chance to manage their products as if they were running their own business.
- **Focus on the customer :** Define quality to demonstrate that the product can do what the customer dictates.
- **Tolerate failure :** Employees in 3 M know that if their ideas fail, they will still be encouraged to pursue other innovative ideas.

Other managerial systems that can facilitate innovation are:

(*i*) ***Cross-functional teams*** to solve problems and create innovative solutions. These ***flat structures*** help to create an environment that encourages collaboration and creativity. Teams focus on present issues and problems as well as future concerns and opportunities.

(ii) ***Learning organisations :*** Teams work with outside partners to bring knowledge into the organisation so that it can be integrated with existing ideas and information to create innovations. Teams are supported by values of egalitarianism, information sharing, openness to outside ideas and positive risk. This will result in destroying the traditional boundaries between functions and departments in order to create less bureaucratic **"learning laboratories"**.

Implementing developmental projects : "Development project" is a powerful tool for managing technology and innovations. It is a focussed organisational effort to create a new product or process through technological advancements. *For example,* development projects were launched by Eastman Kodak to develop the **Fun Saver Camera** and by Hewlett Packard to design a new class of computer printers based on ink-jet technology.

Generally development projects can be categorised as:

(i) ***research or advanced development projects*** designed to invent new science for application in a specific project.

(ii) ***breath-through development projects*** designed to create the first generation of a product or process.

(iii) ***platform development projects*** which establish the basic architecture for a whole set of follow-on projects and

(iv) ***derivative development projects*** which are narrower in scope and are designed to provide incremental improvements to an existing product or process.

Special cross-functional team works on development projects, team frequently interacts with suppliers and customers, works under intense time and budget pressures. For development projects to be successful, they should build on core competencies, have a guiding vision about what must be accomplished and why, have a committed team, instill a philosophy of continuous improvement and generate integrated, coordinated efforts across all units.

2.8 KAIZEN AND INNOVATION

The Kaizen or continuous incremental improvement contrasts sharply with drastic or break-through improvement which is the result of innovation. Innovation improvement is a short term, dramatic improvement resulting from a technological break-through based on individual ideas and efforts. It requires a large initial investment but little efforts to maintain.

Kaizen and innovation are complementary to each other in that, both lead to improvement. Top management of organisations must maintain a balance between the two because both are necessary for the survival and competitive success of an organisation. The major difference between Kaizen and innovation is that **Kaizen is process-oriented, whereas innovation is result oriented**. Whenever a new breakthrough is achieved, Kaizen efforts maintain it and improve it.

Constant innovation is one of the two prerequisites for achieving superior company performance. The ingredients of innovation are – ***persistence, passion, effort, creativity*** **and** ***small research groups***. Failure is a natural ingredient of innovations.

- **Activity B**

Discuss any practical case, where people are encouraged to come out with innovative ideas.

....

....

....

....

....

....

....

....

2.9 THE UNIVERSAL BREAK-THROUGH SEQUENCE

It is imperative to develop the habit of making annual improvements in quality and annual reduction in quality costs, not to lose ground to those competitors who already have it. What is needed is a continuous effort to achieve a breakthrough.

Breakthrough is an organised creation of beneficial change. The main ingredients of this programme are :

- Accept the responsibility for making improvements.
- Understand the universal sequence of events for making the improvements.

- Become familiar with the key concepts and techniques by which the universal breakthrough is carried out.
- Apply the universal sequence to actual company problems.

The universal breakthrough sequence is a road map to success and it follows the following stages in a particular order:

- Proof of the need
- Project identification
- Organisation for improvement
- The diagnostic journey
- Remedial action
- Breakthrough in cultural resistance to change and
- Holding the gains – control at the new level.

These stages are described briefly in the following paragraphs.

(i) ***Proof of the need :*** Middle managers will be the ones to prove to the top management that quality improvement is necessary for survival. The proof of this need is easily provided by quantifying the chronic waste in the language of money wasted. A rough estimation of quality costs can indicate the area in need of improvement and can increase in awareness of opportunities of cost savings.

(ii) ***Project identification :*** General awareness of opportunities need to be converted into specific projects for action. An agreed project provides a way of achieving a breakthrough. It helps to secure the needed budgets, facilities, permission to conduct experiments, needed tools and techniques and adequate personnel. The priority projects can be decided by using ***"Pareto principle"***. The priority projects will be the ones which score highly on their monetary returns on the effort invested, the amount of potential improvement in quality and product saleability, their urgency, ease of technology involved and level of acceptance by the management and workforce.

(iii) ***Organisation for improvement :*** Responsibilities are established for three levels of activities :

(a) Steering or guiding the overall improvement programme.

(b) Steering or guiding each project individually.

(c) Diagnosing or analysing each project.

A broad committee or a team of top managers has to be created to guide the overall improvement programme and to commit funds, personnel and facilities.

Multiple subcommittees or task forces are needed to be set up to guide the individual projects. The choice of the subcommittee members should depend on the skill and capacity to make a useful contribution.

After the completion of the organisation for improvement, the diagnostic journey is ready to begin. This is the journey from symptoms to cause and from cause to remedy.

(iv) The diagnostic journey : The journey from symptom to cause is an essential stage in the breakthrough sequence.

Diagnostic skills are the ability to design experiments or data-sampling schemes, to collect the appropriate data without bias, to interpret the results and to test any theories or propositions on offer scientifically. The two types of defects are :

- Operator – controllable defects and
- Management controllable defects.

Management controllable defects are 80 to 94% of the total. The operators are said to be in a state of "self-control" and to have all the means needed to control any resulting defect when :

(i) They know what is expected of them.

(ii) They know what their actual performance is and

(iii) They have the means to regulate.

Diagnosis of management controllable errors requires a study of current management practices and current technology.

A successful diagnosis can take place by conducting the following :

(i) An analysis of symptoms (to measure and examine the defects).

(ii) A systematic formulation of theories for the causes of symptoms (through brain storming)

(iii) Thorough testing of the theories by analysing prior-in-house data, by studying current operation and processes and by conducting off-line experiments.

The errors are classified as :

(a) *Inadvertent errors* – unintentional, un-predictable errors, occurring randomly, which the operator is unaware of making.

(b) *Technique errors* – errors that arise from lack of knowledge of an essential new technique. They are unintentional, specific and consistent.

(c) *Wilful errors* – errors that the operator makes intentionally and persistently and is aware of making..

(v) ***Remedial action :*** The remedial journey for the management controllable errors has the following phases :

(a) ***Choice of alternatives :*** The choice among many alternative remedies can be made by quantifying for each alternative the cost impact to the company. An optimisation of company costs and customer costs is the criteria for choosing the best alternative remedy. The impact of different cost factors such as materials usage, productivity, energy consumption and market research expenditure should be considered.

(b) ***Preventive maintenance :*** Managers usually try to rectify what has gone wrong, try to make defective work good, which are wasteful and disruptive activities. Instead of fire-fighting, managers should resort to value–added activity such as preventive maintenance of machines, tools, instruments, computers and automated process equipments.

(c) ***Communications :*** Adequate, open communication and feedback between various departments are crucial. Procedures, instructions, corporate policies and objectives should be adequately and clearly documented. Incomplete communication and feed back may lead to errors.

(d) ***Allocation of responsibility :*** Clear responsibilities for quality–oriented decisions and actions are necessary and people available to make decisions and take actions should be identified.

(e) ***Inspection and test :*** Inspection is a necessary evil, which until the time comes when we can do without it, is in a disparate need of improvement. But the fact remains that mass inspection and its associated costs cannot be reduced unless the chronic defect rate is reduced by controlling the quality of production processes by utilising SPC tools and other diagnostic techniques.

(f) ***Separation of problems :*** Pareto principle is applied to the diagnosed problems to separate the *vital few* problems from the *trivial many.* The vital few are the minority of the problems which account for most of the defects and they should be tackled first. The *trivial many* problems which account for a relatively low amount of defects and costs should be tackled either individually or collectively depending on the types of problems.

(vi) ***Resistance to change :*** Beneficial application of remedies for dealing with poor quality may be inhibited by one obstacle – *"resistance to change".* This may take the form of delaying tactics or outright rejection of the remedy by management ranks, supervisors, labour unions and also the workers.

Resistance to technological change is due to social and cultural factors. The company's cultural pattern – a tight system of beliefs, habits, traditional practices etc. may inhibit the implementation of any change, which is seen as threat. Certain actions to be taken to deal with cultural resistance are :

(a) ***Provide participation :*** Participation of all those affected, both in the planning and in the execution of the changes will be helpful to overcome cultural resistance. Every participant should be treated with dignity, so that a favourable social climate if developed, can make the change more acceptable.

(b) ***Provide enough time :*** Adequate time should be allowed for the change to be accepted because it takes time to evaluate and accommodate the merits or threats of a change.

(vii) Holding the gains : This requires that the operating forces engage in control, which consists of evaluation of current performance, comparison of this performance with the desired one and corrective action when the comparison shows a large difference indicating out of control situation. Management can assist the operations to achieve a state of self-control by providing the following :

(a) A process capable of holding the gains

(b) Established new standards

(c) Training and

(d) Established system of control.

When a breakthrough into new levels of performance has been achieved and the resulting gains have been held and established as the new standard, the universal break through sequence of events is ready to start again.

Reengineering means radically changing an organisation's way of thinking and consequently of doing things. It involves changing processes, organisational structures, management style and behaviour, compensation and reward systems as well as relationship with shareholders, customers, suppliers and other external partners. Reengineering is synonymous with innovation. It is rethinking the ways things have always been done. It is different from continuous improvement and it goes beyond continuous improvement, which is considered to be gradual and incremental and is simply doing better what is already being done.

According to Masaaki Imai, improvement can be defined as Kaizen and innovation–innovation calls for radical improvements as a result of large investments in technology and/or equipment.

Actually more total quality practitioners now insist that continuous improvement does include innovation, reengineering or breath-through. Therefore, the term continuous improvement refers to both incremental and breath-through improvements.

2.10 SUMMARY

Both *'maintenance'* function and *"improvement"* function are the concern of management in any organisation 'Maintenance' function is concerned with maintaining the existing standards of all aspects of business while 'improvement' function is concerned with changes for the better and improving the existing standards.

In Japanese industries which practice total quality, two techniques for improvement are *(i) continuous improvement or Kaizen and (ii) innovation or break-through improvement or reengineering*.

There is no need to over emphasise the need for improvement. A firm's ability to survive and succeed now depends on its ability to continuously improve products and services to meet and exceed customer expectations. Continuous improvement is synonymous with continuous process improvement. When the improvement reaches a threshold, incremental improvement, becomes slow and expensive. Then something new and radically different from incremental improvement becomes necessary. This kind of radical improvement is referred to as innovation improvement or break-through improvement or business process reengineering.

Innovation and *creativity* an closely related concepts. Whereas creativity provides new ideas for improvement, innovation puts these ideas into action, converting the useful ideas into useful products, services or processes. Further, innovation includes *change*, which often involves new and better ideas.

There basic types of innovation are *(i)* technical, *(ii)* process and *(iii)* administrative innovation.

The various types of innovation often go hand-in-hand. Also innovation and organisational change go hand-in-hand.

Technology and innovation are closely related. Innovation is a change in technology. Technological innovation is quite complex and is vital for a firm's competitive advantage.

Managing technology requires that managers understand how technologies emerge, develop and affect the ways organisations compete and the way people work. Managers must encourage technological innovations and develop and diffuse new technologies. Technological innovation can support a firm's generic strategies *viz.,* **"low-cost leadership"** strategy and **"differentiation"** strategy. Managers have to make important decisions regarding whether to become a technology leader or a technology follower after considering the advantages and disadvantages of technological leadership.

Technologies are classified as emerging technologies, pacing technologies, key technologies and base technologies. Technologies can evolve rapidly through these categories. Firm's can have a better understanding of how technology is changing within the industry by 'benchmarking' and 'scanning' techniques.

Technical innovation decisions made by a firm are based on the considerations such as *market receptiveness*, *technological feasibility, economic feasibility, competency development* and *organisational suitability*.

Organising for innovation involves *(i)* managing creativity and *(ii)* architecture for innovation. The terms *'creativity'* and *innovation* are often used interchangeably. But in the real sense, creativity is the process of generating new ideas, while innovation relates to the activity of generating new products or services.

Three components of creativity are is *(i)* Expertise, *(ii)* Creative thinking skills and *(iii)* Motivation.

Creativity preceeds innovation. Managers must encourage creativity among employees and help build infrastructures that encourage and support innovation. Architecture for innovation comprises *(a)* learning organisations, *(b)* resilient workforce and *(c)* support for innovation.

Creativity can be encouraged by orienting toward intrapreneurship, having an organisational culture that encourages innovation, celebrating failure, busting bureaucracy etc. Other managerial systems that can facilitate innovation are *(i)* cross-functional teams, *(ii)* learning organisations and *(iii)* development projects.

Kaizen and innovations complement each other in that both lead to improvement. Whereas Kaizen involves continuous, incremental improvements, innovation involves major, radical improvements which are also known as break-through improvements.

To survive and compete successfully, an organization requires both continuous improvement (Kaizen) and break-through improvement (or business process reengineering). The major difference between Kaizen and innovation is that Kaizen is process-oriented whereas innovation is result oriented.

The "universal break-through sequence" is an organised creation of beneficial change. It includes annual improvements in quality and annual reductions in quality costs so that the company stays in competition. What is needed is a continuous effort to achieve a "break through".

In conclusion, we may say that reengineering is synonymous with innovation. It is different from continuous improvement which is gradual and incremental improvement. 'Kaizen' or continuous improvement is simply doing better what is already being done whereas innovation or process reengineering involves rethinking the ways things have always been done.

Nowadays, more and more total quality practitioners insist that continuous improvement does include innovation, reengineering or break-through improvement. Therefore, the term continuous improvement refers to both incremental and break-through improvements.

2.11 Self Assessment Questions

1. Define the term “innovation”. How does it differ firm “creativity”?
2. State the need for improvement in organisations.
3. Distinguish between continuous improvement and innovation or break-through improvement.
4. What is meant by innovation improvement?
5. Discuss the relationship between creativity, innovation and ‘change’?
6. What are the various types of innovation? Elaborate.
7. Discuss the relationship between innovation and technology.
8. What is meant by “diffusion of technological innovations”?
9. Discuss how technological innovation can support the generic strategies *viz.*, “low-cost leadership” strategy and “differentiation” strategy.
10. What is meant by technology leadership and technology followership? State the advantages and disadvantages of technological leadership.
11. How do you assess technology needs? Explain.
12. How technologies are classified? Elaborate.
13. Describe the techniques of bench marking and scanning to understand how technology is changing within the industry.
14. How do you decide about technological innovation?
15. What is meant by “organising for innovation”? Explain.
16. What is meant by “managing creativity”? Explain.
17. What are the three components of creativity in individuals?
18. State the advantages of and obstacles to creativity.
19. List the Do’s and Don’ts for managing creativity.
20. What is meant by “architecture for innovation”? Elaborate.
21. What is meant by “learning organisation”?
22. What is meant by “unleashing creativity”?
23. Discuss the relationship between Kaizen and innovation.
24. “Improvement involves both Kaizen and innovation” – Discuss.

♦ ♦ ♦ ♦ ♦

3 Chapter

BUSINESS PROCESS REENGINEERING – CONCEPTS AND TECHNIQUES

Objectives

After going through this chapter, you would be able to :

- Understand the need for bringing continuous changes in the PROCESS
- Understand the meaning of PROCESS and PROCESS MANAGEMENT
- Learn about core elements of Process Reengineering

Structure

3.1 INTRODUCTION

For the survival of any organisation, improvement is not an option but it is a compulsion. For organisations which seek to thrive, dramatic improvement is often the only key to success. Eventhough small incremental improvements are always essential, sometimes, quantum leaps are needed for an organisation to grow and sustain global competition.

Many processes in an organisation may need reengineering because:

(i) Old ways of doing things need to be changed.

(ii) Your customers are demanding a change.

(iii) Competitors are taking over your market share.

(iv) It takes too long for your organisation to move products from conception to the market place.

(v) Your manufacturing process may be too costly and time consuming.

(vi) Your budgeting process may be too complex and

(vii) your services are not compatible with your customer's needs.

Then it is time for starting process reengineering.

Process reengineering is a new approach to doing a business. Over a period of time, it has been observed that it works well and some reengineered processes have provided gains of 100 to 300 percent.

Process reengineering defined : Process reengineering is defined as ***"the fundamental rethinking and reengineering of existing process tasks and operating structure to achieve dramatic improvements in the performance of the process"***.

The word 'dramatic' improvement means 'radical' improvement. In global competitive business environment, marginal or incremental improvements in some of the key business processes may not be adequate. Eventhough small, incremental, continuous improvement in the way business is conducted may be helpful to bring about substantial improvement in the long-run, major, dramatic or radical improvements (changes for the better) in the key business processes are necessary for Indian firms to survive and grow in globally competitive market.

3.2 NEED FOR PROCESS REENGINEERING

Many manufacturing companies suffer from the problems in product development due to long lead times, a large number of design changes, manufacturing problems and ultimately excessive costs to satisfy customer requirements. **"Product improvement"** is an area which is given more attention to in regaining the company's competitive position. Product improvement means improving product features to make it more attractive to the customer. But at the same time, the effectiveness and efficiency of the engineering, manufacturing and/or business processes that support development and delivery of the products or services are often neglected. Many firms are not competitive, not because of product or technology related problems, but because of the process – the way the firms carry out the design and development of a product and the way their teams spend their time. *For example,* when a firm might have updated its technology, its engineers might not have changed corresponding design processes or work habits accordingly. Design process means how a set of design-tasks is performed. Work-process means how a set of work tasks or job functions is performed. A **process** is defined as a set of tasks arranged in a particular manner so as to transform a set of inputs into a specified set of outputs. There can be many process possibilities of performing a set of design tasks, manufacturing tasks or work-tasks. Some could be more efficient or effective than others.

Many progressive firms are interested in maintaining a competitive edge in the world market and in producing high quality products and also keep their net cost of production at a lower level than their competitors. There are six parts (5 W 1 H) to achieve competitiveness.

- What (tasks, objects, inputs, outputs and process steps)
- Who (talents, team work, customers, suppliers)
- Why (technique, purpose, function and rationale for decision making)
- When (time, process order and structure)
- Where (technology gaps, space-process relationship)
- How (tools, method-process boundaries and process flow)

Knowing what information is required or task to perform and how this information or task satisfies the corporate goal is important to win the battle for competitiveness. The other questions to be addressed to are:

- Who makes up the team?
- Who needs it?
- Why this process or technique will not work?
- Why is this information be used?
- What is the optimum time to do it?
- Where are the right places to use this technology?

Process management is a concept often used to accomplish many **lean production goals**. In many organisations, process improvement is often perceived as a functional service referred to as **productivity improvement**. In some other organisations it is perceived as **process restructuring** rather than a process of **workforce productivity improvement (continuous process improvement)**. Process restructuring is targeted at achieving ***"one-at-a-time improvements"*** due to incremental or "add-on" approach of continuous improvement in manufacturing process, product quality etc. However, in firms following lean production principles, process improvement is seen as a pervasive set of renovation activities.

Process reengineering means one or more of the process modification strategies, which take into consideration the needs of the company as a whole. The term "reengineering" implies that the change or effort is directed toward an array of process modification strategies. More frequently, reengineering implies either starting with a clean state (a new process) or radically overhauling – which means replacing the old processes with completely new ones. Reengineering generally provides companies with opportunities to do things differently and creatively and to distinguish themselves from their immediate competitors.

3.3 UNDERSTANDING AND MANAGING CHANGE

Changes are an essential part of any improvement. When we introduce new steps or new tools in a process, we require change in the processes or workhabits.

Steps in the change process

Step 1 : The first step before we introduce a change is to understand the change process. Understanding the change process requires knowing:

(i) ***When to change,*** *(ii)* ***How to change,*** *(iii)* ***How to cause change,*** *(iv)* ***Where to change,*** *(v)* ***What to change,*** *(vi)* ***How to promote change so that the improvement cycle repeats.***

The key factors that influence the change process are **7 'T's** – ***tasks, talents, team work, techniques, technology, time*** and ***tools***. Sometimes the change process (where to change, what to change) has involved performing a strategic review which is *competitiveness analysis process* known as ***SWOT analysis***. SWOT stands for strengths, weaknesses, opportunities and threats.

Step 2 : The second step is to manage the change. There are six steps to managing change:

(i) Leading the change process, (ii) Setting the direction, (iii) Creating the environmental for change, (iv) Challenging past practices and excuses, (v) Removing the barriers and road blocks to change, (vi) Rewarding the right things so that change continuous to evolve.

Setting the direction involves method of data collection and determining the change frequency and change complexity. Challenging past practices and excuses involve understanding the sources of waste. Waste exists in all work activities, all tasks, all processes and at all levels in the organisation. 7 types of wastes reported by Taiichi Ohno are commonly found in manufacturing work-site.

They are: *(i)* ***waste of over production***, *(ii)* ***waste of correction***, *(iii)* ***waste of material movement***, *(iv)* ***waste of processing***, *(v)* ***waste of inventory***, *(vi)* ***waste of waiting*** and *(vii)* ***waste of motion***.

One more type of waste added to the above seven types is ***waste of information movement***. Removing business and roadblocks to a large extent involves eliminating waste and associated reworks.

The product improvement efforts can be categorised into four primary reengineering strategies:

(i) A set of continuous process improvement (CPI) tactics.

(ii) A set of restructuring tactics.

(iii) A set of organisational traits.

(iv) A set of renovation tactics (*e.g.*, best industry practices)

Benchmarking is a strategy that is common to all four **reengineering strategies**. Other strategies are *"as–is" flow charting, value engineering* and *value analysis* which will be discussed in later chapters.

3.4 UNDERSTANDING "PROCESS"

Before understanding what "Business Process Reengineering " or "Process Reengineering " or simply "Reengineering" means, it is necessary for one to understand the meaning of **"process"** itself and of **"process management"** and **"process improvement"**.

A ***"process"*** is a system composed by operators, machines, work methods, materials, tools and their immediate environment. The process consists of a certain number of activities or operations which are used in a given sequence to transform a set of inputs into useful outputs.

Process management includes the management of processes and management by processes. The **management of process** means that all the activities or operations of a process are required, are carried out correctly, at the right time, in the right place by the right person.

Management by process is organising and managing around a process (say order fulfillment) rather than around a function (marketing, production, purchasing etc.,) as is traditionally the case. Management by process requires cross-functional teams to perform the process.

Process management involves the design of processes to develop and deliver products and services that meet the needs of customers and control so that they perform as required and their continued improvement. Well designed processes lead to better quality products and services and less waste and rework.

Process management activities strongly emphasise on prevention of defects which is best achieved by designing quality into products and services and also into the process that produce them.

In an organisation, the processes that are being carried out serve some need. These processes result from efforts to meet customers' needs, the vision, mission and objectives of the organisation, the need for cost-competitive products and the desire to provide the best product and service for the least possible cost. Common processes include the following.

(i) **Assessing** customer requirements for goods and services.

(ii) **Defining** customer desires for goods and services.

(iii) **Designing** quality goods and services to meet needs and desires.

(iv) **Producing** quality goods and services as designed.

(v) **Marketing** goods and services that are produced.

(vi) **Stocking** shelves with goods.

(vii) **Billing** for goods sold or services provided.

(viii) **Serving** customers.

(ix) **Satisfying** customers by redressing their complaints.

Planning these processes is crucial to quality because process planning and design determines the end capability of the process. All processes have the same level of built-in capability. People who design the processes are responsible to determine this capability of the process. Often the process is designed to meet some specific performance capability which was outlined as part of the design goals.

Processes are covered by various rules, operational procedure and standards. The absence of such guide-lines generally cause deterioration of performance to a level far below the process is capable of producing.

In designed processes, the actual process performance is measured against its potential capability. Actual processes are continuously evaluated by the organisations that strive to achieve excellence in performance. These evaluation processes reach the operator level so that immediate real-time results provide real-time process and performance improvement.

Process as an evolution : Process is a two cycle evolution : *(i)* the process is controlled and *(ii)* the process is improved. Each cycle has several steps that must be understood in order to achieve continuous process improvement.

Box 3.1 illustrates two cycle evolution of a process.

Box 3.1 : Two cycle evolution of process	
Control cycle	**Improvement cycle**
• **Define** the process	• **Determine** causes
• **Establish** ownership	• **Develop** solutions
• **Identify** customer requirements	• **Develop** action plans
• **Develop** standards and measures	• **Implement** plans
• **Audit** for conformance	• **Assess** results
• **Identify** improvement opportunities	• **Prevent** recurrence
• **Develop** improvement objectives	• **Reward** participants

3.5 PROCESS CONTROL

Process control is a seven step cycle:

(i) Define the process

(ii) **Establish** ownership

(iii) **Identify** customer requirements

(iv) **Develop** standards and measures

(v) **Audit** for conformance

(vi) **Identify** improvement opportunities

(vii) **Develop** improvement objectives.

These steps are briefly discussed in the following paragraphs.

(i) **Define the process :** The process definition includes process boundaries, inputs or suppliers, outputs or customers, subprocesses and major activities.

Box 3.2 illustrates process definition

Box 3.2 : Process definition		
Input/supplier	**Process**	**Output/customer**
• List all inputs to the process • List vendors • List suppliers	Define boundaries ----------- Process begins ----- Process ends ----- Major groups are : ---- Subprocesses include -----	List all outputs of the process List all customers who receive this output

- **Activity A**

Take any process in your organisation and define it completely into three parts i.e., input, process and output.

....

....

....

....

....

....

....

....

(ii) **Establish ownership :** Ownership for a process establishes accountability with one person. This is helpful in controlling the process, establishing long-term customer satisfaction and achieving continuous process improvement. The person selected has the responsibility for the process, its results, process improvement and people involved in carrying out the process. Also the owner of the process has the authority and responsibility to effect appropriate changes and accountability for doing so.

(iii) **Identify customer requirements :** Process performance and improvement is driven by customer satisfaction. Specific customer needs and wants that determine customer satisfaction must be addressed based on priority of such requirements. Customer specification identify customer requirements.

- **Activity B**

Take any process or product in your organisation and identify its internal customers and their requirements from this process or product.

....

....

....

....

....

....

....

....

....

(iv) **Develop standards and measures :** To control the process, appropriate standards must be established and measurements developed for each process. They provide the means to establish targets and determine how well the process is performing against the targets.

(v) **Audit for conformance :** Standards and measures are only useful if audits and assessments are made continuously to determine the level of conformance. The audit should include the process itself, customer feed back and market data. Attention should be given to variations and their causes. Effort must be continually applied to remove abnormal variations in all process areas.

(vi) **Identify improvement opportunities :** Improvement opportunities arise from the specific problems identified during conformance audits and process assessments. Opportunities for simplifying the process, reducing costs, improving quality, increasing customer value etc., should be investigated. Specific attention should be given to causes of rework, redundancy, waste and bottle necks.

(vii) **Develop improvement objectives :** Based on the improvement opportunities identified, problems should be prioritised and corrected accordingly. The criteria for improvement priority are safety issues, customer requirements, business concerns, profit potential, cost of improvement, resource availability and potential for success.

3.6 PROCESS IMPROVEMENT

Once the process is under control, the improvement process begins. The steps involved in the process improvement cycle are as follows:

(i) **Determining causes :** The symptoms that are present in the process are listed, the reasons for the presence of symptoms are discovered and the root causes are ascertained.

(ii) **Developing solutions :** Potential solutions are listed, possibilities are combined and tested for correction and the best solution is selected.

(iii) **Developing action plans/implementation plans :** The action plan/ implementation plan developed must address ***what must be done, when*** **and by** ***whom***. The method of implementing the plan must be decided by the team along with measures to determine success.

(iv) **Implementing the plan :** The plan for improvement is carried out as intended.

(v) **Auditing or verifying results :** The obtained results are compared against the standards and measurement criteria which was established as part of the plan.

(vi) **Preventing recurrence :** This is the control to the new level step and begins the cycle all over again.

(vii) **Rewarding participants :** Some rewards or benefits are given to the workers to motivate them to work for continuous process improvements.

3.7 CORE ELEMENTS OF PROCESS REENGINEERING

Process reengineering is more complex than CPI. It results in drastic improvement because it affects change in more than one area. To achieve break-through organisational performance, process reengineering drives change in three areas

(i) **Organisational structure**, *(ii)* **People/Jobs** and *(iii)* **Technology**.

Three core elements of process reengineering are

(i) Organisational restructuring

(ii) Work redesigning and

(iii) Technological retooling

These three elements are briefly discussed in the following paragraphs.

(i) **Organisational restructuring :** Some from of organisational restructuring is often a key ingredient of reengineering effort. The considerations involved in restructuring are

(a) reducing organisational layers

(b) realigning functions/work groups around the customer

(c) driving accountability to the front line.

(ii) **Work redesigning :** Redesigning of work is necessary to assign responsibility (and possibly accountability) to a particular employee to carryout a portion of an entire work process. When redesigning the work, the following activity must be considered.

(a) Conducting a **"customer value-added"** process analysis of job tasks.

(b) Expanding job scope and ownership.

(c) Building cross-functional teams.

(iii) **Technological retooling :** Technological retooling for gaining optimum performance through reengineering requires the following considerations.

(a) Increasing the emphasis on process tasks that happen parallely.

(b) Gathering and communicating data related to customers.

(c) Expediting access to information and data for all employees.

Understanding the improvement opportunities and challenges that underlie process reengineering happens to be the first step in discovering whether it can work successfully or not in your organisation.

3.8 THE REENGINEERING PROCESS

Process engineering is an innovative process for which a disciplined approach to the effort is essential. It involves a six-step plan. These steps are :

Step 1 : State a case for action.

Step 2 : Identify the process for reengineering.

Step 3 : Evaluate enablers for reengineering

Step 4 : Understand the current process.

Step 5 : Create a new process design and

Step 6 : Implement the reengineered process.

These steps are explained below.

(i) **State a case for action :** The need for change should be effectively communicated to the employees of the organisation through educational and communication campaigns. Two key messages to be articulated are: *(i)* a need for action and *(ii)* a vision statement.

The objectives of reengineering must be in the form of a qualitative and quantitative *vision statement.* These objectives include goals for cost reduction, time-to-market, quality and customer satisfaction levels and financial indicators. *For example,* the vision statement by Federal Express (a US courier company) in its infancy was "we will deliver the package by 10 30 a.m. the next morning".

Box 3.3 : Steps Manufacturers Take When Reorganising

	Steps	Percentage of Manufacturers
(i)	Outsourcing one or more operations	31%
(ii)	Eliminating a product line	34%
(iii)	Reducing the number of suppliers	34%
(iv)	Reducing the number of production workers	41%
(v)	Flattening the layers of management	56%
(vi)	Organising operations by customer or product line	60%
(vii)	Investing in automated equipment	76%
(viii)	Significantly improving process flows in the factory	87%

Source : Richard B. Chase, Nicholas J. Aquilano, F. Robert Jacobs, *Production and Operations Management,* Eighth Edition, Irwin McGraw-Hill Publications, p. 772.

The CEO of the company is responsible for communicating the vision statement first to the senior management and then to the rest of the firm. A senior management *steering committee* that includes the CEO typically champions the change process, sets goals, assigns resources and expedites progress.

- **Activity C**

Get information about vision statement for any three reputed companies.

....

....

....

....

....

....

....

....

(ii) **Identify the process :** All the major processes in the firm should be initially identified and few processes should be selected for reengineering. The following questions define the criteria for selecting processes for reengineering:

- Which processes are currently more problematic?
- Which processes are critical to accomplishing company strategy and have the greatest impact on the company's customer?
- Which processes are most likely to be successfully redesigned?
- What is the scope of the reengineering project and what are the costs involved?
- What is the strength of the reengineering team and the commitment of process owners and sponsors?
- Can continuous improvement deliver the required improvements?
- Is the process antiquated or is the technology used outdated?

Response to these questions can be weighted in accordance with the company's need for improvement. The selected process should have a manageable reengineering project scope with well-defined process boundaries.

(iii) **Evaluate enablers :** Information technology and human/organisational issues act as enablers of the reengineering process. Technology evaluation has now become a core competency required of all companies. Companies should develop the ability to evaluate current and emerging information technology and identify creative application to redesign their existing processes.

The current organisational culture should also be evaluated in light of the impending change to be brought about by reengineering. Participative and customer-oriented cultures that have evolved from the quality revolution provide a suitable environment for further change. But the magnitude of change created by process redesign makes the management of change a necessity. Issues of measurement and compensation, career paths, work enrichment and new skills training should be addressed.

(iv) **Understanding the current process :** The current process must be understood by making use of process evaluation techniques such as flow charts, fishbone diagrams and quality function deployment. The purpose is to create a new, radically better process. The current process must be studied to understand the activities which are essential to completion. All activities can be classified into three types :

(a) *Value-adding work* – work for which customer is willing to pay.

(b) *Non-value adding work* – work which creates no value for the customer but is required in order to get the value adding work done.

(c) *Waste* – work that neither adds nor enables value.

Value adding work consists of all of the activities that create the goods and services that customers want. *For example,* if a customer's order has to be executed, value adding activities include inventory allocation, picking, packing, route planning and shipping. Waste work is work whose absence would not be noticed by the customer. Waste work needs to be eliminated.

Non-value adding work is the glue that binds the value-adding work in conventional processes. It is mainly the administrative overhead – the reporting, checking, supervising, controlling, reviewing and coordinating. Michael Hammer argues that it is necessary to design non-value adding work by reorganising the value-adding tasks into a new and more efficient process.

(v) **Create a new process design :** Process redesign requires beginning with a clean slate. Reengineers should suspend current rules, procedures and values so as to create new process design. They also need to utilise the principles of reengineering.

The first emphasis in reengineering a process is to *eliminate all waste work.* Next, the focus is on the elimination of non-value-adding work. Hammer has found that less than 10 percent of the activities in a process are value-adding activities.

(vi) **Implement the reengineered process :** Leadership is critical to the implementation process as well as to the entire reengineering effort. Process engineering teams are typically responsible for implementing the new designs. However, support and buy-in from line managers are crucial to success. Training employees in additional skills needed to perform in the new environment is also essential.

3.9 SOME ISSUES IN BUSINESS PROCESS REENGINEERING

Business process reengineering comprises several issues which are discussed in the following paragraphs.

(i) **Downsizing :** Also known as right sizing or man power rationalisation, downsizing in considered as the shortest route to cut costs. Employees in many organisations work under the threat of losing their jobs any time owing to the management policy of downsizing. Because of this feeling of insecurity, their productivity in affected. The impact of downsizing on the financial performance of a firm is temporary because

it can not go on reducing its manpower for ever. Besides, the image of the firm in the market may suffer and when there is a need to increase man power, competent people may hesitate to join such firms. When an organisation is going through a bad patch, instead of downsizing, the top management should consider reengineering . A few key processes can be identified and reengineered to reduce the costs. The implementation of the reengineered process may be quite inexpensive, thereby eliminating the need for downsizing. Usually reengineering should precede downsizing.

(ii) **Human resources :** Human resources are the most valuable of all the resources in an organisation. In a process-driven organisation, the employees at all levels play a major role. They act as **intrapreneurs** capable of offering valuable suggestions for process improvement. They should be provided with opportunities to play their roles effectively. The employees must be trained to develop capability to apply their skills as members of reengineering teams, gain more experience and move to the next assignment with better skills and experience. In process-oriented organisations, management should regard employees training as an investment which far exceeds the cost incurred for their training.

(iii) **Leadership :** The leader of reengineering team should be from the top management, preferably with technical background. The leader should have personality characteristics needed for the assigned job. Also the leader should be able to handle overt or covert resistance from employees at any level in the organisation.

(vi) **Quantitative objectives :** For successfully reengineering processes, one or more major objectives should be expressed quantitatively so that the employees can be motivated.

(v) **Resistance to change :** Human beings are resistant to change by nature itself. When the change is major or radical, employees at middle and junior levels of management resist change. While Kaizen involves minor changes in work practices, business process reengineering is concerned with radical changes in current business practices and hence the resistance to business process reengineering is more. Since managers are uncertain about their performance when the processes are redesigned, they are afraid of losing power, authority and even job as a result of implementation of reengineered process. The employees resist change indirectly by participating with out enthusiasm and commitment in the implementation of reengineered process. Hence, to implement business process reengineering, the top management must be totally committed to it and they should be able

to deal with resistance from employees of different departments at different hierarchical levels.

(vi) **Implementation time :** The success of BPRE greatly depends on the time taken to implement it and the benefits derived from it within that time period. According to Hammer and Stanton, it should not take more than 12 months from the time of starting to think about a process to be reengineered until some substantial benefits are achieved from the change. In this short period of one year, the reengineering team must be able to clearly understand the existing process to be reengineered, examine its sub processes/tasks and evolve ways and means of performing them in a radically improved way, design and evaluate the prototype of the new process and successfully implement the process.

(vii) **"Out-of-the-box" thinking :** In BPRE, the emphasis in on "out-of-the-box" thinking or lateral thinking or divergent thinking to generate creative or innovative ideas. People are required to deviate from their traditional paradigms and offer creative or innovative ideas to reengineer a business process. Encouragement and reward from top management sustain the motivation of employees even though few of their ideas may not be successful and find a place in the reengineered process.

(viii) **Organisational culture :** BPRE brings about major changes in organisational culture. There is a paradigm shift in the way organisations are managed – from the traditional way of exercising command and control to emphasis on business processes and team work. Vision and mission of the firm are no more confined to top management only, but are shared by middle and junior level managers.

The strategic decision of BPRE should percolate down to reach the lower levels of hierarchy and also to reach every employee of the organisation. Employee participation is crucial for the success of BPRE. The top management should create a culture that enables every employee to have role clarity in the reengineered processes so that they can play their role effectively.

(ix) **Concept of human capital :** In a process oriented firm, the concept of assets is not limited to capital assets such as machinery and equipment and cash, but encompasses human resource also. People represent the most valuable asset in a firm practicing BPRE along with knowledge capital (*i.e.,* knowledge of key business process, quality and quantity data base etc.). These assets add value to business in terms of higher customer satisfaction, bigger market share, high profitability etc.

(x) **Behavioural change :** BPRE not only involves technological change, but also behavioural change of employees. The management of behavioural change is more difficult than management of technological change. It in the responsibility of managers who are leaders of BPRE to convince employees about the need for change for the survival of business in a competitive business world.

3.10 SUMMARY

Dramatic or radical improvement in often the only key to success for any organisation that seeks to thrive. Eventhough small incremental improvements are always necessary, quantum leaps are also essential. Reengineering is needed because customers demand change and competitors snatch a firm's market share. Also, the manufacturing process may be too costly or the time to market may be too long. Reengineered business processes can bring about dramatic gains of even 100 to 300 percent.

Process reengineering is *the fundamental rethinking and reengineering of existing process tasks and operating structure to achieve dramatic improvements in the performance of the process.*

Process reengineering is needed because

(i) the firm may suffer from problems in product development due to long lead times, a large number of design changes, excessive costs, quality problems etc.

(ii) the firm may have product or technology related problems.

(iii) when a firm might have updated its technology, its engineers might not have changed the design process or work processes accordingly.

(iv) the firm may have to maintain a competitive edge in the world market by producing high quality products at low costs.

Process management is helpful in achieving lean production goals and process improvement which in turn improve productivity.

Understanding and managing change is essential in process reengineering because changes are essential in any improvement. Product improvement efforts can be categorised into four primary reengineering strategies *viz., (i)* continuous improvement tactics, *(ii)* restructuring tactics, *(iii)* organisational traits and *(iv)* renovation tactics based on bench marking.

To have a better understanding of business process reengineering (BPR) it is necessary to understand the meaning of process, process management, process control and process improvement.

Process has evolved in two cycles *viz.,* the control cycle and the improvement cycle. The process control cycle has seven steps *viz., (i)* defining the process, *(ii)* establishing ownership, *(iii)* identifying customer requirements, *(iv)* developing standards and measures, *(v)* auditing for conformance, *(vi)* identifying improvement opportunities and *(vii)* developing improvement objectives.

The process improvement cycle has the following steps:

(i) Determining causes, *(ii)* Developing solutions, *(iii)* Developing action plans/ implementation plans, *(iv)* Implementing the plan, *(v)* Auditing or verifying results, *(vi)* Preventing recurrence and *(vii)* Rewarding participants.

The core elements of process reengineering are: *(i)* Organisational restructuring, *(ii)* Work re-designing and *(iii)* Technological retooling.

The reengineering process has six steps. They are: *(i)* State a case for action, *(ii)* Identify the process for reengineering, *(iii)* Evaluate enablers for reengineering, *(iv)* Understand the current process, *(v)* Create a new process design and *(vi)* Implement the reengineered process.

Some issues in business process reengineering are : *(i)* downsizing, *(ii)* human resources, *(iii)* leadership, *(iv)* quantitative objectives, *(v)* resistance to change, *(vi)* implementation time, *(vii)* "out-of-the-box" thinking, *(viii)* organisational culture, *(ix)* concept of human capital and *(x)* behavioural change.

3.11 Self Assessment Questions

1. State the reasons for process reengineering.
2. Define the term "Process Reengineering ".
3. What is a "Business Process"?
4. What is "Process management"?
5. What is meant by "change"? Discuss the steps involved in the change process.
6. Name the seven types of wastes found in manufacturing work-site.
7. Define the terms "process", "process management", "process control" and "process improvement".
8. Describe the evolution of process in terms of "control cycle" and "improvement cycle".
9. Discuss the core elements of process reengineering.
10. Write short notes on:

    (a) Downsizing

    (b) Resistance to change

    (c) "Out-of-the-box" thinking

    (d) Organisational culture

    (e) Concept of human capital and

    (f) Behavioural change.

◆ ◆ ◆ ◆ ◆

4 Chapter

RELATIONSHIP BETWEEN BPRE AND TQM

Objectives

After going through this chapter, you would be able to :

- Understand relationship between BPRE and TQM (Total Quality Management)
- Learn about common features of BPRE and QFD (Quality Function Deployment)
- Understand relevance between BPRE and Benchmarking
- Learn about relevance between BPRE and ISO Standards

Structure

4.1 INTRODUCTION

The management of all organisations have one common objective viz., "*to improve the performance of the organisation.*" Improvements can be brought about either in the form of *continuous, incremental improvements* (as envisaged in **Kaizen**) or in the form of drastic and dramatic improvement *i.e.*, ***innovation*** or **"*breakthrough improvement*"** (or ***Business Process Reengineering***). In case of continuous improvement, the improved level of performance becomes the standard which should be maintained till it is replaced by a new standard of higher level of performance. In some organisations, both incremental and drastic improvements are carried out simultaneously. This view holds that dramatic improvements (BPRE) can be sustained only when they are supported by incremental improvement on a continuous basis.

4.2 REENGINEERING AND TOTAL QUALITY MANAGEMENT

When reengineering is implemented in an organisation, the objectives of total quality must be kept in mind as the foremost to ensure success of reengineering. Otherwise, implementation can be costly and may not yield acceptable or long term results. BPRE emphasises radically changing the existing processes, assuming that those changes will improve the firm's global performance or the performance of one of its specific processes. A firm's internal processes should be directly linked to enhancing profitability through the fulfillment of its customers' needs. Reengineering could be one of the best tools to achieve total quality and it will significantly improve a company's performance. *For example,* in a large manufacturing firm, there were lot of delays in procuring some critical materials which would affect the progress of production. These days were attributed to the faulty purchasing system. The process of preparing the purchase requisition was too lengthy and the entire purchasing process was cumbersome and prone to errors. The firm's declining sales was attributed to the delays in production which were due to the inefficiency of purchasing system. The management appointed a business process reengineering team to solve this problem. The team worked on rethinking the purchasing process from scratch. As a result, they could reduce the cycle time, eliminate some procedures entirely and computers were used for some operations and errors were eliminated.

Total quality management comprises both continuous process improvement (CPI) and business process reengineering (BPRE) for achieving improvements in quality in all areas of operations of a business, right from inputs, through processing to outputs.

A comparison between BPRE and TQM is given in the following paragraphs:

(i) Both BPRE and TQM primarily focus on customers. Success of BPRE and TQM is reflected in adequate response to the changing needs of customers in a competitive business environment. Even though BPRE does not explicitly high-light the concept of internal customers like TQM, its success very much depends on satisfaction of internal customers.

(ii) Both BPRE and TQM are process-oriented concepts involving cross-functional activities. While TQM may or may not involve break-through improvements, BPRE always attempts to achieve major or dramatic improvements in the existing business processes. For process improvement, TQM and TQC tools such as Pareto analysis, cause-and-effect diagram, control charts etc., to identify the root causes of problems and to eliminate them. BPRE aims at drastic changes to improve the processes which are markedly different from the existing processes.

(iii) Both BPRE and TQM emphasise cultural changes in the organisation and behavioural changes in employees by introducing ***customer focus*** and ***process-orientation*** in the minds of employees. Employees are motivated to behave not just as job holders in the organisation but as part of the whole process of the business.

(iv) Both BPRE and TQM require top management support. The chief executive of the company has to play the role of a leader for successful implementation of BPRE and TQM. Since both BPRE and TQM are supporting processes to achieve business goals, it is necessary that the top management must take initiative in these processes, rather than delegating the responsibility to middle management.

(v) Both BPRE and TQM are not "one-time" experiments. Both need to be implemented on a continuous basis.

(vi) Every employee in every department is directly or indirectly involved in BPRE and TQM.

The common features of BPRE and TQM are listed in *Box 4.1*.

Box 4.1 : Common features of BPRE and TQM
(i) Customer-focus
(ii) Process-orientation
(iii) Cross-functional activity
(iv) Emphasis on cultural change
(v) Top-down approach
(vi) Continuous improvement
(vii) Employee involvement at all levels
(viii) Stress on quality enhancement

- **Activity A**

Collect data about any company which has adapted Total Quality Control technique for improvement.

....

....

....

....

....

....

....

....

4.3 BPRE AND QUALITY FUNCTION DEVELOPMENT

One of the keys to achieving continual improvement is getting customers involved as early in the product development process as possible. This is the main focus of quality function deployment (QFD).

QFD is a practice to design a process in response to customer needs. It translates what the customer wants into what the firm produces. It enables manufacturing firms to prioritise customer needs, find innovative responses to those needs, and improve processes to maximum effectiveness. QFD leads to process improvements which enable a firm to exceed customers' expectations.

Quality function deployment is a TQM tool for process design and process management.

Comparison between BPRE and QFD is summarised in the following paragraph:

(i) Both BPRE and QFD concepts have the same focus, *i.e.*, ***focus on customers***.

(ii) Both BPRE and QFD can be applied to a wide variety of business processes in both manufacturing and service organizations.

(iii) In both BPRE and QFD, inputs are converted into outputs having added value to customers.

(iv) Both BPRE and QFD have cross functional approach in their implementation.

4.4 BPRE AND BENCH MARKING

Bench marking involves partnering with the owner of a best-in-class process so that a firm might adopt or adapt that process in its operation without having to spend time and energy to design a duplicate of the superior process. BPRE requires the firm to do the latter on its own. Therefore, BPRE should only be considered when it is impossible to use bench marking approach to process improvement. That could happen because:

(i) No known process available for bench marking even though such cases may be very rare.

(ii) Best-in-class not willing to partner with the firm.

(iii) Best-in-class not accessible due to geography or costs.

If a firm's subject process is not satisfactory, and the firm cannot bench mark because of any of the above reason. Then it may have to resort to reengineering. If the process is not satisfactory because either it may be a wrong process for the job or it may be out of statistical control. Either of these problems can not be solved by reengineering. If the process is appropriate and is in statistical control, but it is still not producing the desired result, then it means the process is not capable. Then redesigning the process through reengineering is a good approach.

In case of process reengineering there is no guarantee that after spending the time and resources, the process will be a competitive process. With bench marking, it is evident that a competitive process exists and is implemented in a firm which is best-in-class.

In process improvement by bench marking, a firm normally prepares the flow chart to understand how the process really works (*i.e.*, the steps, people and functions involved are studied. Then the process is improved by changing or eliminating activity in the process that does not add value or consumes too much of time or resources. An alternative way of doing process improvement is to abandon the current process and replace it with a brand new process that provides the same functionality but better, faster or cheaper. This approach to process improvement is known as process reengineering.

If an organisation could achieve the same results by either continuous improvement route (with bench marking) or the process reengineering, which one would stand the best chance for success in the work place? Obviously, the answer is – "continuous improvement" route because it would be more readily accepted by the work force and hence more likely to succeed. Continuous improvement will not be perceived by employees as something being forced on them whereas process reengineering tends to be radical and sudden and not readily accepted by employees because often consideration is not given to the human issues in process reengineering. Process reengineering is widely perceived today as a management tool for laying off workers.

In summary, we may say that if there is a very good process to begin with, the firm must use continuous improvement techniques to make it better. On the other hand, if the process is clearly inferior to some used by other firms, then bench marking should be tried by the firm. When the firm can not achieve the kind of improvement it needs from either continuous improvement or bench marking, then process reengineering may be the choice to achieve the needed improvement.

- **Activity B**

Take few parameters like sales figures, manpower, product cost, technical specifications etc. of your organisation and prepare a comparative statement with any other market leader at national or international level.

....

....

....

....

....

....

....

....

....

4.5 BPRE AND ISO STANDARDS

ISO 9000 standards represent a group of international standards of International Organisation for Standardisation (ISO) for the management of quality systems in organisations. It was first introduced in 1987 and later revised in 1994 and 2000. At present, it includes ISO 9000:2000, ISO 9001:2000 and ISO 9004:2000. ISO 9001:2000 lays down the requirements of a "Quality Management System" (QMS). It provides requirements for compliance with standards. ISO 9000:2000 and ISO 9004:2000 provide guidelines for the achievement of standards.

Quality Management System (QMS) is defined as ***"the process of management of the systems of an organisation with regard to its quality related activities for meeting and enhancing customer satisfaction and also taking care of all other interested parties such as legislative and regulatory bodies, shareholders, suppliers, employees etc."*** The Quality Management Principles are given below:

(i) Customer focused organisation, *(ii)* Leadership, *(iii)* Involvement of people, *(vi)* Process approach, *(v)* Systems approach to management, *(vi)* Continual improvement, *(vii)* Factual approach to decision making and *(viii)* Mutually beneficial supplier relationship.

The ISO 9000:2000 is based on Quality Management Principles as well as "Plan-Do-Check-Act" Improvement Cycle.

The ISO 9000 standards are used for *(i)* Internal audit, *(ii)* Vendor assessment and *(iii)* Supplier capability.

Internal audit : An organisation can audit its existing systems with reference to the standard to provide feed back to management regarding the deficiencies of the system.

Vendor assessment : To assess and ensure a vendor's capability to consistently meet the quality standards for product standards desired by the organisation.

Supplier capability : To provide confidence to its customers regarding its capability to consistently meet the quality standards desired by the customer.

Contents of ISO 9000: The ISO 9000 is a family of standards comprising:

(i) ISO 9000:2000 — Quality Management Systems – Fundamentals and vocabulary.

(ii) ISO 9001:2000 — Quality Management Systems – Requirement.

(iii) ISO 9004:2000 — Quality Management Systems – Fundamentals and vocabulary.

In ISO 9001:2000 is the most comprehensive standard in the series: It specifies system requirements in purchase, design and development, production, installation and servicing. This is the only contractual situational standard for which organisations can be certified.

The ISO 9001:2000 standard recommends that an organisation should:

(i) ***Decide its quality policy*:** Determine how the policy is to be implemented and design a system accordingly.

(ii) ***Implement the system*:** Review the system regularly to gauge its effectiveness. Review the system regularly to gauge benefits from continuous improvement of product, process, and customer satisfaction. ISO 9004:2000 provides guidelines to the organisation on all the above activities.

- **Activity C**

Collect data about number of clauses in ISO-9001 : 2000 standards.

....

....

....

....

....

....

....

....

....

4.6 PROCESS APPROACH IN ISO 9001:2000

The International Standard promotes the adoption of a process approach when developing, implementing and improving the effectiveness of a quality management system, to enhance customer satisfaction by meeting customer requirements.

To function effectively, an organisation has to identify and manage various linked activities. A **process** is an activity which uses resources and is managed in order to enable the conversion of a set of inputs into a set of outputs.

The application of a system of processes within an organisation together with the identification and interactions of these processes and their management can be referred to as the **"process approach."** The process approach provides control over the linkage between the individual processes within the system of processes as well as over their combination and interactions.

Such an approach when used in a quality management system, emphasises the importance of:

(i) understanding and meeting requirements.

(ii) the need to consider processes in terms of added value.

(iii) obtaining results of process performance and effectiveness and

(iv) continuous improvement of processes based on objective measurement.

Quality systems have to be tailor-made to suit the requirements of the organisation in order to be effective. Therefore the standard only provides the basic frameworks for the system (*i.e.*, what to do) and offers unlimited scope within the basic framework. *For example*, if we take the "quality policy," the standard does not specify the contents of the policy, which could be anything between producing zero defects or to produce within a certain level of defects. The standard specifies that whatever be the quality policy, the management should ensure that it is understood and implemented at all levels in the organisation.

The salient aspects of the ISO 9001:2000 standards are:

(i) The standard specifies that the quality system be documented through quality manuals, work instructions, organisation charts, process charts etc.

(ii) In any customer-supplier relationship (internal/external) the onus is on the supplier to fully clarify and comprehend all customer requirements, stated as well as implied.

(iii) The standard does not specify requirements of cost of quality and does not dwell upon employee participation, morale attitudinal change etc.

A comparison between BPRE and ISO 9000:2000 reveals that:

(i) Both BPRE and ISO 9000 are driven by top management. The CEO should take initiative to introduce them. Since these activities include company wide cross-functional activities, only the CEO of the company can assume the leadership and exercise control to ensure the compliance of various departments involved in improvement activities.

(ii) Sustained efforts are needed to maintain both BPRE and ISO 9000 standards.

(iii) For organisations where the existing quality management system in quite close to ISO 9000, the benefits of ISO 9000 certification are marginal. But even in organisations which are having ISO 9000 certification, the potential benefits from implementing BPRE are quite enormous.

(iv) Both BPRE and ISO 9000 are process oriented. BPRE is concerned with process redesign to achieve dramatic improvements in critical business processes. ISO 9000 focuses on processes to be followed for compliance with international quality standards.

(v) Both BPRE and ISO 9000 certification are essential for the survival and growth of an organisation in a globally competitive market.

To summarise, it may be noted that the common factors of BPRE and ISO 9000 quality standards are: *(i)* top-down approach, *(ii)* need for sustained efforts, *(iii)* process orientation and *(vi)* driven by market forces for the survival and growth of the firm in the global market.

In conclusion, we may say that BPRE focuses on customer needs. It is a process centred approach which discards non-value adding tasks and adds value to customers. It helps in improving the efficiency and effectiveness of the organisation which implements BPRE. Therefore it is similar to other approaches such as TQM, QFD, ISO 9000 standards etc., in helping the organisation to achieve highest efficiency and effectiveness.

4.7 SUMMARY

An organisation can strive to bring improvements in the form of continuous incremental improvement or drastic, dramatic, innovation improvement (through Business Process Reengineering). These two improvement processes can be taken up simultaneously.

Reengineering (or Business Process Reengineering referred to as BPRE in short) is closely related to Total Quality Management (TQM) because it can be one of the best tools to achieve total quality and to improve a company's performance significantly. TQM comprises both continuous improvement and BPRE to achieve improvements in quality. Both TQM and BPR primarily focus on customers, both are process-oriented and both involve cross-functional activities. While TQM aims at process improvement, BPR aims at drastic changes to improve a process, if possible discarding the existing process and developing an entirely new, improved process.

Both TQM and BPRE emphasise cultural changes in the organisation and behavioural changes in employees. Both require top management support. Both are to be implemented on continuous basis. Both stress on involvement of employees at all levels and on quality enhancement.

BPRE and Quality Function Development (QFD) are related. QFD is a practice to design a process in response to customer needs. Both BPRE and QFD focus on customers, are applied to a wide variety of business processes, add value to customers and cross-functional in approach.

BPRE is related to bench marking. In TQM practice, process improvement is carried out continuously, bench marking the best-in-class business practices of other world class companies.

But BPRE is considered only when it is impossible to use bench-marking approach to process improvement. The continuous improvement route is more acceptable to employees than BPRE because they perceive that continuous improvement forced on them. Process reengineering is perceived as a management tool for laying off workers.

BPRE and ISO standards (ISO 9000:2000) are also related because both have top-down approach, have need for sustained efforts, process orientation and are driven by market forces for the survival and growth of the company.

BPRE and TQM focus on customer needs, strive to improve customer satisfaction, add value to customers and improve the efficiency and effectiveness of the organisation which implements them.

4.8 SELF ASSESSMENT QUESTIONS

1. Discuss the relevance of BPRE as a part of TQM.
2. Discuss the features which are common to BPRE and to each of the following (a) TQM, (b) QFD and (c) ISO 9000 standards.
3. What are ISO 9000:2000 standards?
4. What is "Quality Management System?"
5. Discuss the areas of application of ISO 9000:2000 standards.
6. What are the contents of ISO 9000?
7. Discuss the salient aspects of ISO 9000:2000.
8. Discuss how BPRE enhances the efficiency and effectiveness of a firm.

♦ ♦ ♦ ♦ ♦

5 Chapter

IMPLEMENTATION OF BPRE

Objectives

After going through this chapter, you would be able to :

- Understand, how to identify a Business Process.
- Learn about various types of Business Processes.
- Understand meaning of Business Process Management.
- Learn how to apply a Process Reengineering model to bring in break through improvements.
- Learn about various phases and steps involved in the Process-Reengineering model.
- Learn about potential benefits from BPRE as well as risk associated with BPRE projects.

Structure

5.1 INTRODUCTION

Proper implementation of management concept like Business Process Reengineering (BPRE) requires a clear understanding of the concepts amongst all the employees. Hence some basic concepts of BPRE are discussed in this chapter to give the reader a clear understanding of the same.

What is a Business Process?

A process takes inputs and performs value-added activities on those inputs to create an output. Every business, whether related to manufacturing or services, has key processes that it must absolutely perform well in order to attract and retain customers to whom to sell their products or services. A business process starts with the first event that initiates a course of action. Organisations have many processes that enable them to provide products and services for the customers. Some of the processes typically found in any organisation include financial management, customer service, equipment installation and maintenance, production and inventory control, employee hiring, training, performance appraisal, payroll, software development, product or service design, creation, inspection, packaging, delivery and improvement etc. The key or critical business processes work together within an organisation so as to achieve the organisation's mission and objectives. If an organisation's processes are not integrated properly or if they work ineffectively, then the organisation cannot optimise its performance. Hence in order to be effective and to supply what the customer needs, wants and expects, an organisation must focus on maintaining and improving its business processes that enable them to meet these needs, wants and expectations.

Exhibit 5.1 : Illustrates the Business Processes

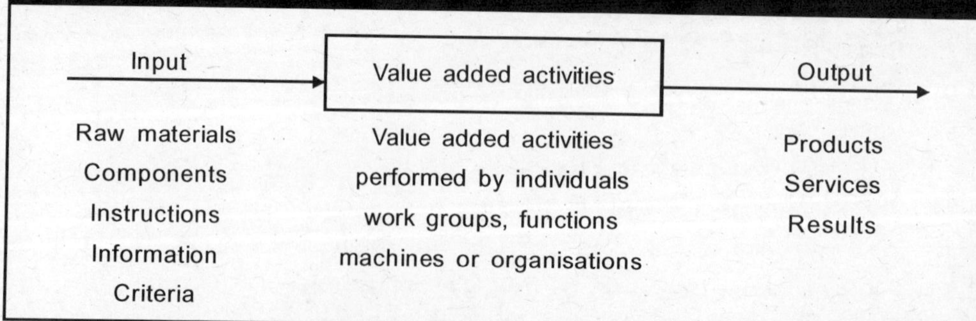

Identification of key processes : Key processes are the business processes which have the greatest impact on customer's value perceptions about the product or service and the greatest impact on customer retention. To increase their competitiveness, effective organisations focus on system and process improvement efforts on business processes that increase their competitiveness. Today's organisations face the challenge of implementing systems which reduce the frequency of human errors and of devising ways of limiting the consequences of errors which do occur. Effective organisations design systems which investigate and analyse process performance so as to facilitate detection of root cause problems and taking corrective action. Organisations which manage their business processes effectively, realise significant improvements which make an impact on the profitability of the organisation.

5.2 TYPES OF BUSINESS PROCESSES

Business processes are sequences and combinations of business activities. They can be classified into *(i)* ***external customer facing processes*** which deliver products and services of value, *(ii)* ***management processes*** which control and coordinate the business activities and ensure that business objectives are achieved and *(iii)* ***support processes*** which provide infrastructural and other assistance to business processes.

Business processes can further be differentiated into *(i)* ***knowledge based processes*** and *(ii)* ***operational processes***.

Knowledge based processes include product development, research activities, advertisement and management consulting. These processes rely on the knowledge and creativity of the people involved. They are not dominant in BPRE projects.

Operational processes are at the heart of most BPRE efforts. They are classified by their relative stability, standardisation and repeatability. Examples of operational processes are – customer service, procurement and manufacturing. Operational processes are further classified into key processes and secondary processes. Key processes directly support the mission and the strategies of the company.

5.3 WHAT IS BUSINESS PROCESS MANAGEMENT?

Business process management is a process which ensures continued improvement in an organisation's performance. Business process management needs leadership and guidance. At times, it means taking a ***radical-change perspective*** which involves reexamination and perhaps renewal of the fundamental tenets of the process. At other times, the process may undergo a cycle of continuous review and enhancement considering minor adjustments in the process. But at all times, the process management team should understand, examine and challenge the fit of the process under review with other processes in the organisation.

Exhibit 5.2 : Process Management Hexagon

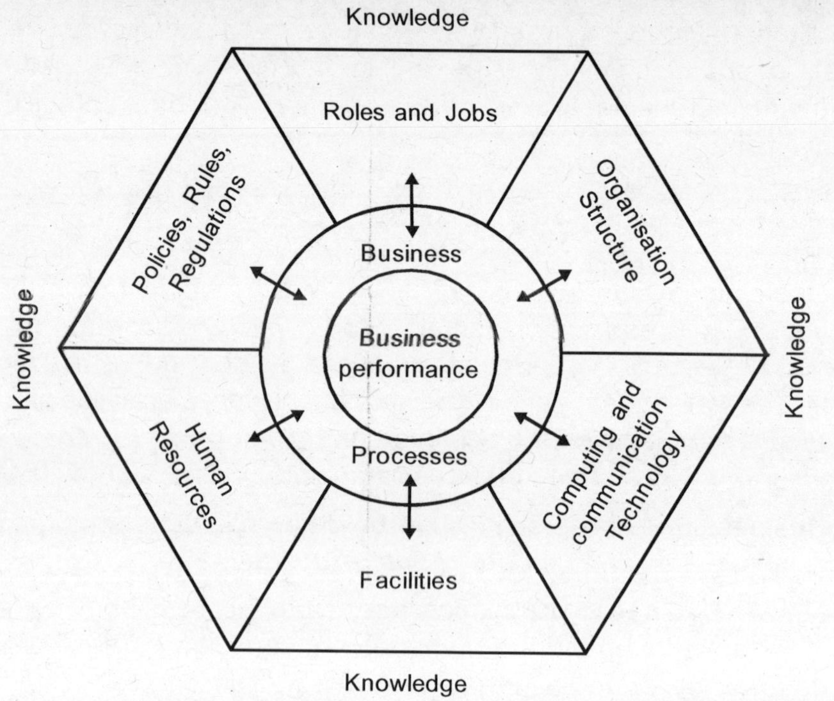

Much like people, facilities and information, processes are also considered as assets of an organisation and hence they need to be managed well. Well-managed processes will pay-off in terms of performance to the organisation. Processes are instrumental for synchronisation of other assets and aspects of change. They are the organising framework for all other components of the organisation shown in *exhibit 5.2*.

Process management ensures that all other factors shown in *Exhibit 5.2* are in sync to deliver performance. The workflow from input through transformation to output aligns with the desired results. The technology, people and facilities enable the process to deliver repeatedly. The policies, rules, regulations and organisational structure provides the controls to execute the process well. Knowledge and intellectual capital are embedded in the physical and technological assets of a business and embodied in its human abilities.

Principles of Process Management

A number of fundamental principles must be honoured in order to deliver business results to customers and to satisfy the needs of the organisation's other stake holders. These principles are

1. Business change must be performance driven.
2. Business change must be based on stake holders.
3. Business change decisions must be traceable to the stake holder criteria.
4. The business must be segmented along business process lines to synchronize change.
5. Business process must be managed holistically.
6. Process renewal initiatives must inspire shared insight.
7. Process renewal initiatives must be conducted from outside in.
8. Process renewal initiatives must be conducted in an iterative, time-boxed approach.
9. Business change in all about people.
10. Business change is a journey, not a destination.

5.4 PROCESS - REENGINEERING MODEL

In the chapter 4, we discussed the need for process reengineering and the core elements of process-reengineering. Before discussing the process reengineering model, we need to clear the confusion caused by some organisations using the terms *work process reengineering, business process reengineering* and *business reengineering* synonymously. To avoid confusion, it is better to consider reengineering at three levels which will make the implementation of Business Process Reengineering or Process Reengineering easier.

The three levels of reengineering are

(i) **Work process reengineering** which deals with any process in a firm that describes the sequence of activities through which a major function is performed, *for example,* packing a finished product, processing a customer order or processing a purchase requisition, hiring a new employee, carrying out preventive maintenance of a machine etc.

(ii) **Business process reengineering** is concerned with the whole process of an organisation. It describes the entire sequence of activities directly or indirectly connected with satisfying the needs of a firm's customers while generating quality return on investment for share holders. The **business process** is made up of all the

work processes in the firm. It includes the processes of the business partners such as suppliers of materials or services upstream or a distributor downstream.

(iii) **Business reengineering** goes beyond Business Process Reengineering (BPRE). It deals with all aspects of running the business. It includes the management style, the organisational structure, the business philosophy and marketing strategies, production and operations, human resource management, purchasing, organisational structures, accounting concepts, information systems and global business strategy.

However, we limit our discussions to business process reengineering (BPRE) which is a part of business reengineering.

5.5 APPLYING A PROCESS REENGINEERING MODEL

There is no only one **"right"** way to approach process reengineering. But we can use guidelines to approach our process reengineering effort. The process-reengineering model illustrated in the *exhibit 5.3* gives us guidelines that will pave the way for our reengineering effort.

Exhibit 5.3 : "Process-Reengineering" Model

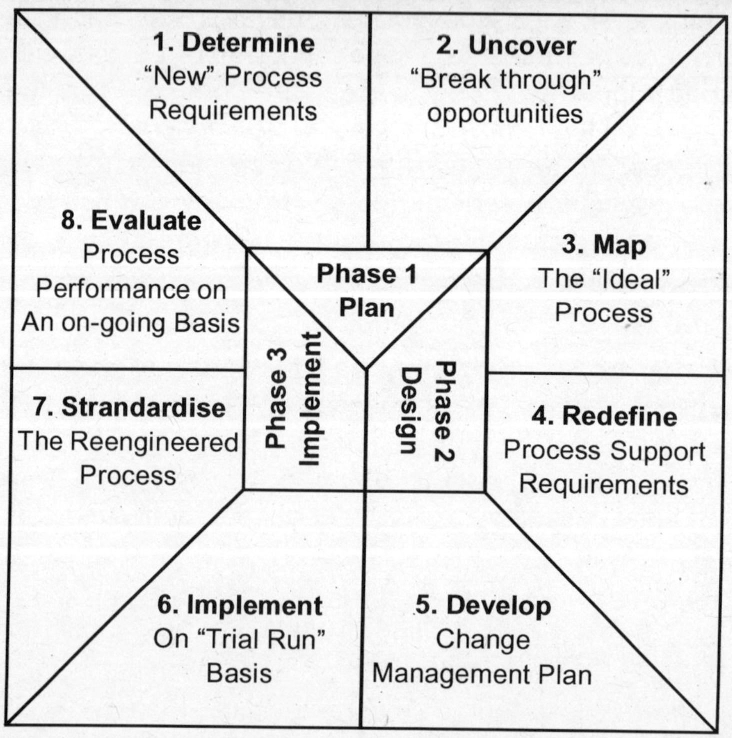

The Process Reengineering Model is structured around three phases namely : *(i)* Planning, *(ii)* Designing and *(iii)* Implementing.

Each of the three phases contains major steps which provide direction toward making the efforts more effective. The three phases and their major steps are listed in *Box 5.1*.

Box 5.1 : Phases and Steps involved in the Processes-Reengineering Model

Phase	Steps
Phase 1 **Plan**	*(i)* **Determine** "New" Process Requirements *(ii)* **Uncover** "Break through" opportunities • Analyse **"as is"** capability • Envision desired state • Identify process performance gaps
Phase 2 **Design**	*(i)* **Map** The "Ideal" Process • Complete preliminary work • Set new goals and establish measures • Create a new process flow chart *(ii)* **Redefine** Process Support Requirement *(iii)* **Develop** Change Management Plan
Phase 3 **Implement**	*(i)* **Implement** on "Trial Run" Basis *(ii)* **Standardise** The Reengineering process *(iii)* **Evaluate** Process Performance on An ongoing Basis

PHASE ONE : PLANNING PHASE

A close look is taken at the process to be reengineered. The requirements for the "new" process are forecasted by focusing on the current and future needs of customers, analysing what is currently accomplished by the old process, creating a vision of what is to be achieved by the reengineered process and zeroing in on the differences between the two. At the end of this phase, the reengineering team should have a good grip on reality. If the planning results in a great desire to change, the reengineering team will process to the next phase.

PHASE TWO : DESIGN PHASE

This phase involves designing a reengineered process which starts with actual mapping of the new process and moves to the development of a change management plan. In between these two steps, the jobs are redefined and redesigned, taking a careful look at the technology available and considering the organisation's resources.

PHASE THREE : IMPLEMENTATION PHASE

This phase involves implementing a reengineered process. The new process is tested and its success is gauged. An atmosphere of continuous process improvement is promoted in which employees strive to make improvements that make a difference to the customer.

5.6 SELECTING A PROCESS REENGINEERING TEAM

A process reengineering effort begins with the formation of a team of people who drive the reengineering effort. The factors to be considered when designing a team and selecting the members are:

(i) Should there be an **interim** team with the responsibility for looking at the need for reengineering?

(ii) Should the team manage the process reengineering effort from the beginning to end?

(iii) Should team members be assigned to the team on a full time or part time basis?

(iv) Should team members be selected for their first-hand knowledge of the process being reengineered, their level of authority or for other reasons?

(v) Should the team be made up of small core group or a large group of people who can contribute to the group?

(vi) How much autonomy should the team have?

The answers to these questions depend on the scope of the process being reengineered, the effort involved and who needs to have input. The decision regarding the size and structure of the team is taken at this stage.

Two broad options regarding team size are *(a)* "core team", *(b)* "Full team".

The **"core team"** is a small team consisting of three or four members who have strong commitment toward reengineering, who devote full or nearly full time for reengineering effort. These members are selected based on their ability to manage themselves. Others may be added to the core team as and when needed. The "full team" is a larger team having, eight to twelve or even more members. It comprises those involved in the process, as well as process suppliers and customers. The participation of members is usually part time (approximately 10 to 25% of their time is committed to reengineering effort).

The members are selected for their ability to make a specific contribution to the team and they stay on the team as the reengineering effort continuous.

Advantages and disadvantages of "core team" and "full team" are listed in *Box 5.2*.

Box. 5.2 : Advantages and disadvantages of core team and full team

Core team	Full team
Advantages	
(i) A small team can achieve results faster than a larger team. *(ii)* Members are more committed to the task because of deeper involvement. *(iii)* Others who need to contribute need not be pulled from their regular job positions until they are actually needed.	*(ii)* Most or all of the skills and input are built into the team when it is formed. *(ii)* The team has contacts and resources available in various parts of the organisation.
Disadvantages	
(i) The team may not have all the skills required. *(ii)* The team may become isolated from the rest of the organisation.	*(i)* It may not move as quickly as a smaller team. *(ii)* When reengineering task is handled by a "committee" type of group, some team members may take it lightly. *(iii)* Managing and coordinating a larger team is more difficult.

The phases and steps involved in the process reengineering model are briefly discussed in the following section.

5.7 PHASE ONE

STEP 1 : DETERMINE "NEW" PROCESS REQUIREMENTS

The following activities are involved in this step.

(a) **Planning the reengineering effort :** Since reengineering a process should result in benefits to the organisation and change will improve

the performance of the organisation, it is necessary to thoroughly plan for, design and implement this reengineered process. This phase is critical because it may reveal that reengineering a particular process won't add value, or it does not address customer needs or that the required resources may not be available.

Determining *"new"* process requirements involves uncovering what customers and the market place require of this process and focusing on the own requirements of the organisation.

(b) **Knowing what the customers want :** Successful reengineering projects realign processes to satisfy customer demands. Organisations that undergo process reengineering believe in the standard credo of ***"the customer comes first"***.

(c) **Identifying the customers :** Before determining what the customers want, it is necessary to know who the customers of the process are. The customers include both external customers and internal customers of the firm. Two key questions to be answered while identifying the customers are;

(i) Who is affected by this process?

(ii) Who depends on this process for information, products or service?

(d) **Zeroing in on customer concern :** Once the customers are identified, it is necessary to zero in on what concerns them. Customer requirement areas from the process to be reengineered are determined by brainstorming with the team members. *For example,* some of the customer "requirement areas" could be: *timeliness, cost, accuracy, functionality, reponsiveness, quantity, dimension, yield, price, availability* etc.

(e) **Soliciting customer input :** Interview or survey questions are developed to solicit customer input, once the customers are identified and their areas of concern are zeroed in. Questions that related to the areas of customers' concern are designed. Key information that will aid the process reengineering effort is collected from the customers using interview method or a survey.

A knowledge of the customers' want is helpful to reengineer the process correctly. After all, reengineering is not taken up just because the CEO of the firm wants it or a major competitor is reengineering a process, but because the customers' want has to be met.

(f) **What is the market place providing? :** A firm should compare its position in the market with that of its competitor. The firm should have a good look at what its competitors offer. If the customers have found

some discrepancy in what the firm offers and its customers are preferring competitors' offers then the firm might opt for process reengineering so that it can offer some benefits to its customers in the form of superior products or services. Even if the customers are quite satisfied with the process the firm is considering for reengineering, they won't remain satisfied for long because competitors are doing better.

New product development is a process that lends itself well to reengineering. If a firm's competitors continually offer new products much faster than the firm does, then the firm must start looking at process reengineering.

To keep up with what the market place offers, a firm must:

(i) Know what is out there in the market place.

(ii) Keep a close watch on its competitors.

(iii) Be open to new ideas, services and/or products.

(g) **Using Benchmarking :** It is not enough for a firm to know that some other firm is doing better than it, but also it should know which is the other firm that does better. Bench making can provide a firm with the inside information it needs to reengineer a process. Benchmarking involves learning and discovering how other work groups within a firm perform common processes and how other competitive or world class firms operate. The firm must choose successful operations and try to adapt the processes of "best-in-class" firms to its own processes.

Benchmarking is critical to any process-reengineering effort because it provides goals to achieve and aids in helping a firm envision and design its new process.

(h) **What are the firm's operating requirements?**

When a firm knows what its customers want and it has identified what the market place offers, it is ready to look at what it needs to achieve to meet the wants and demands of those driving its reengineering effort. The questions posed are:

(i) Does the firm need to reduce costs so that it can offer price reductions to its customers?

(ii) Does it need to become more technology based so that it can improve its process?

(iii) What does the firm expect the reengineered process to do?

(iv) How much costs be reduced?

(v) What new equipments or machines or computer hardware and software to be purchased?

Determining new process requirements involves researching what the customers of a firm want and what the market place offers and determining what operating requirements are needed to set for the new process to meet those demands. Completing this step of the planning phase should provide insight into the forces behind the effort exerted by the firm and prepares it to move forward.

PHASE ONE – STEP 2 : UNCOVER "BREAK THROUGH" OPPORTUNITIES

This step in the planning phase enables the firm to find out the possibility of great improvement in performance if process reengineering is taken up by the firm. The firm will look at its current process to determine what it is accomplishing, create a vision of what the "new process" should be like and figure out the difference between the two.

To uncover break through opportunities, the firm will need to do the following.

(i) Analyse "As Is" capability

(ii) Envision desired state and

(iii) Identify process performance "Gaps"

These are discussed in the following paragraphs.

(a) Analyse "As Is" Capability

Unless the reengineering team knows how the process is currently performing, it can't be sure whether or not process reengineering will benefit the firm. In the reengineering process, all major aspects a process must be defined and then measured to achieve the greatest breakthroughs.

To start with, the **"as is"** process is documented. All the tasks in the process selected for reengineering are defined and mapped out to have a clear and realistic view of the process. This will provide the information that will help the reengineering team in the beginning of the designing phase.

Two basic steps involved in documenting a process are:

(i) List the major process tasks and decisions required to translate inputs into outputs.

(ii) Create a process flowchart which shows how the process currently works. This is to be used as an ongoing working document.

These two steps are discussed below.

(i) **List the major process tasks :** First the reengineering team determines what is the input and output involved in the process. Every

thing in between the input and the output would be the tasks involved in the process. Next, the major tasks and their decision points are listed. After the major tasks are identified, the team should determine what smaller subtasks and decisions link the major tasks together. The following questions should be answered to analyse **"as is"** capability.

(a) What really happens next?

(b) Does some-one need to make a decision before this task?

(c) What approvals are required before proceeding?

(d) Is there anything missing in these tasks?

(ii) **Create a process flow chart :** The process flow chart helps to visually see what happens at each step of the process. The details in the flow chart are limited. Some of the common symbols used in flow charts are shown in *Exhibit 5.4*.

Exhibit 5.4 : Symbols used in Flow Charts

Symbol	Name	Explanation
	Elongated circle	Shows the starting and ending points of a flow chart.
	Box	Indicates any work flow task.
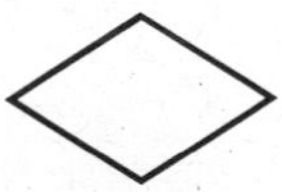	Diamond	Any decision point, each diamond should contains a question that can be answered "yes" or "no".
	Connector	A small circle with a letter is used to connect one task of a flow chart to another.
	Document	A transfer (or output) of a hard copy document.
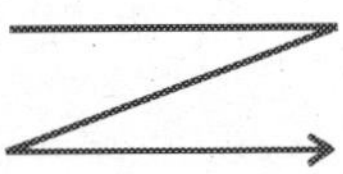	Zig zag arrow	Shows an electronic data transfer.
	Straight arrow	Shows direction of process flow

After the process is documented, it should be measured. Gathering performance data will show where improvement is needed or that the process is not deficient as it was originally thought.

Measurement clears up any discrepancies and provides an opportunity for comparison after the engineered process has been implemented. Data are gathered for each necessary task or section of the process. The data gathered depends on what has to be measured - whether the cost of the whole process has to be measured or the amount of time each task takes has to be measured or how accurately some tasks are performed. It is necessary to measure the "as is" capability of the current process in order to compare the actual process performance to the "new" process requirements. *Exhibit 5.5* illustrates a process flow chart for order fulfilment process.

Exhibit 5.5 : Process chart for order - fulfillment process

(a) Process : Order fulfillment

Task	Major process tasks	Sub tasks/Decisions	Symbol
1.	Customer service executive receives order		
1a		By phone?	
1b		Customer service executive writes information on order form	
1c		By mail or fax?	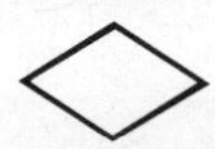
1d		Customer service executive verifies order form	
1e		Appropriate corrections made	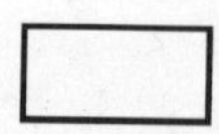
2.	Forward order form to order-entry clerk		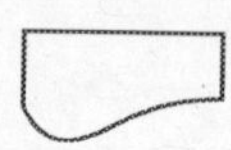
3.	Order-entry clerk enters data		
:	:		
14.	File copy of invoice		

(b) Process Flow chart

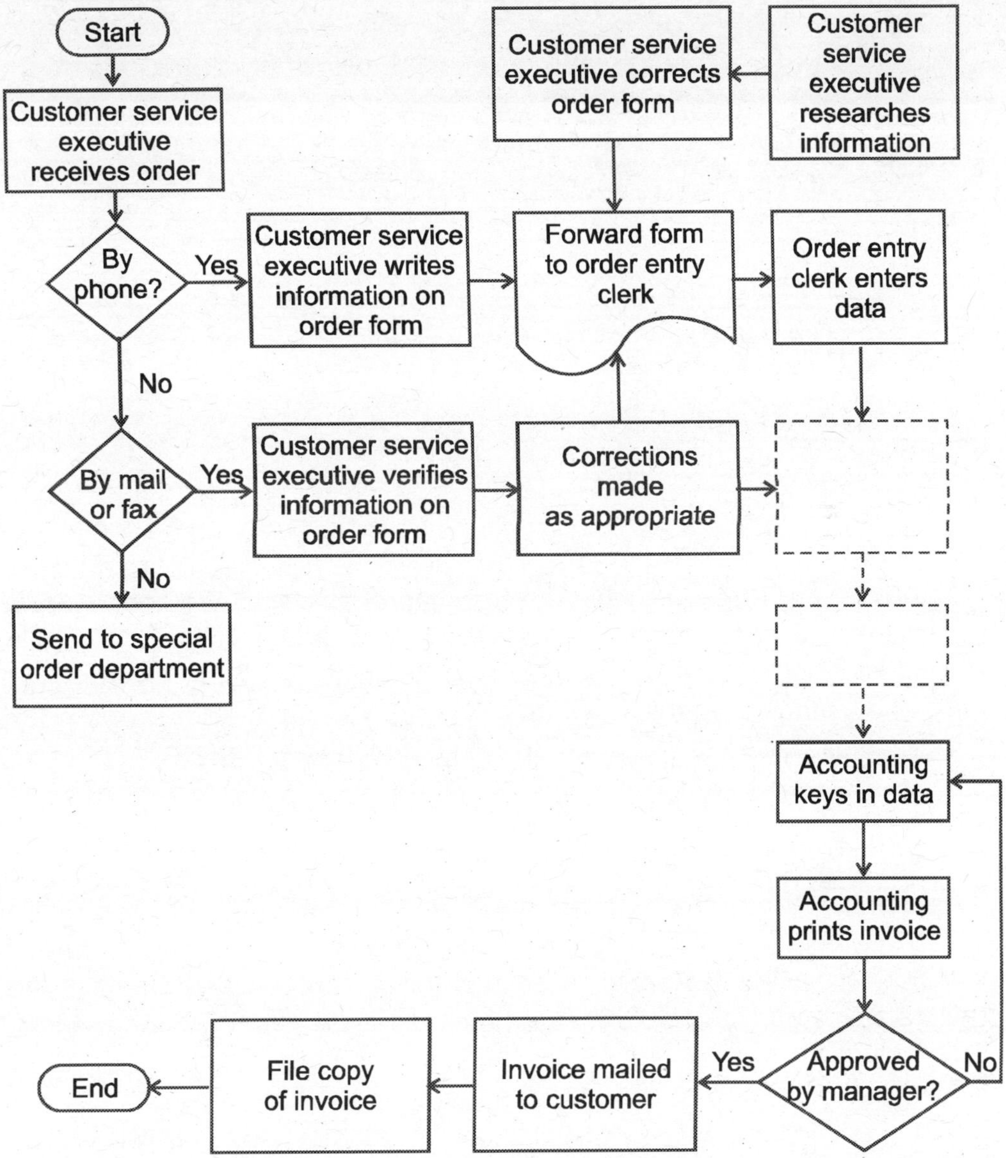

(*Source :* Richard Y. Chang, *"Process Reengineering in Action"*, Wheeler publishing, p.41)

- **Activity A**

Prepare a flow chart for any activity being performed by your department.

....

....

....

....

....

....

....

....

(b) Envision Desired State

This means forgetting what the current process looks like and focusing on what the new process could be and what it could accomplish. The team should look beyond the new process and consider what the environment around the process should look like.

The following questions should be answered by the team.

(i) How will the new process help the customer?

(ii) How will it help the firm?

(iii) How will the environment of the firm change?

It may be helpful for the team to come up with a *"current limitations list"* which details all the factors that constrict the current process. Some of the factors are: organisational structure, technology, regulations and the like. The factors which may limit the potential of the process are examined by the team members who will then start to envision their new process not having any limitations. The envisioning of team members may provide certain benefits or values beyond the expectation of customers. At this stage, any measures or factors identified during bench marking as positive characteristics are included in the new process. The team members and the employees of departments that will be impacted by the process reengineering effort are included in the brainstorming so that their insights will serve to enlarge the picture of the desired state. The brainstorming may address functions of the new process that had not even been considered by the team.

(c) Identify Process Performance "Gaps"

This step helps to decide whether the process is the one to be reengineered or not. The data gathered to is used to measure the current process and compare it with the ideal process. The difference between the two is referred to as a process performance **"gap"**. If the gap is small, there is no need for reengineering, instead, continuous improvement may be considered. But if the gap is big, then a major effort is required in the form of reengineering.

Some of the tasks of the current process may work very well and may meet the identified requirements of the new customers. These tasks need not be changed and can be included **"as is"** in the reengineered process. Other tasks which are detrimental to the firm are discarded and not included in the new process.

Uncovering breakthrough opportunities is a challenging task. If the team is successful in this phase and is more sure than ever that process reengineering will work for the firm, then the team should head for the designing phase.

5.8 PHASE TWO

PHASE 2 – STEP 3 : MAP THE "IDEAL" PROCESS

This step of the designing phase involves mapping the "ideal" process. To map the ideal process, the following substeps are to be followed:

(i) Complete preliminary work

(ii) Set new goals and establish new measures and

(iii) Create a new process flow chart

These steps are briefly discussed below:

(i) **Complete preliminary work :** The process performance gaps identified by the team in the previous step needs to be closed and the team must decide how to close these gaps before drawing an actual map of the new process. The following has to be considered.

(a) Can we make the process simpler?

(b) Are we asking for unneeded reports or data?

(c) Can technology help?

(d) Is new computer hardware or software necessary for the reengineering effort?

(e) Can we reduce time and/or cost?

These considerations apply to most organisations looking to improve processes. The team should not attempt to reengineer a process unless it realises the existence and extent of the deficiencies of the current process. Also the team members should share their ideas and/or conclusions with employees who will be affected by the reengineering effort.

(ii) **Set new goals and establish new measures :** The effort to bridge the gaps will be helpful for setting new goals and establishing new process measures. The team should set goals and establish measures worthy of reengineering effort but also should be realistic. The goals set and the measures established must at least meet customer requirements. From there, the team must try to meet or beat what the competitors provide.

(iii) **Create a new process flow chart :** Starting with a clean slate, the team should work on designing a flow chart for the new process. Reengineering the process should involve something new, not just reducing the old. After preparing the flow chart, each section of the process must be checked with the employees working directly with the process.

Mapping the **"ideal"** process results in a practical application of the planning effort of the team.

- **Activity B**

Set the new performance goals for the activity for which flow process chart was made as activity A and modify the flow process chart.

....

....

....

....

....

....

....

....

....

PHASE 2 – STEP 4 : REDEFINE PROCESS SUPPORT REQUIREMENTS

After mapping the **"new"** process by creating a flow chart that identifies the steps in the process, and establishing new measures for the process, the team has to decide what the new process requires to support it. The team should decide what will be required for the reengineered process to operate as designed.

Three different areas of support with in an organisation that need to be redefined whenever a process is reengineered are:

(i) People, *(ii)* Technology/support tools and *(iii)* Finance.

People or human element is an important element of process reengineering because if the process is completed by people, they will be affected by the reengineering effort. The reengineering may involve redesign of the way people do a portion of their jobs, elimination of some of their work and even a total change in what they are required to do. Hence a **"Role-Transition Work Sheet"** for each position is prepared and the present and future job responsibilities of each position in the firm are listed in it.

The second area of support is technology support tools required for reengineering process. Technology required can be complicated and costly or it can be simple and inexpensive. The technological tool identified to support the reengineered process must be included in the new design of the process.

Benchmarking can be helpful at this stage. If other firms are using certain technology to meet their customer demands, then the team may decide to go for it.

Technology in often an essential ingredient of process reengineering but more support is needed for success. If a technology is a must for the reengineered process, a type of technology needed for the firm must be chosen. Also other support tools such as furnitures, fax machines, telephones etc., may be required - Even more people may have to be hired and additional work space may be required for the reengineered process.

The third area of support is finance. A cost/benefit analysis of the reengineering project helps to determine whether it is advisable to move forward. Cost/benefit analysis can be described as ***"a complete, realistic comparison of costs and resulting benefits associated with implementing a decision"***.

Redefining the process requirements provides a greater knowledge of what reengineering the process entails. If the benefits appropriately out weigh the costs, then the team can go ahead with the change management plan.

PHASE 2 – STEP 5 : DEVELOP CHANGE MANAGEMENT PLAN

This step involves developing a change management plan that will help the firm execute a quantum leap forward toward radical improvement, as flawlessly as possible. This step requires the following activities.

(i) **Designing the change management plan :** This is the final segment of the designing phase *i.e.,* phase two, after the reengineering team has mapped the **"ideal"** process, redefined the process support requirements and analysed the organisational impact. It is done by

(a) Identifying change management plan requirements.

(b) Choosing a planning process and format and

(c) Deciding how to move the action plan forward.

These are briefly discussed in the following section.

(ii) **Identifying change management plan requirements :** This involves deciding what will be needed to get from the old process to the new process and what it will take – time, money, acting managers, consultants, new roles etc.

Decisions have to be taken regarding:

(a) What the change management plan will require?

(b) Will it be necessary to hire people for training employees?

(c) Will consultants be in charge of training?

(d) How much time will it take to complete each step in the plan?

(e) Will it be necessary to form new teams to choose the best machinery or computer system for the firms?

(iii) **Choosing a planning process and format :** The reengineering team will need to devise an action plan that is both detailed and specific. The action plan should include project time tables, contingency plans, feed back and communication systems.

(iv) **Deciding how to move the action plan forward :** Since the action plan will impact a number of employees of the firm, it is necessary to include them in the plan. The team should decide how to start the reengineering effort, get progress updates and keep employees excited about the changes.

Developing change management plan for the reengineered process completes the designing phase. The next phase is the implementation phase.

5.9 PHASE THREE

STEP 6 : IMPLEMENT ON "TRIAL RUN" BASIS

The "trial run" will determine whether the team should be permitted to proceed with its process reengineering effort. Even though the "trial run" may take upto six months, it is a vital step in the implementation phase.

This step involves two activities:

(a) Conducting a pilot test to ensure that the proposed changes will dramatically improve the process.

(b) Assessing the results and making necessary adjustments in the flow chart.

PHASE 3 – STEP 7 : STANDARDISE THE REENGINEERING PROCESS

Standardising means that the new process becomes an accepted and established process within the firm. The new process might be documented and new guidelines are written down. Also the job descriptions are revised to accurately reflect the new process and the copies of the new job descriptions are distributed to the employees. Employees are encouraged to participate. The customer - survey data is shared with all employees and the process-reengineering effort is kept focused on the customer.

PHASE 3 – STEP 8 : EVALUATE PROCESS PERFORMANCES ON AN ONGOING BASIS

As implementation progresses, the team needs to gather and evaluate data. Measurement results should indicate movement towards the goals of the team for the new process. The process performance should be evaluated on an ongoing basis to determine the extent of progress of the team.

This step of the implementation phase requires the team to hold regular meetings and celebrate progress.

The process reengineering team should not disband as soon as implementation begins or even after it is over. The meetings should continue because the team has to evaluate progress and solve any problems that may arise.

To evaluate progress, the team must analyse measurement data. Use of tools such as a **"run chart"** to compare one period data to another helps the team to verify whether the engineered process has improved performance and if so by how much.

The team should use meetings to discuss any problems. The team members should be encouraged to discuss the problems with the employees. Depending on the process reengineering effort, the team may meet for quite sometime (two years is not uncommon). After sometime the team may feel that the process can be evaluated and continuously improved by the process owners. When the new process is firmly established the organisation has achieved its goals of dramatic improvement, the reengineering team and its leader can be moved else-where for more effective use. Knowing when to disband is also crucial to the effective process reengineering team.

A successful process-reengineering effort deserves commendation. All the persons who took part in achieving a quantum leap towards radical improvement must be rewarded. A formal celebration or informally recognising the winners is desired.

The implementation phase is both exhilarating and exhausting. It takes time but it can bring new life to the organisation which will enhance the competitiveness of the organisation.

5.10 BUSINESS REENGINEERING PROJECTS

A ***project*** is a well organised development of a tangible or intangible end-product that has a discrete beginning, a discrete end and a discrete deliverable.

A ***Business Reengineering Project*** effects revolutionary change to an organisation. The project deliverables are radically improved business processes, which satisfy customer requirements much better than before, and which achieve drastic improvements to the operational results of a company.

Organisational change is not "happening" but intentional, usually triggered by external events to the organisation. Planned change can be effected incrementally or revolutionary. The action roles in the change process are: *(i)* The **Initiator**, usually, though not always the responsibility of top management, *(ii)* The **Change Implementers**, the project team or change agent, often represented by middle-management, and external consultants and *(iii)* The **Change Recipients** or **Change Targets**, all people affected by the change. Organisational change is effected through projects.

Project management is the discipline, that cultivates the expertise to plan, monitor, track and manage the people, the time, the budget and the quality of the work on projects.

Project management of a Business Reengineering project is a set of principles, methods, tools and techniques for effective management of the introduction of new or drastically changed business processes in a corporation.

Box 5.3: The Principles of Business Reengineering
1. Externally focus on end customers and on the generation of greater value for customers. 2. Internally focus on harnessing more of potential of people and applying it to those activities which identify and deliver value to customers. 3. Encourage learning and development by building creative working environments. 4. Think and execute as much activity as possible horizontally, concentrating on flows and processes (including communication) through the organisation. 5. Give customers and users a single and accessible point of contact through which they can harness whatever resources and people are relevant to their needs and interests. 6. Remove non-value added activities, undertake parallel activities, speed up response and development times. 7. Concentrate on outputs rather than inputs and link performance measures and rewards to customer related outputs. 8. Give priority to the delivery of value rather than the maintenance of management control. 9. Network related people and activities. 10. Move discretion and authority closer to the customer and re-allocate responsibilities between the organisation, its suppliers and customers. 11. Encourage involvement and participation through error-tolerant leadership. 12. Wherever possible people should assume full responsibility for managing and controlling themselves. 13. Ensure people are equipped, motivated and empowered to do what is expected of them. 14. Work should be broadened without sacrificing depth of expertise in strategic areas. 15. Avoid overspecification. Don't replace creative thinking with software tools. 16. Keep the number of core processes to a minimum (approx. 12). They all should be directed to external customers. 17. Build learning, renewal and short feedback loops into business processes. 18. Ensure that continuous improvement is built into implemented solutions.

BUSINESS REENGINEERING PROJECT MANAGEMENT

One way to classify Business Reengineering Projects is based on their ***organisational scope*** which can be narrow or broad. Another way is to classify by ***objective***. The Box 5.4 combines both views, matrix rows describe organisational view and columns describe the objectives view.

Box 5.4: Classification of Business Reengineering Projects

Project Type	**Process Improvement** Cost– Reduction	**Achieving Best-In-Class** Competitive Parity	**Break-Point** Rewriting the Rules
Intrafunctional Projects are aimed at single and isolated tasks, activities or single function	**Example:** Eliminate costly paper work by introducing an e-mail system to internal communication	**Example:** Reengineer the sourcing process to ensure that the lowest cost suppliers are being selected	**Example:** A company uses a digital voice recording system to streamline its acquisition process and to improve communications
Interfunctional Projects target cross-functional business proce -sses, but are contained within a business unit	**Example:** A bank has created a simplified, one page form for loan applications for those customers seeking up to ₹ 20 lakhs	**Example:** Introduce self-directed work teams to the order management process in a manufacturing firm	**Example:** A bank dissolves al existing branches and introduces an extremely user-friendly direct banking system on the Internet
Interorganisational Projects bridge between two or more business units such as the firm and its customers and suppliers	**Example:** Link up with one particular vendor for cost saving purposes in product design and parts delivery (single source concept)	**Example:** Reengineering the delivery process between a German machine manufacturer and all its European automotive parts suppliers (just-in -time processes)	**Example:** An automotive company extern-alises all employ-ees, except a staff of 30 people Former employees turn into entrepreneurs and form a network of suppliers to gether with other vendors

BUSINESS REENGINEERING APPROACHES

Business Reengineering can achieve the potential success only if it is deployed strategically and linked to business goals. There is a large number of different project management methodologies available for Business Reengineering. Information technology and Team Work can be considered key to most methodologies. One key methodology referred to as "The Hammer/ Champy Methodology" is discussed in the following paragraphs.

5.11 THE HAMMER/CHAMPY METHODOLOGY

The steps involved in this methodology and their objectives are illustrated in *Box 5.5* below.

Box 5.5: The Hammer/Champy Methodology

Project Steps	Objectives
(i) Introduction into Business Reengineering	The CEO initiates the project. He/she describes briefly and pragmatically the current business situation to start actions. He/she introduces his/her vision to the employees of the company.
(ii) Identification of Business Processes	This step looks at the broad picture, of how processes interact within the company and in relation to the outside world. The deliverable is a geographical display of all processes.
(iii) Selection of Business Processes	This step serves to select such processes, which once reengineered – will lead to high value for the company's customers. Also processes that lead themselves to easy reengineering are being selected.
(iv) Understanding the selected Business Process	This step does not dwell on a detailed analysis of the functioning of the selected business processes, rather concentrates on the performance of the current processes as opposed to what is expected from them in the future.
(v) Redesign of the selected Business Processes	This step is according to Hammer/Champy the most creative of all. It is characterised by imagination, lateral thinking etc.
(vi) Implementation of redesigned Business Processes	The last step covers the implementation phase of the Business Reengineering project. Hammer/Champy do not talk about implementation as much as about project planning. They believe in the success of the implementation, once the five preliminary steps have been properly performed.

5.12 POTENTIAL BENEFITS FROM IMPLEMENTATION OF BUSINESS REENGINEERING PROJECTS

The success of Business Reengineering projects is measured by the real achievement of project objectives. Companies undertaking Business Reengineering projects expect drastic improvements in business process results.

A study of Business Reengineering projects in 30 Mexican businesses all from the target 500 businesses in Mexico showed impressive results. Business Reengineering had impacted mainly in management costs (82%), production costs (57%) and distribution cost reduction (39%).

Box 5.6 lists the areas of reported achievements and improvements in percentage.

Box 5.6: Achievements of 30 business reengineering projects in Mexico

Areas of reported achievements	Improvements in % age
1. Cost reduction	69%
2. Time optimisation	62%
3. Better service efficiency	59%
4. Productivity increase	59%
5. More precise information for decision making	52%
6. Quality improvement	45%
7. Better financial control	41%
8. Better profitability	38%
9. Hierarchical levels reduction	38%
10. Technology update	34%
11. Personnel motivation	34%
12. Sales increase	28%
13. Market survival	28%
14. Reduction of business losses	21%
15. Environmental impact	17%
16. Increased market penetration	14%

5.13 RISKS ASSOCIATED IN BUSINESS REENGINEERING PROJECTS

The success of Business Reengineering projects is largely dependent on the knowledge management of Business Reengineering project risk factors. The various project risk categories are:

(i) **Financial Risks:** The project does not yield high return-of-investment expected.

(ii) **Technical Risks:** Business process oriented information technology solution either are not available or not working.

(iii) **General Project Risks:** The company is looking for solutions outside its competence or the project team is not performing well.

(iv) **Functional Risks:** The company is confronted with a reorganisation plan which is not applicable to the kind of business the company is in.

(v) **Political Risks:** People confront the project (resistance) or the project gradually loses commitment by top management.

5.14 BUSINESS REENGINEERING IMPLEMENTATION BARRIERS

Barriers which are severe, unexpected and unplanned for problems in Business Reengineering project, increase the impact of project risk factors. For example, middle management resistance against the objective of introducing self-directed work teams increases the political project risk. Barriers hinder implementation efforts such that without intervention the project faulters or even fail altogether. There are other problems which are not considered as barriers, but they may present obstacles on a day to day basis. For example, illness of project members, malfunction of computer equipment etc., are considered as problems and not as barriers.

Hard and Soft Barriers: Barriers to Business Reengineering can be classified as hard barriers and soft barriers. *Exhibit 5.6* illustrates hard and soft barriers along with areas which contain root causes for barriers to Business Reengineering implementation success.

Hard barriers are those, which have to do with things and regulations. Soft barriers are people problems. Hard barriers can be broken into *(i)* ***Information Technology problems****, (iii)* ***Resource problems*** *and (iii)* ***Legal obstacles****.*

Information Technology (software and hardware) which is not suited to support a process based organisation can evolve as a barrier. One typical resource problem is non availability of space for a work team to get together on a regular basis. Team members who are physically separated should have easy access to electronic communication equipment such as teleconferencing. Legal obstacles can become severe barriers. In some countries, various federal and state regulations hinder several Business Reengineering projects. For example, in Germany, Siemens Corporation could not reap as much success from its reorganisation efforts as it originally planned for because work place regulations did not support work time flexibility.

Exhibit 5.6: Relationship between potential barriers and potential causes of barriers

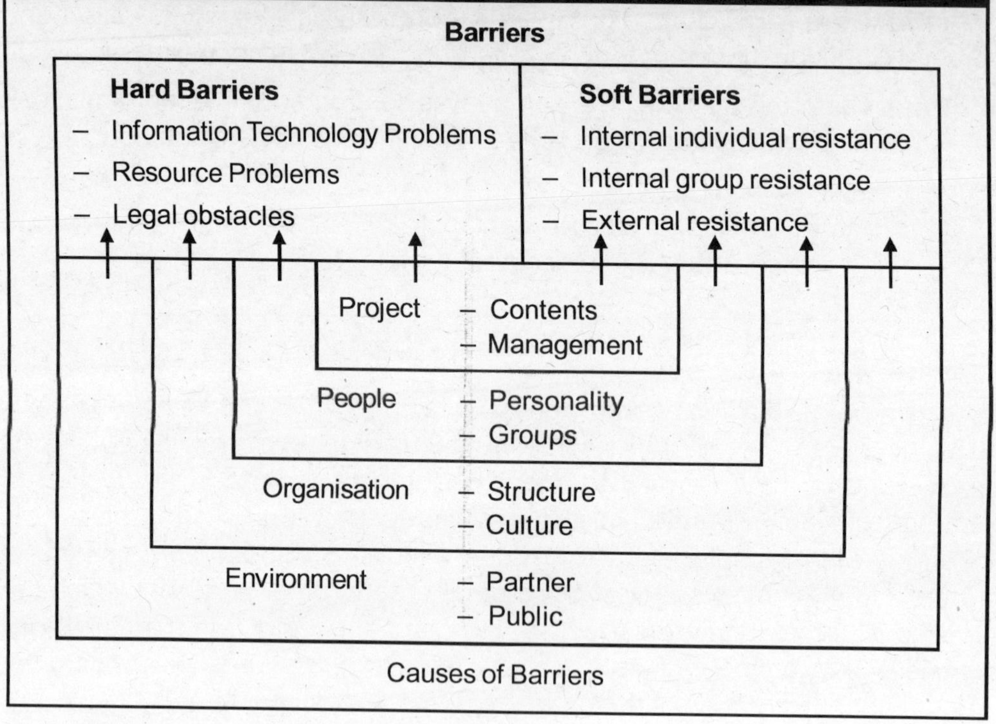

Soft barriers are related to people problems. People resist organisational changes. Resistance to Business Reengineering can be differentiated into internal individual resistance, internal group resistance and external resistance. Resistance of type A describes resistance against reasonable thinking and actions. From the perspective of the initiators and the project team, affected people demonstrate type A resistance. Four most common reasons people resist organisational changes are *(i)* a desire not to loose something of value, *(ii)* a misunderstanding of the change and its implications, *(iii)* a belief that the change does not make sense in the organisation and *(iv)* a low tolerance for change.

Resistance of type B describes resistance against indoctrination and power usage. Affected people don't call themselves resisters and consider their resistance as of type B. Resistance is an indirect way for subordinates to say 'No' to a change.

Resistance is viewed by initiators and project members as a necessary evil. ***"No change without resistance"*** and ***"Innovations represent a history***

of resistance". People resist change most when they have not been asked to change, or have not been told how the change is going to take place and how they personally will be affected by the change.

Internal group resistance describes group behaviour in the organisation. These groups may be formally or informally organised. For example, a group of electronic engineers may resist the plan of being split up into work teams where they have to work side by side with mechanical engineers, because they consider their status superior to that of mechanical engineers.

External resistance is put up by people outside the organisation. Customers, suppliers, the public may develop considerable resistance against plans which interfere with their interests.

Areas generating barriers to Business Reengineering implementation

All barriers to Business Reengineering implementation success are the result of some underlying causes, some of which may not be self-evident. Hence it is necessary to study the areas for potential causes of barriers to Business Reengineering implementation success in sufficient detail.

The areas generating barriers to Business Reengineering implementation success are:

(i) Project related causes, *(ii)* People related causes, *(iii)* Organisation related change and *(iv)* environment related causes.

***(i)* Project related causes:** The Business Reengineering project set up may lead to barriers which have to be dealt with. Project contents and project management can cause both hard and soft barriers. Project contents are represented by project objectives, the selected business processes and the introduction of new Information Technology. The project content may lead to considerable resistance and hard barriers. For example employees of a firm may resist against the implementation of change which they fear may lead to loss of their jobs. People who have doubt or fear, do not take action towards attaining the project objectives. Also the attitudes, values and methods of external consultants may cause considerable resistance on the part of employees.

***(ii)* People related causes:** People affected by the organisation change constitute the main source of potential barriers. This is true for people on all level in an organisation. People behaviour is based on their personality and norms of the groups to which they belong. Managers may resist a change, which jeopardises their job; workers may fear unemployment by being replaced by a computer system. Managers may pay lip service to the change and behave in autocratic ways not to suffer any personal draw lacks from the change. Workers want to be told what exactly is expected from them.

***(iii)* Organisation related change:** An organisational structure which is inflexible towards a drastic change in operations may cause barriers. Large bureaucratic organisations tend to wither changes which potentially destroy the existing structure – Also the embedded culture of the organisation is another cause for barriers because culture unconsciously influences the thinking, decisions and actions of people working in a given firm. Thus culture may dictate the inability to forget the past and the inability to invent the future.

***(iv)* Environment related causes:** The environment of an organisation may yield barriers to the implementation success of Business Reengineering project, by withstanding through the means of laws, regulations and public resistance. The organisation's business partners i.e., vendors and customers may resist the objectives and content of a Business Reengineering project undertaken by the organisation. Also, the environment may rapidly change in a way that makes the Business Reengineering project redundant.

5.15 SUMMARY

To enable proper implementation of business process reengineering, it is essential that all the employees have a clear understanding of the concepts such as *"business process", "key process", "business process management"* etc. Also the "principles of process management" must be honoured to deliver business results to customers.

The **"process reengineering model"** has three levels namely *"work process reengineering", "business process reengineering"* and *"business reengineering"*. It has three phases namely – *(i)* Planning, *(ii)* Designing and *(iii)* Implementing.

The planning phase has two steps namely

(a) Determine new process requirements and

(b) Uncover break-through opportunities

The Design phase has three steps namely

(a) Map the ideal process

(b) Redefine process support requirements and

(c) Develop change management plan

The implementation phase has three steps namely

(a) Implement on "trial run" basis

(b) Standardise the reengineered process and

(c) Evaluate process performance on an ongoing basis.

A process reengineering team should be formed either on part time or full time depending on the scope of the process being reengineered. Either a core team having 3 to 4 members working on a full time basis for reengineering or a "full team" having 8 to 12 members working on part time basis will be required.

In the **first step of phase 1** namely "determine new process requirements", the sub steps involved are:

(a) Planning the firm's reengineering effort

(b) Knowing what the customers want

(c) Identifying the customers

(d) Zeroing in on customers' concern

(e) Soliciting customer input

(f) Finding what the market place is providing

(g) Using bench marking

(h) Finding the firm's operating requirements

Step 2 of phase one namely "uncover break-through" opportunities has the following substeps.

(a) Analyse **"as is"** capability

(b) Envision desired state and

(c) Identify process performance gaps

To start with, in this step, the "as is" process is documented. Two basic steps involved in documenting a process are:

(i) Listing the major process tasks and *(ii)* Creating a process flow chart.

Phase 2. Step 3 involves mapping the ideal process which has three sub steps namely : *(i)* Completing preliminary work, *(ii)* Setting new goals and establishing new measures and *(iii)* Creating a new process flow chart.

Phase 2. Step 4 involves redefining process support requirements. Three different areas of support within an organisation that need to be redefined are: *(i)* People, *(ii)* Technology/support tools and *(iii)* Finance.

Phase 2. Step 5 involves developing change management plan which has the following activities.

(i) Designing the change management plan

(ii) Identifying change management plan requirements

(iii) Choosing a planning process and format

(iv) Deciding how to move the action plan forward

Phase 3. Step 6 involves implementing on "trial run" basis

Phase 3. Step 7 involves standardising the reengineering process and

Phase 4. Step 8 involves evaluating process performance on an ongoing basis.

5.16 SELF ASSESSMENT QUESTIONS

1. What is a business process?
2. How are key processes identified?
3. What is business process management?
4. State the principle of process management?
5. What are the three levels of reengineering?
6. Discuss briefly the various phases and steps involved in applying a process reengineering model.
7. What are the factors to be considered when designing a team and selecting the members?
8. Distinguish between a core team and a full team. Compare their advantages and disadvantages.
9. What is meant by "as is" capability?
10. List the symbols used in creating flow process charts.
11. What are Business Reengineering projects?
12. Discuss the principles of Business Reengineering.
13. Describe the Hammer/Champy methodology used in Business Reengineering approaches.
14. Discuss the potential benefits from implementation of Business Reengineering projects.
15. Discuss the risks associated with Business Reengineering projects.
16. Describe the Business Reengineering implementation barriers.
17. Describe the areas generating barriers to Business Reengineering implementation.

♦ ♦ ♦ ♦ ♦

6 Chapter

ORGANISING FOR BPRE

Objectives

After going through this chapter, you would be able to :

- Understand, how to identify a Business Process.
- Learn about various types of Business Processes.
- Understand meaning of Business Process Management.
- Learn how to apply a Process Reengineering model to bring in break through improvements.
- Learn about various phases and steps involved in the Process-Reengineering model.
- Learn about potential benefits from BPRE as well as risk associated with BPRE projects.

Structure

6.1 INTRODUCTION

While a company may not need a formal structure to carryout minor improvements (*i.e.*, incremental improvements on a continuous basis) which are confined to a particular work centre or a department, major improvements through Business Process Reengineering (BPRE) can not be implemented in an *adhoc* or unstructured manner. An incremental improvement can be effected by the departmental heads or managers who have the authority for the same. BPRE deals with interdepartmental and cross-functional issues and several departments are actively involved in BPRE. *For example,* quality circles require a formal structure consisting of circle members, circle leaders/deputy leaders, facilitators, coordinators and steering committee members for achieving the desired quality improvements. Eventhough BPRE and quality circles have different objectives, their scope and applications are companywide. Therefore there is a need to have proper organisational structure to implement both quality circles and BPRE. *Exhibit 6.1* indicates the general structure of BPRE.

Exhibit 6.1 : General structure of BPRE

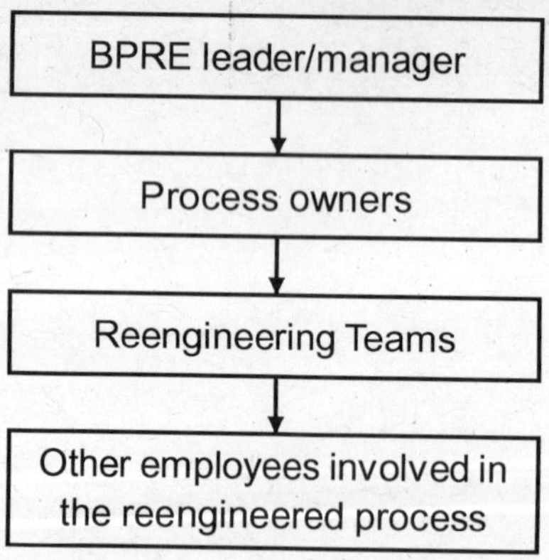

How the above structure of BPRE functions will be described later in this chapter.

6.2 PROCESS-FOCUSED ORGANISATION

A process focused organisation or process organisation is arranged according to processes or product lines. The organisation focuses on key business processes that it must absolutely do well in order to gain, satisfy and retain customers. In a process oriented firm, traditional departmental boundaries are blurred or non existent. A process-oriented organisation is flexible. Individuals work toward completing an overall process rather than one particular activity. People have multiple skills and they are cross-trained so that they are aware of all the steps in the process of providing a product or a service to the customers. Process managers are responsible for the overall process and what it produces. Some characteristics of process-oriented organisation are listed in *Box 6.1*.

Box 6.1 : Characteristics of a Process-oriented Organisation

(i) Broad competencies
(ii) Improvement efforts focus on processes
(iii) Cross-functionally trained employees
(iv) Focus on organisation' mission and objectives
(v) Better utilisation of employees and equipment
(vi) Increased communication with appropriate departments/areas
(vii) Shared accountability and responsibility
(viii) Optimising organisational performance
(ix) Use of feed-back from customers
(x) Seamless or boundary less organisation

- **Activity A**

Prepare process focused organisation structure for your department.

....

....

....

....

....

....

....

....

6.3 BENEFITS OF PROCESS FOCUSED ORIENTATION

Process orientation forces people to become aware of the links between the activities in the process. It enables an organisation to achieve its overall mission and objectives more easily. Process orientation enables every one in the organisation to be aligned with the key business process that absolutely must take place in order for the company to attract and retain customers. People understand how the entire process they are working on operates. They are also aware of how their day to day activities support the process.

A process focus supports the use of problem-solving and self-directed work teams. Since individuals in the organisation can see the links between activities, they are more likely to work together to enhance their activities and the links between them.

6.4 DIFFERENCES BETWEEN A FUNCTIONALLY STRUCTURED ORGANISATION AND A PROCESS-FOCUSED ORGANISATION

In a functionally structured organisation, the activities are grouped together and managed as separate entities. The machines, equipments and human resources which are used to carryout similar activities are grouped together and a manager is placed in charge of these activities. *For example,* in a manufacturing firm, different functional activities such as marketing, purchasing, storing, finance, planning, production, quality control, maintenance, personnel etc., are grouped under separate departments each headed by an individual manager. In a functionally structured organisation, management boundaries are set clearly and there is no overlapping of function between any two departments.

A process focused organisation or a project organisation groups all the functions such as research and development, manufacturing, marketing, finance etc., under each project headed by a project manager who in turn report to the project director who is at the top management level. There are other functional directors such as director-marketing, director-manufacturing, director R&D, director-finance etc., at the top management level along with the director-projects. All these directors report to the president or managing director or chairman of the organisation.

Process focused organisations deviate from traditional vertical functional structure in that they use cross-functional teams (temporary or permanent), task forces or project teams. **Cross-functional teams** consist of employees from various functional departments who are responsible to meet as a team and resolve mutual problems. Team members report to their functional departments, but they also report to the team leader of the cross-functional team to which they belong.

A **task force** is a temporary team or committee formed to solve a specific short-term problem involving several departments. A **project team** is a group of participants from several departments who meet regularly to solve ongoing problems of common interest or to work on a specific project (a complex task) assigned to them. The project team is headed by a project manager who is responsible for coordinating the activities of several departments for the completion of a specific project.

Since Business Process Reengineering approach involves a complete rethinking and transformation of key business processes, there is a need for a strong horizontal coordination and greater flexibility in responding to changes in the environment. Because work is organised around process rather than function, reengineering often involves a shift to a horizontal structure based on teams.

Organising around key business processes also may lead to redesigning information systems to cut across departmental lines. This will enable managers to share information throughout the organisation to make their companies more competitive and more responsive to customers.

The increasing shift toward more horizontal versus vertical structures reflect the trend toward greater employee empowerment, broad information sharing and decentralised decision making. Such organisations are referred to as **learning organisations**. In such organisations, every one in engaged in identifying and solving problems, enabling the organisation to continually experiment, change and improve. The learning organisations are characterised by horizontal - team based structure, open information, decentralised decision making, empowered employees and a strong adaptive culture.

6.5 ORGANISING THE PROCESS REENGINEERING TEAM

As discussed earlier, process reengineering requires organisational structuring with reduced organisational layers (a change from vertical structure to a horizontal structure), realigning functions/work groups around business processes or customers, and decentralising decision making by empowering employees.

The various components of the organisation for Business Process Reengineering are discussed in the following section.

1. Leader of BPRE Team: The team leader should be a top management level executive because the outcome of process reengineering effort depends greatly on the quality of leadership. Ideally the chief executive officer (CEO) would be the most suitable person for leading the BPRE team. But it may not be possible for the CEO to lead the BPRE team because of his/her inability to devote much of his/her time to the process reengineering effort. The leader of the BPRE team may be designated as chief operating officer (COO). He/she may be incharge of the overall internal activities of the company and therefore has the power and authority to ensure that the concerned departments strictly abide by his/her instructions to carryout activities required for a reengineered process.

In large organisations consisting of several divisions involved in different types of businesses, the head of a strategic business unit (SBU) may head the BPRE team, but he or she can reengineer only those processes which are confined to his or her SBU.

In addition to holding a top management level position, the BPRE team leader should possess some personal attributes such as ***conviction, commitment, persuasiveness, sternness*** and ***optimism***. The experience and gut feeling may play a vital role in taking decisions to carryout the reengineering exercise.

Basically, the team leader must be convinced that old ways of doing things are no longer tenable in the modern business world and some key business processes need drastic improvements. These processes may have to be partially or completely changed, some tasks may have to be modified or replaced by radically improved ones.

In addition to conviction, the leader should be able to demonstrate his/her commitment to BPRE and convince the employees about the need for reengineering the business process. The leader should identify the process owners for the processes to be reengineered and must be accessible to them. He or she should exhibit personal interest in monitoring the activities of the process owners by meeting them from time to time. Also the leader should provide the necessary resources to the team members for the successful implementation of a reengineered process. The leader should identify and pick up high performers from different departments to form the BPRE team. The leader should have the vision to foresee the need for a change in the business processes and should be able to persuade the top management to take necessary proactive steps even if some top level managers may oppose such moves.

The leader must have instinctive feelings to initiate changes for dramatic improvements and he/she has an uphill task of convincing the top management about the need for drastic changes which may apparently look as not called for and status-quo is good enough to carryon.

Also, BPRE is unlikely to succeed in an organisational climate characterised by skepticism, doubts and frustration among most of the employees. The leader must be highly optimistic and should be able to exert relentless efforts to convince the employees that old ways of doing things are no longer valid or productive in the fast changing business world. The leader should be able to bring about changes in the organisational culture which would be supportive of the reengineering efforts that the team will be exerting. The leader should have a very strong determination to succeed in his/her endeavour.

The leader should be constantly aware of the initiatives taken by the competitors to bring about major improvements in some of their key areas of business processes. The leaders must be able to bench mark the business processes which are best-in-class and reengineer the process of his/her firm in order to bring them on par with that of the best-in-class firms.

The leader must be firmly determined to succeed eventhough he/she may face many challenges and problems during the implementation of the reengineered process. He/she should have the perseverance to see it through and achieve radical improvements in business processes.

2. Process Owners : Because the leader of BPRE team has many other responsibilities apart from process reengineering, he or she should appoint **"process owners"** who are responsible for reengineering individual processes in the reengineering project.

The objectives to be achieved by the reengineered processes are set by the leader in consultation with the process owners. The process owners are directly involved in the tasks pertaining the processes to be reengineered and hence they are in a better position to offer valuable suggestions to improve the processes, for which they are appointed as "process owners". By participating in objective setting, (*i.e.,* setting the standards of performance) the process owners feel the ownership of the processes and become committed to them. Also the performance standards set based on the consultation between process owners and the BPRE leader will be more realistic and achievable because the process owners participate in the decision making process to set these standards. This would increase the chances of success of BPRE.

The process owners should have undergone adequate training to acquire the knowledge and skills necessary for reengineering a process. In addition to technical knowledge and skills, they should possess certain behavioural characteristics such as leadership, communication ability, team work, positive attitude, less resistance to change etc., which they can acquire through appropriate training. Also the process owners should be highly optimistic about the success of BPRE projects. They should work like team leaders in their area of operation and motivate the members of their teams and resolve problems faced by the team members during implementation of changes in their tasks.

The process owners should conduct meetings with their team members, arrange for brain storming sessions to solicit creative ideas from the team members and quantity the benefits derived from them.

3. Reengineering Teams : Each process owner has to work with a reengineering team to implement the reengineered process. The reengineering team is a cross-functional team having members with expertise in different parts of the process.

The objective of the team is to integrate the fragmented tasks or sub processes into a complete process that brings about radical improvements. In a manufacturing firm, the reengineering team may include a cost accountant in addition to engineers to work out the cost-benefit analysis of reengineered process. The composition of the team may be very much different in a service organisation when compared to a manufacturing organisation. The experts from various departments related to the process to be reengineered are selected as members of the reengineering team. The leader of the BPRE team must ensure that the departmental heads release the best persons from their departments to work as members of the reengineering team so as to ensure the success of reengineering projects. These team members must be appraised based on their performance as members of reengineering teams and not based on their performance in their previous positions in their parent departments. These team members may have to work in reengineering teams for quite a long period (say several years) and even if they successfully complete a BPRE project, they may be assigned to another BPRE project to work in another newly formed BPRE team. Hence they have a total change in their career path as BPRE experts. They may experience an improved quality of life, higher job satisfaction and higher level of motivation because of substantial rewards for their significant constitution.

The members of BPRE team have to be high performers with process orientation, holistic perspective, creativity, enthusiasm, high need for achievement, optimism, persistence, tact and communication skills, They should be able to view their jobs not in isolation, but as a part of the entire process. (*i.e.,* holistic view). They should be able to think creatively and generate innovative ideas which can bring about drastic improvements in the existing processes.

Unforeseen set backs or failures are not uncommon in the BPRE projects. In such adverse situations the members of BPRE team and the process owners should be enthusiastic and optimistic without becoming desperate or losing their initiative. They should have the conviction that failure is the stepping stone to success and ultimately they are bound to succeed in their endeavour. They should have persistence and tact and also the communication skills to convince other non-member employees who directly contribute to the improvement of the processes.

4. Non members (other employees) involved in the reengineered process: The process owners and their team members are supported by other employees who are not members of the reengineering teams but can assist the members or process owners to successfully implement a reengineered process. These employees may be required to acquire new skills through adequate training. A successfully implemented process requires their cooperation and active involvement in the tasks assigned to them. The process owner and his/her team members are responsible to ensure that the tasks are carried out smoothly and efficiently by the other non-members who are involved in the reengineered process.

In some organisations, some middle level or junior level managers may play the 'role of catalysts' to initiate the reengineering projects. They may be highly capable and creative thinking persons who are not just satisfied to do their routine jobs and discharge the assigned responsibilities in a routine manner. They do "out-of-the box" thinking and come out with innovative ideas to make significant contributions to the BPRE efforts.

6.6 TEAMS

Team working is a feature of product and service delivery to customers. Work teams as opposed to large departments are responsible for as much business as possible. Team work is more than friendly people located in a single room or office. ***A team is a special group of people with complementary skills, highly dedicated to a common process objective***. A functioning team does not necessitate management control. Hence middle management position often become redundant in reengineered organisations with work teams at the execution level. Box 6.2 shows important factors that differentiate winning teams from losing teams.

Box 6.2 : Winning Teams Vs Losing Teams	
Winning Teams	**Losing Teams**
• Are clear about their goals.	• Bring people together only because they like one another.
• Are in touch with what is going on outside the team.	• Focus more on the team itself than the outcome.
• Are small in size, but large enough to master the process.	• Are too small or too large in size.
• Have and increase complementary skills.	• Do not have the necessary skills available for the tasks. Do not train their capabilities.
• Value input, regardless of rank.	• Fight is common
• Are confident in overcoming conflict.	• Accept ideas only from suppliers.
• Support each other in achieving more than they ever thought, possible.	• Flight is common. Do not support each other.
• Celebrate their success.	• Ignore the need for individual recognition.

Types of Teams: Most teams can be classified as being one of the following three types:

(i) ***Department improvement team*:** This is the most common type of team. It consists of people who make up a specific unit, department or function within the organisation, for example a *quality circle* which is a team of workers and supervisors that meet regularly to address work place problems involving quality and productivity.

(ii) ***Process improvement team*:** This type of team has a mission of improving an entire process. Consequently it is made up of people from each individual phase in the process, for example, business process reengineering team.

(iii) ***Task force*:** Some times called a *project team*, a task force is a temporary team formed for a specific, well-defined mission. Special project teams and problem-solving teams fall into this category. Task forces are composed of the people who are most likely to be able to accomplish their specific missions and are disbanded once the mission has been completed. Other than the above three categories of teams, other types of teams are:

(a) *Management teams*: Teams consisting mainly of managers from various functions like sales and production that coordinate work among teams.

(b) *Work teams*: Teams which are organised to perform entire jobs rather than specialised, assembly line type works. When work teams are empowered, they are called ***self-managed teams***. Self-managed teams or self-directed teams are defined as groups of people who work together continuously and who plan, execute and control their work to achieve a defined output.

(c) *Cross-functional teams*: Also known as cross-departmental teams, these teams provide the best vehicle for linking business process improvement activities such as procurement, billing, recruiting, record keeping, design, sales, etc., to the key business objectives of the organisation for improvement of quality.

(d) *Virtual teams*: Relatively a new concept in team work, virtual teams consist of team members who communicate by computers, take turns as leaders and jump into and out of the team as necessary.

6.7 FUNCTIONS OF TEAMS

Problem solving drives the team concept. *Exhibit 6.2* illustrates the process by which teams usually operate. The three basic functions are to identify, analyse and solve quality and productivity problems.

Exhibit 6.2 : Functions of Teams

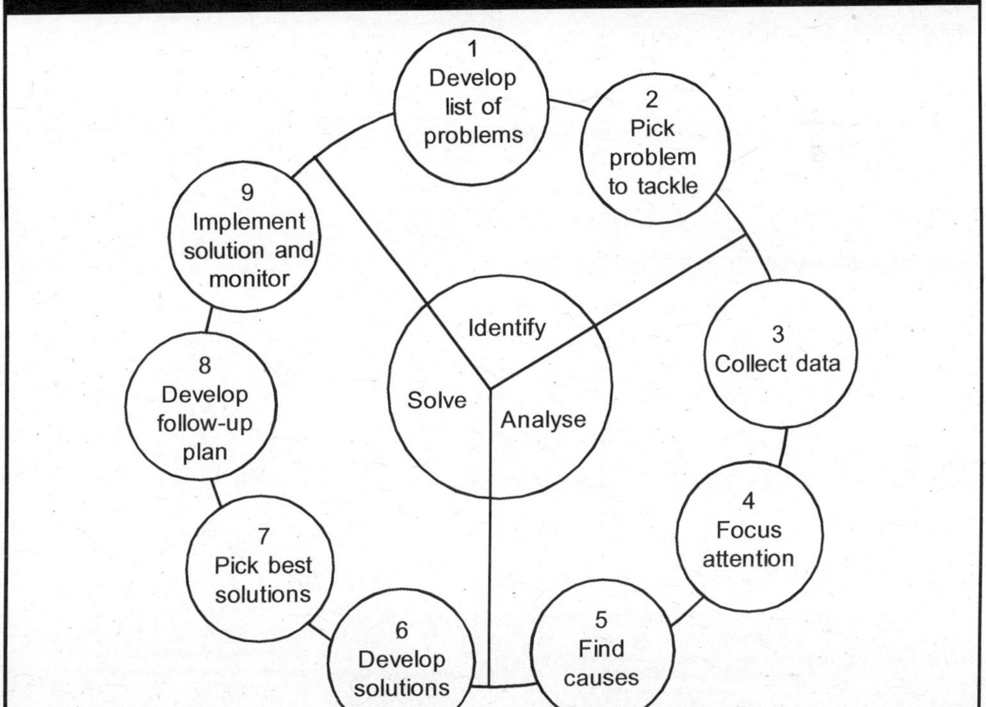

Source : James R. Evans, *et. al, op. cit,* p. 298.

6.8 DEVELOPING SUCCESSFUL TEAMS

Team approaches need adequate planning. A certain period of investigation, reflection and soul searching is necessary before plunging into any team initiatives. Some companies may form the wrong kind of teams for a specific job in a hurry. Managers should examine their organisation's goals, objectives and culture to evaluate its readiness to develop and support team-based initiatives.

Most organisations benefit by establishing a steering committee made up of a group of interested, committed line and staff managers together with a union representative if a union exists. The steering committee establishes initial policies and procedures and choose a person or persons to be the facilitators. If employees choose to join the team, they are given 8 to 16 hours of initial or concurrent training before or during the first few group meetings. Usually, the facilitator or group leader will conduct the training. Teams are taught to use brainstorming and problem solving tools as well as skills in presentation techniques, group leadership and motivation. Ten ingredients for a successful team for quality improvement are :

(i) Clarity in team goals
(ii) An improvement plan
(iii) Clearly defined roles
(iv) Clear communication
(v) Beneficial team behaviours
(vi) Well-defined decision procedures
(vii) Balanced participation
(viii) Established ground rules
(ix) Awareness of group process and
(x) Use of the scientific approach.

Self-managed teams (SMTs) represent the greatest challenge because the teams are empowered :

(i) Creating a work unit responsible for an entire task
(ii) Establishing specific measures of the work units' output
(iii) Designing multi-skilled jobs
(iv) Creating internal management and co-ordination tasks
(v) Creating boundary management tasks
(vi) Establishing access to information and
(vii) Establishing support systems.

6.9 SUMMARY

While continuous improvement may not require a formal organisational structure to be implemented, major improvements through Business Process Reengineering (BPRE) require a formal structure. While continuous improvement can be effected by departmental managers, several departments have to be involved in BPRE.

The general structure of an organisation for BPRE includes a BPRE leader or manager, the process owners, reengineering team and other employees involved in the reengineered process.

BPRE requires a process-focused organisation which focuses on key business processes which must be carried out efficiently to satisfy its customers. A process focused organisation is flexible and does not have departmental boundaries. The employees of such organisations are multi-skilled, cross-trained and knowledgable about all the steps in the process they carry out. Process orientation helps the organisation have its employees aligned with key business processes and achieve its overall mission and objectives.

Functionally structured organisations are traditional and they perform specific functions grouped under specific departments such as production, marketing, finance, R&D, personnel etc. Process focussed organisations deviate from vertical functional structure and use cross functional teams, task forces or project teams. Such organisations are also referred to as learning organisations which are characterised by greater employee empowerment, broad information sharing and decentralised decision making.

The various components of the organisation for BPRE are : *(i)* BPRE team leader, *(ii)* Process owners, *(iii)* Reengineering teams and *(iv)* Other employees involved in the reengineered process.

The BPRE team leader must be a top management level executive (usually a chief operating officer) who has the required authority over internal activities and departments to carryout the activities for a reengineered process. He or she should have characteristics such as conviction, commitment, persuasiveness, sternness and optimism. He or she should have the experience and gut feeling to take decisions to take up BPRE projects and their implementation. He or she should have instinctive feelings and should act as a change agent. He or she should be aware of competitors's effort regarding BPRE in their firms and should be able to benchmark the best-in-class and reengineer the processes of his/her firm in order to bring them on par with that of the best-in-class firms.

Process owners are the persons who are ultimately responsible for seeing that a process is completed in a manner that results in customer satisfaction. These individuals are in a position to make and have the necessary power to make changes to the process.

Reengineering team is a cross-functional team having members with expertise in different parts of the process. They are drawn from different departments based on their ability and expertise and they work in the BPRE team for quite some time (even several years) and after completing their task as members of a certain BPRE team, they may be assigned to another BPRE team and project. They should be high performers with process orientation, holistic perspective, creativity, enthusiasm, high need for achievement, optimism, persistence, tact and communication skills.

The other employees involved in the reengineered process support the process owners. They are not members of the BPRE team. Their cooperation and active involvement in the tasks assigned to them are essential for the successful implementation of reengineered process. Apart form them, some middle management level or junior level managers may also act as "catalysts" and initiate reengineering projects. They are highly capable and creative in their thinking.

6.10 SELF ASSESSMENT QUESTIONS

1. Discuss the general structure of an organisation of BPRE.
2. What is a process-focused organisation? What are its characteristics?
3. State the benefits of a process focused organisation.
4. Differentiable between a functionally structured organisation and a process focused organisation.
5. What are *(a)* cross-functional teams, *(b)* task forces and *(c)* project teams?
6. Describe briefly how a process reengineering team is organised?
7. Discuss the characteristics and role of team leaders in BPRE.
8. Who are process owners? What is their role in BPRE?
9. How is a reengineering team formed? What are the characteristics of its members?
10. Discuss the role of other employees who are involved in the reengineered process.
11. What is meant by a "team"?
12. Distinguish between winning teams and losing teams.
13. What are the various types of teams? Elaborate.
14. Describe the functions of teams.
15. Explain how successful team are developed.

♦ ♦ ♦ ♦ ♦

7

Chapter

PROBLEMS IN BPRE

Objectives

After going through this chapter, you would be able to :

- Get information about limitations of BPRE process.
- Learn about common pitfalls of BPRE process.

Structure

7.1 INTRODUCTION

Business Process Reengineering brings radical changes in the organisational structure, work methods, procedures, processes, performance, appraisal systems, behaviour and altitude of employees and therefore, successful implementation of BPRE in quite difficult. Because organisations vary widely in their culture and characteristics, their employes vary in their behaviours, it is not easy to identify the pitfalls that management should avoid while implementing BPRE.

BPRE can be easily introduced in organisations that have people who are receptive to new ideas and keen to accept change in their ways of doing things for the benefit of the organisation. The employees in these organisations understand the short-comings of some of the existing processes and have open mind and are prepared to contribute significantly for implementing radical improvements for the survival and growth of their organisations in a competitive market.

The employees of TQM organisations are willing to learn and acquire new skills and use their knowledge and skills to reengineer the processes to improve the performance of the organisation and quality of work life.

On the country, if the employees of an organisation are pessimistic, sceptical, defensive and have complacent mind set, it is difficult to implement BPRE in such organisations. Eventhough top management may take initiative and try to convince the employees about the need for reengineering, they are reluctant to change their mind set for the better. They feel quite comfortable in their present method of doing their jobs and they have fear of the unknown when they are asked to change their ways of doing things. They even try to justify their ways of doing things as good and feel that they do not need to be changed.

Resistance to BPRE usually occurs at junior and middle management levels. They suffer from the feeling of insecurity when they are asked to examine their tasks for the purpose of improvement. They have an unfounded fear that process-oriented thinking would result in the loss of power, control and authority for them. In some organisations, even top managers exhibit resistance to change and are not supportive of BPRE.

Many problems that arise in BPRE are due to the limitations of BPRE and the pitfalls in BPRE. The limitations are:

(i) BPRE is not a panacea to achieve instant competitive advantage.

(ii) BPRE is not simple or easy to implement. Also it may not be appropriate for all processes for all organisations.

(iii) Many organisations may not be able to invest the time and resources required to implement a radical, clean state approach.

(iv) Significant process improvement requires the use of information technology.

(v) Improvement within each functional areas is necessary in addition to improvement in the firm's cross-functional processes.

(vi) People who perform the work each day, have the best understanding of the processes they use, and also know to improve them, rather than cross-functional teams or top management.

(vii) The core-business processes are designed to satisfy a particular customer need in the **"one best way"** particular customer need. Most BPRE efforts do not seem to consider what will happen if that customer need changes.

7.2 COMMON PITFALLS OF BPRE

Same of the common pitfalls of BPRE are:

(i) Improper knowledge of reengineering.

(ii) Reengineering too many processes at initial stages.

(iii) Lack of training for process owners and team members.

(iv) Improper monitoring of a reengineered process.

(v) Wastage of time due to detailed process analysis.

(vi) Fear of failure.

(vii) Unfavourable organisational environment.

(viii) Delay in achieving results.

(ix) Unsatisfactory appraisal system.

(x) Inability to quantity improvement.

(xi) Complacency of management.

(xii) Non-availability of adequate resources.

(xiii) Limited employee awareness and

(xiv) Discontinuance of BPRE after achieving bench mark.

These pitfalls are discussed in the following paragraphs.

1. Improper Knowledge of Reengineering

Continuous improvement or Kaizen is concerned with small incremental improvements in business processes. *For example,* if an order fulfillment process which usually takes two weeks is reduced by one or two days, there is an improvement which is quite small. This kind of minor improvements should not be considered as reengineering (*i.e.,* BPRE). In BPRE, *for example,* a process may be radically changed and the time taken to complete this process can be reduced drastically, say from two weeks to two days.

If a firm is unable to generate break-through or innovation ideas to change the ways the tasks are being performed at present and bring about dramatic process improvement, then the firm's effort to reengineer the process has failed. Even if the firm achieves minor improvement, such process can be implemented, but it should not be considered as reengineering.

Another example of improvement may be introduction of computers in various departments of an organisation for reducing clerical work by people. Also computers carry out the task with greater speed and accuracy. But such an improvement can not be treated as business process reengineering.

- **Activity A**

List out various steps which can be taken to avoid above pitfall of improper knowledge of Reengineering.

....

....

....

....

....

....

....

2. Reengineering too many processes at Initial Stages

Top management of an organisation may be highly enthusiastic about BPRE and may initiate reengineering of too many processes simultaneously. A firm may be carried away by the success stories of its competitors and try to catch up with them as early as possible. This may prompt them to take up many reengineering projects at a time. Eventhough such initiatives may be appreciable, they are not practicable, because the firm may encounter too many unforeseen problems which may be difficult to resolve when too many processes are taken up for reengineering.

The leader of the reengineering team may not be in a position to devote enough time to guide many process owners and keep track of their activities. Also the computer facilities may not be adequate to handle too many

IT-enabled processes. Hence in the initial stages, only a few key processes should be reengineered. The advantages are:

(i) The leader will be able to spend enough time to interact with the process owners and offer his suggestions for improvement.

(ii) The members of the team gain in-depth experience from handling few processes and this will be useful in the execution of other processes in the future.

(iii) The team leader and members can sense the attitudes and behaviours of people toward BPRE at the initial stages of introducing BPRE and they can take necessary steps to motivate people towards BPRE and create an environment conducive to BPRE.

3. Lack of Training for Process Owners and Team Members

The firm planning to introduce BPRE, should arrange for training programs to members of reengineering team to provide technical skills needed for reengineering a process. Also the training program should stress on transforming task-oriented mind set of trainees to process-oriented thinking. Many BPRE projects will fail because of inadequate training. Hence the management should give proper attention to train the process owners and BPRE team members adequately for the success of BPRE.

The trainers must have a fairly clear knowledge of the way the company works and the attitude of its employee towards change. The training should be focused at changing the attitude of employees towards BPRE and change.

The training materials should help the participants to relate the inputs of training programs to their organisational environment and the kind of work they are doing. The training programme should include detailed discussion of behavioural issues like team work, creativity, leadership, motivation, organisational culture, communication and the like.

In the beginning of the training program, the tentative action plans for reengineering a chosen business process must be prepared. In this action planning exercise all the participants must be actively involved. For this, the participants may be divided into small groups and each group may be asked to prepare its action plan. The action plan must include the following:

(a) *Line of action (What) :* What action to be taken? *i.e.,* what are the tasks to be performed for reengineering a process?

(b) *Time (When) :* When to complete each of the task involved in the line of action? This gives a time horizon for the action plan.

(c) *Concerned agency (Who) :* Who should carryout what tasks? This specifies, the individual, group or department to be given the responsibility of carrying out the specified tasks within the stipulated time.

(d) *Mode of action (How) :* How to complete the tasks involved in reengineering the process?

This stipulates the way in which the tasks must be carried out.

Each group prepares the plan according to the above format and each group presents their action plan. After all the groups involved complete their presentations, a combined overall action plan is prepared. In this exercise of preparing the over all plan, the trainers and all the trainees must be involved. The overall action plan is then submitted to the leader of the BPRE team for his/her approval.

Exhibit 7.1 : Process of action planning in BPRE

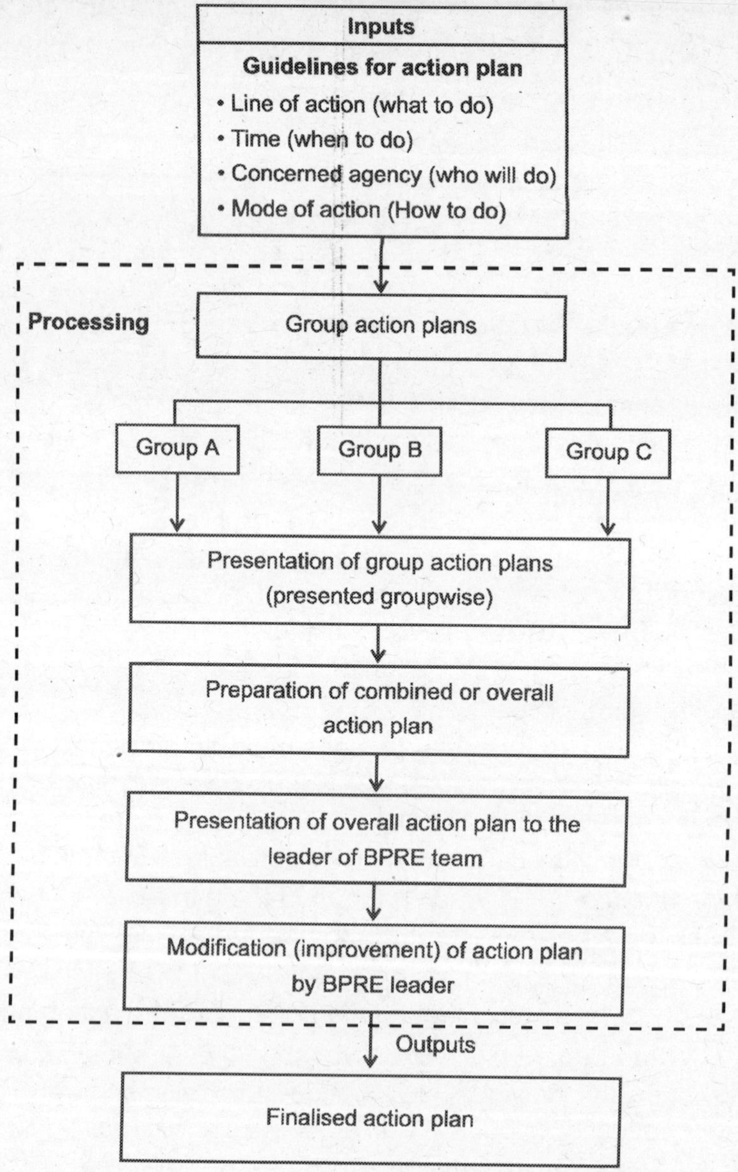

The leader may make some valuable suggestions to change and improve the plan. The leader consults with those who are involved in the preparation of the overall action plan before incorporating the changes or modifications. This participatory approach ensures the commitment of all concerned (*i.e.,* the team leader and team members, process owners and other employees who are involved in reengineering the process) to the successful implementation of the reengineered process. *Exhibit 7.1* illustrates the process of action planning in the business process reengineering project.

The execution of the training program need not be entrusted to external training organisations. Instead, a few core groups of individuals who have been already trained in the training programmes organised by the management using the external training agencies or training experts may be given the responsibility to act as facilitators for the training programmes conducted companywide. These core group persons (resource persons or groups) need not conduct formal training programmes. Instead they may act as consultants and interact with other employees to:

(a) Highlight the limitations of the existing processes and their adverse effect on the performance of the company.

(b) Explain the objectives of BPRE and the benefits that can be achieved by reengineering the problematic processes.

(c) Clarify the doubts and the queries of those who are affected by the introduction of reengineering.

4. Improper Monitoring of Reengineered Processes

Reengineering a process requires innovative or break through ideas on which to base the reengineering project. Even though a process or system can be dramatically improved initially, it has a tendency to deteriorate if adequate efforts are not put to maintain and improve the process further (*i.e.,* continuous incremental improvement must succeed break through improvement). This requires proper monitoring of the implementation of a reengineered process. Otherwise there will be an adverse impact on the reengineered process and the benefits may not be significant.

In Japanese firms, the break through improvement achieved by BPRE will be followed by kaizen (*i.e.,* continuous incremental improvements), not only for maintaining the high level of performance, but also for achieving further improvement.

Exhibit 7.2 illustrates the ideal pattern of implementation of a reengineered process.

Exhibit 7.2 : Ideal pattern of a reengineered process

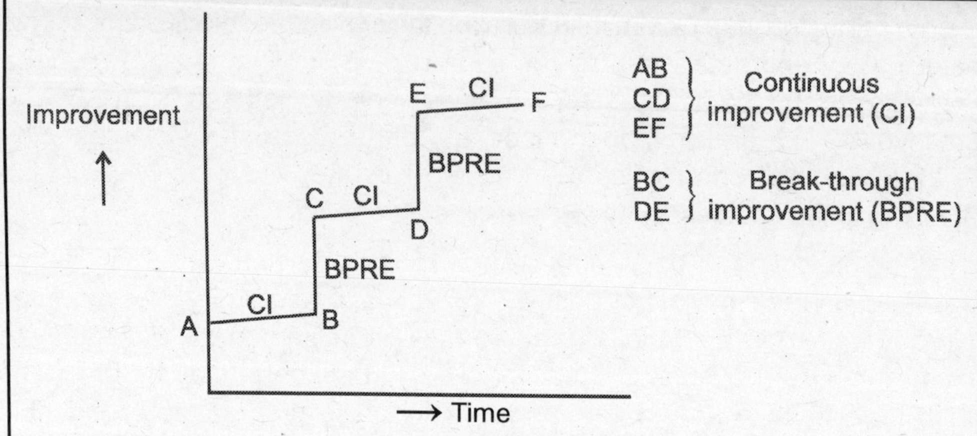

In actual practice, it is observed that processes or systems, if not monitored after reengineering, tend to deteriorate over time. Hence continuous monitoring is required to maintain the desired level of process performance. This will ensure that the desired performance level is maintained and also adequate effort is put to improve the process further through creative ideas and suggestions.

Because people have a tendency to be used to old ways of doing things, it is essential that regular monitoring of the reengineered process is a must. People need to unlearn many of their old practices and adapt themselves to the new ways of performing tasks. Reengineering demands new ways of thinking and doing work.

5. Wastage of Time due to Detailed Process Analysis

For process owners and team members to understand the process before reengineering it, detailed analysis of the process is not necessary. A detailed analysis of the process consumes lot of time. But it doesn't mean that the reengineering team members attempt to reengineer a process with superficial knowledge of the process. What they need to understand is the overall knowledge of the tasks and their relevance to the process as a whole. Detailed knowledge of the tasks may condition the thinking of the team members and they may feel that all the tasks are necessary for carrying out the process and therefore, none of the tasks can be modified or eliminated. This kind of thinking is detrimental to generate creative and innovative ideas.

Some managers who oppose BPRE insist that the BPRE team must carryout a detailed analysis of a process selected for reengineering before they try to change it. But if the BPRE team takes up detailed analysis, they will be entangled in that and will not be able to reengineer the process.

What is important for the team members is to understand why some tasks are being performed in an existing process and if these tasks are found necessary or relevant, what should be done to improve their execution drastically. A detailed knowledge of how these tasks are performed is not necessary for reengineering the process.

6. Fear of Failure

In BPRE, failure is not condemned, but celebrated because failure is the stepping stone to success. Fear of failure curbs creativity and innovation. Any drastic change is always associated with certain degree of risk of failure. There is no guarantee that everything will work well when a reengineered process is being implemented.

There are many uncertainties in BPRE. There is lack of past experience while a process is reengineered. Also there is no guarantee that every person who is involved in the process will extend his/her support to the team and cooperate with it. Further the resources needed may not be available in time. The BPRE project can not be planned well in advance like other conventional projects.

Because of fear of failure, the BPRE team may try to play safe and instead of going for the best solution, they many choose a suboptimal solution, which may be satisfying. This will affect the quality of the outcome of reengineering effort.

The BPRE team leader has the responsibility of driving out the fear of failure in the team members. Also, the leader should encourage the team members even if they fail in their reengineering venture. He or she should ask the members to investigate the cause of failure instead of questioning them for failure. However, the leader may advise the team members to learn from failure and take necessary action to avoid failure in future.

7. Unfavourable Organisational Environment

Although the BPRE team leader, process owners and members of the reengineering team are committed to the success of BPRE projects undertaken by them, if the majority of employees in the firm are sceptical and apprehensive about the success of BPRE projects, it is very difficult for BPRE to be successful in such firms.

Before introducing BPRE, the top management must inform all the employees at all levels in the organisation that the management is determined to improve many of its existing business processes drastically. Top management should communicate to inadequacies and deficiencies of the existing process to employees to ensure their support for reengineering. Also the management should communicate the benefit of BPRE in quantitative terms to the employees.

It is very important that top management convinces middle and junior level managers about the need to reengineer certain business processes because these people are those who are directly affected by BPRE. They are apprehensive about BPRE bringing in drastic changes such as process-orientation and team based organisational culture, which would result in their loss of power and control.

Many middle and junior level managers have reached their present position in management by performing their jobs in the traditional ways and not through process-orientation. Hence they may oppose reengineering covertly. They may not depute their high performing staff for becoming members of BPRE teams. Since the whole-hearted support of managers at all levels is essential for the success of BPRE, they must be told to change their attitude and accept and support the new initiatives. They must be asked to either change and adapt to the new culture or to quit.

Once the reengineering idea is accepted by middle and junior managers, they must be asked to convince the supervisors and employees at lower levels. This will create a conducive organisational climate which is favourable for introduction and implementation of BPRE.

8. Delay in Achieving Results

If there is undue delay in realising significant improvements in concrete terms (*i.e.,* measurable improvements), the reengineering initiatives will be adversely affected. In such cases, people will begin to doubt about the capabilities and benefits of reengineering and will look at it as a fad. If reengineering takes a very long time to yield the expected or desired results, even the top management may get disappointed and lose interest in reengineering.

Hence to overcome this problem, it is advisable to focus on key processes which can be reengineered with little investment and within short time. According to Hammer and Stanton, from the time of starting to think about a process to be reengineered till some concrete benefits are realised, it should not take more than twelve months. However, this does not mean that the whole new process will be installed and become fully operational within twelve months. On the other hand it does not mean reengineering can stretch for ever. What is important is that majority of the tasks of the reengineered process operates at high performance level within a period of one year so that, there is enough evidence about the newly designed process actually working well in practice.

9. Unsatisfactory Appraisal System

The process owners and BPRE team members work hard to reengineer a process and make it a success to meet the expectation of the team leader. They should ensure that the reengineered process should have dramatic improvements over the existing process. To achieve this, they have to work very hard and even work extra hours in office. When the reengineered process is successfully implemented and the results and benefits are dramatic, it is quite natural that they expect rewards proportionately to the efforts they have put and the gains of the organisation due to reengineering.

In order to motivate the people who have really worked hard and effected dramatic changes and improvements through their efforts must be correctly assessed by top management. Their performance should not be rewarded in the routine manner by giving them nominal rewards which may not meet their expectations. This will demotivate them and they may not put all their effort in the subsequent reengineering tasks assigned to them.

When high performers are adequately rewarded, they are highly motivated and others also show keen interest in getting involved in reengineering projects. Hence proper performance appraisal and suitable rewards worth the effort of employees will create a favourable altitude in the employees which is conducive to the success of BPRE.

The members of reengineering team, process owners and others who contribute significantly to the success of reengineering should not only be rewarded monetarily substantially, but also their contributions should be recognised and appreciated by publishing their performance in house magazines, special functions etc. The members of the BPRE team must be appraised by the BPRE team leader and not by the heads of the departments from which they have come.

It is important that the team members who have achieved drastic improvements and significant financial gain to the organisation must be rewarded a percentage of that gain rather than being rewarded with some extra increments in their salary or a promotion in recognition of their performance. The traditional method of rewarding for good performance may not be quite effective.

10. Inability to Quantify Improvement

Improvement from reengineering must be measured and shown in quantitative terms in order to show its importance (*for example,* the amount of money saved due to cost reduction by modifying a process). Even then, the improvement should be dramatic quantitatively. Alternatively, if reengineering results in improved communication systems, or improved accounting practices or improved organisational culture, all these improvements can not be quantified but only expressed quantitatively. These results are interpreted subjectively.

However, when the reengineered process yields significant quantitative benefits, simultaneously there can be some qualitative improvements such as improved quality of service leading to higher customer satisfaction or improved quality of work life. Such qualitative improvements are also welcome in addition to the quantitative improvements which are the main objectives of reengineering projects.

- **Activity B**

Discuss what can be effect of failure to quantify the improvement or outcome for any improvement project.

....

....

....

....

....

....

....

....

11. Complacency of Management

Top management of some organisations are complacent when the business is going on well and they are not having any concern for reengineering their key business processes. But sooner or later, they may feel the pressure of competition and by the time they realise the need to improve, it may be too late. Hence, some visionary at the top management level may have to take initiative to take up reengineering projects or some junior level manager may act as a catalyst and take initiative to convince top management about the need for taking up reengineering projects. The middle and junior level managers must exert relentless effort to impress upon the top management about the need for reengineering some of the existing key business processes which are inefficient and non productive. This approach is essential for any organisation to survive and grow in the face of fierce competition. Two ways of convincing top management about the pressing need for BPRE are:

(i) Bench marking the firm's key processes with other organisations who are best-in-class.

(ii) Bringing to the knowledge of top management the growing customer dissatisfaction due to some of the existing business processes.

Reengineering should not be treated as a one-time improvement process. After achieving dramatic improvements in some of the key business processes, BPRE should not be discontinued. Rather, the company should go into depth of the reengineered processes and also try to reengineer as many key processes as possible and continue to improve the processes already reengineered (*i.e.,* incremental or continuous improvement after break through improvement).

Ultimately, the organisation should create a process-oriented organisational culture where the focus of every employee should be on the whole process rather than on the specific task performed by him or her, which is a part of the whole process.

12. Non-availability of Adequate Resources

Eventhough a BPRE team may suggest an innovative idea to reengineer a process, design and evaluate the process prototype successfully, at the stage of implementation of the reengineered process if adequate resources are not available, the organisation can not realise the benefits of the reengineered process. This would lower the enthusiasm of the team members and demotivate them in their subsequent reengineering projects.

When a reengineered process could not be implemented due to lack of funds, those who are opposed to BPRE may try to convince others that it is a difficult goal for the company to achieve because it cannot afford it from financial point of view. In such situations, the BPRE leader must ensure that adequate resources needed for BPRE projects are made available as and when needed.

The team members must assess the correct requirement of resources for reengineering in terms of technology, man power etc. The resource requirements must be submitted to the BPRE leader for approval. The reengineering project must be taken up only after all the needed resources are made available to the BPRE team. *For example,* if an expert has to be released from a department to work as a member of a BPRE team, the team leader must ensure that the expert employee is spared by the concerned department head.

13. Limited Employee Awareness

Process-oriented thinking has to be institutionalised by communicating the message of the need for reengineering the business processes to all the employees of the organisation. The employees must realise that the organisation needs to conduct its business on the basis of business processes and not the tasks. They should be able to understand the difference between a task and a process. They need to understand their roles in the whole process and also their roles in implementing the process.

BPRE concepts should not be restricted to only managerial levels, the supervisors and workers also need to understand the same. They should know how their present tasks are related to BPRE concepts because their active involvement is required during the implementation of reengineered processes.

Since the BPRE leader can not meet every employee individually or in groups to make them aware of the concepts and implications of reengineering, he or she can perform the task of making the departmental managers aware of reengineering. These managers in turn meet their supervisors and workers and explain them in detail what is meant by process-oriented thinking and reengineering. Sometimes the help of external experts may be sought to introduce reengineering and conduct awareness programmes to all the employees of the organisation in batches of employees.

14. Discontinuance of Reengineering after Achieving Bench Mark

In BPRE, to start with, a company may bench-mark its key processes with those of its competitors or other companies which are best-in-class. While it is a correct approach, it is a big mistake if the company discontinues reengineering once it achieves the bench-mark. The reengineered process may have the capability to exceed the bench-mark and the company should explore this possibility. Efforts should be put to reach a level above the existing bench mark. To achieve this, the BPRE leader is expected to play a key role in motivating his team members to increase the level of the process further.

7.3 SUMMARY

Because of the complex nature of business process reengineering and the radical changes that have to be brought about in organisational structure, processes, procedures, behaviour and attitude of employees etc., its successful implementation becomes quite difficult. To over come this problem, it is necessary to understand the pitfalls and avoid the same while implementing BPRE.

The implementation of BPRE requires employees who are receptive to new ideas and who accept changes in their ways of doing things. They should be able to identify the short comings of the existing processes and have open mind to effect changes in their work methods.

In organisations having pessimistic, sceptical, defensive employees who have complacent mindset, implementation of BPRE becomes difficult. Even though top management takes initiative to introduce BPRE, employees who have negative attitude towards BPRE can become a road-block in the path of improvement and progress. Also resistance to BPRE may occur in the middle and junior management level due to the feeling of insecurity and fear of loss of power.

Some of the limitations of BPRE are:

(i) BPRE is not a panacea to achieve instant competitive advantage.

(ii) BPRE is not easy to implement. Also it may not be appropriate for all processes for all organisations.

(iii) Many organisations may not be able to invest the time and resources needed for BPRE.

(iv) Need for information technology.

(v) Improvement in each functional areas is necessary in addition to improvement in cross-functional processes.

(vi) Improvements must come from those who do the work themselves as they only understand the processes best.

(vii) BPRE may aim at "one best way" to satisfy a customer need, but may not consider what will happen if that customer needs changes.

Some of the pitfalls of BPRE are:

(i) Improper knowledge of reengineering.

(ii) Reengineering too many processes at initial stages.

(iii) Lack of training for process owners and team members.

(iv) Improper monitoring of a reengineered process.

(v) Wastage of time due to detailed process analysis.

(vi) Fear of failure.

(vii) Unfavourable organisational environment.

(viii) Delay in achieving results.

(ix) Unsatisfactory appraisal system.

(x) Inability to quantity improvement.

(xi) Complacency of management.

(xii) Non-availability of adequate resources.

(xiii) Limited employee awareness and

(xiv) Discontinuance of BPRE after achieving bench mark.

7.4 SELF ASSESSMENT QUESTIONS

1. State the limitations of BPRE.
2. List the pitfalls of BPRE.
3. What kind of organisational climate is: *(a)* favourable to BPRE and *(b)* unfavourable to BPRE?
4. "Reengineering too many processes at initial stages of BPRE has some disadvantages". What are they? Elaborate.
5. State the advantages of reengineering a few key processes at the initial stages of BPRE.
6. "Successful implementation of BPRE is affected by unclear knowledge of reengineering". Elaborate.
7. Discuss the steps involved in action planning in BPRE with a block diagram.
8. Describe the ideal pattern of a reengineered process with a diagram.
9. "In Japanese industries, break-through improvements are always accompanied by continuous improvement" – comment.
10. Discuss the disadvantages of carrying out detailed analysis of a process before it is reengineered.
11. How does fear of failure affect the successful implementation of a reengineered process?
12. How awareness of BPRE can be created among the employees of an organisation?
13. How does delay in realising the benefits of a reengineered process affect BPRE? How do you resolve this problem?
14. Discuss the differences between a traditional appraisal system and an appraised system needed for process-oriented organisation.
15. Discuss the need to measure the major results of BPRE and express them quantitatively.
16. Discuss the possible behavioural improvements that can be brought about by successful reengineered processes.
17. How does complacency of management of an organisation becomes visible in BPRE?
18. Discuss the procedure that should be followed for ensuring availability of the needed resources during the implementation of reengineered processes.
19. Why is the discontinuance of reengineering after achieving bench-mark regarded as a pitfall in BPRE?

◆ ◆ ◆ ◆ ◆

8 Chapter

CHANGE MANAGEMENT IN BPRE

Objectives

After going through this chapter, you would be able to :

- Learn about various aspects of CHANGE PROCESS associated with BPRE.
- Understand various sources and forces for bringing in CHANGE.
- Learn about sequence of steps for a CHANGE PROCESS.
- Get knowledge about various factors which cause resistance to a CHANGE PROCESS and approaches to reducing these resistance.
- Learn about relationship and difference between terms, CHANGE and INNOVATION.
- Get knowledge about various strategies tobe followed for implementing CHANGE successfully

Structure

8.1 INTRODUCTION

Business Process Reengineering is a major break-through initiative which calls for drastic changes or innovation improvements in the ways business processes are carried out and organisations function.

Organisations continually evolve, whether by expanding, contracting, exploring or eliminating which means that over a period of time, some changes would have occurred making the difference between the status of the organisation at the beginning and at the end of this time period. Any organisation that desires to improve or to keep up with its competitors has to change, change is invertible, *change is the one constant in any organisation*.

Managing change is not easy, but it can be done, or done well by following a change management process. By managing change effectively, the managers can control change instead of letting it control them.

BPRE deviates from traditional function oriented vertical organisational structure to process focused, team work based horizontal organisational structure consisting of cross-functional teams, task forces or project teams. In BPRE, many old practices are dramatically modified or totally changed or replaced by new practices. Implementation of reengineered business processes necessitates managers and employees to forget what they have been doing for years and learn new ways of doing things. The problem encountered not with paucity of creative ideas or innovative technology, but with attitudes and belief of people who are involved in the reengineered process or those who are affected by implementation of BPRE projects. Therefore, proper management of human resources in dramatically changing work-environment is the greatest challenge to be faced by the BPRE team and the organisation implementing BPRE projects.

In today's highly complex world, organisations need to continuously adapt to new situations if they are to survive and prosper. This process of change is termed **"organisational change"**, which is defined as the adoption of a new idea or behaviour by an organisation. The current trend in organisational change is toward development of **learning organisation** which is the epitome of continuous organisational change and growth.

Before discussing various aspects of change process associated with BPRE such as structure of change, nature of change, process of change, role of change, resistance to change, commitment to change, culture and change, synergy and change, resilience and change etc., we will discuss "change management" as a topic of general interest in the following section.

8.2 CHANGE MANAGEMENT

The 21st century managers are facing inescapable and inevitable pressures from many sources to change their organisations. In the 1980s, managers have witnessed significant and irreversible changes in organisations to respond to global competition, diversity in the workplace, the drive for quality and responsiveness etc.

Organisations are encountering a wide variety of dramatic changes. Organisations face government regulations or deregulations, expanding or shrinking markets, merges or hostile acquisitions, downsizing programs, business process re-engineering programs and the like. The faster pace of change required by the electronic age, of the shift to a service economy and the growth of the global competition have made change mandatory and resistance to change-a problem to be solved. The problem for managers is that even if they use their logical arguments and persuasive skills to support a change, the employees remain unconvinced of the need for it. Hence, managers must be able to understand the ***nature of change, reasons for resistance to change*** and ways to ***introduce change*** more successfully.

8.3 NATURE OF CHANGE

Change is any alternative in the current work environment. The shift may be in the way things are perceived or in how they are organised, processed, created or maintained. Change is experienced by every individual and organisation. Some times external events cause change beyond the control of a person on an organisation. Some times change results from planning. *For example*, a company plans to reduce the price of its products or services to increase market penetration. But one simple change may trigger a series of changes. For instance, a company lowers prices to increase sales. If sales increase, the production should increase for which the company may need more production capacity, additional staff or equipment etc. to handle the volume of orders. A more efficient technology may have to be adopted to meet the needs and so on.

Sources of Change: Change originates in either the external or internal environments of the organisation. **External sources** include the political, social, technological or economic environment, externally motivated change may involve government action, technology development, competition, social values and economic variables. Managers must adjust to developments in the external environment.

Internal sources of change include managerial policies or styles, systems and procedures, processes, methods and employee altitudes.

Types of Change: Change can be understood on the basis of its focus, which can be ***strategic, structural, process oriented*** **or** ***people centred***.

These changes have considerable impact on organisational culture.

Strategic change is a change in the strategy or mission of the organisation. *For example*, diversification of business, acquisition of new business or merging with another company are strategic changes which in turn may require a change in organisational culture.

Structural change is a change in the organisational structure such as ***team building*** or ***downsizing***. These changes are made to make operations run more smoothly, improve overall coordination and control or empower individuals to make their own decisions in the area of their work.

Process-oriented change are changes related to technology, automation, robotics, computerisation and the like. If process-oriented change takes the form of ***reengineering,*** it, may have dynamic effects on the organisation's culture.

People-oriented change include changes directed at the **attitudes, behaviours, skills** or **performance** of the employees of the organisation. It is very crucial for managers to change their employees in order to change their organisations. People-oriented changes can be achieved through retraining, replacing current employees or increasing the performance expectations of new employees.

- **Activity A**

Prepare a list of few structural and process-oriented changes you have observed in your organisation in last few months/years.

....

....

....

....

....

....

....

....

Rates of Change: Change can be viewed as ***evolutionary*** or ***revolutionary*** based on its pace. ***Evolutionary change*** focuses on the incremental steps taken to bring about progress and change. It is a gradual continuous change. ***Revolutionary change*** focuses on bold, major break-through; discontinuous advances. The revolutionary changes ("leaps") bring about dramatic transformations in organisational strategies and structures. These changes are brought about by the practice of **"outside-of-the-box thinking"**. *For example*, "Business Process Reengineering" is a tool of revolutionary change which is immediate rather than incremental.

Forces for Change: The various forces for change are listed in *Exhibit 8.1*.

Exhibit 8.1 : Forces for Change

Force	Examples
(i) Nature of the work force	• More cultural diversity • Increase in professionals • Inadequate skills of new entrants
(ii) Technology	• More Computers and automation • TQM programs • Re-engineering programs
(iii) Economic shocks	• Security market crashes • Internet rate fluctuations • Foreign currency fluctuations
(iv) Competition	• Global competition • Mergers and consolidation
(v) Social trends	• Increase in college attendance • Delayed marriage by young people • Increase in divorce rate
(vi) World politics	• Collapse of Soviet Union • U S occupation of Iraq

(i) **Nature of workforce:** Every organisation is having to adjust to a multicultural environment. Human resource policies and practices have to change in order to attract and keep more diverse workforce.

(ii) **Technology:** Technology is changing jobs and organisations. The substitution of computer control for direct supervision is resulting in wider spans of control for managers and flatter organisations.

(iii) **Economic shocks:** From early 1970s, with the steep rise in oil prices, economic shocks have continued to impose changes in organisations.

Interest rates have become highly volatile and economics of individual countries have become more interdependent.

(iv) **Competition** is changing in the global economy. In such environments, establishing organisations need to define themselves against both traditional competitors who develop new products and services as well as small entrepreneurial firms with innovative offerings. Successful organisations will be those that can change in response to the competition.

(v) **Social trends:** Past social trends suggest changes that organisations have to adjust for. For instance, there has been a change in the trend of marriages and divorce over a period of time.

(vi) **World politics:** The recent changes in the world politics were: the fall of the Berlin Wall, the reunification of Germany, invasion of Kuwait by Iraq and the consequent Gulf War, break up of the Soviet Union, and the recent invasion of Afghanistan and Iraq by US forces etc. The changes in world politics will have an impact on global economy and on the demand for certain products. It also results in increase or decrease of defence budgets of some countries.

8.4 THE CHANGE SEQUENCE

The sequence of events that is needed to bring about change in an organisation is referred to as the **change sequence.** Whether the intended change is from a less participative to a more participative corporate culture or along some other dimension, the process tends to follow a certain pattern. *Exhibit 8.2* illustrates the sequence of events as identified by social psychologist Kurt Lewin.

First the management should recognise a need for change. Then the specific change method should be identified. Finally, the following steps should be carried out:

(i) Unfreezing the status quo.

(ii) Moving to a new condition

(iii) Refreezing to create a new status quo.

Feedback is provided to determine whether the change has recurred or whether further change is needed. The steps involved in the change sequence are discussed in the following paragraphs:

Step 1: Recognising the need for change: The question that should be asked is: **"Is the change necessary?"** Changes should not be made merely for the sake of change. Organisations and people want some degree of stability in order to accomplish their assigned tasks. Yet there are times when changes become necessary and the failure to be quick and decisive can prove disastrous for the firm.

Exhibit 8.2 : The Change Sequence

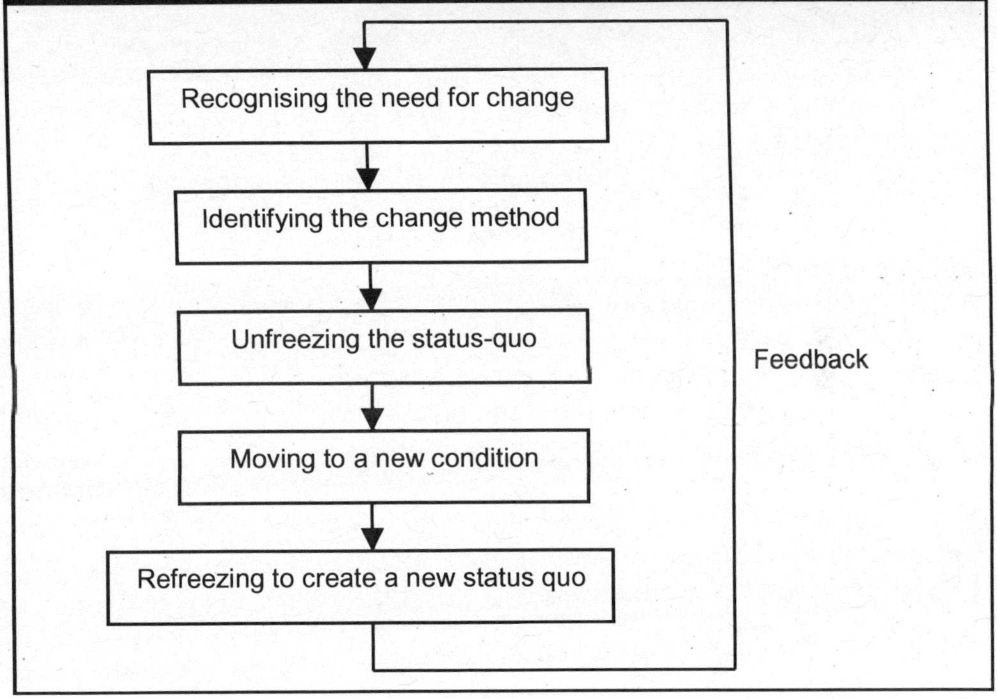

It has been found by many firms that cultural change is not only feasible, but necessary. At times, firms may need to change their culture or go out of business. Five reasons for imposing rapid cultural change are:

(i) If your company has strong values that don't fit a changing environment.

(ii) If the industry is very competitive and moves with lightening speed.

(iii) If your company is mediocre or worse.

(iv) If your company is about to join the ranks of the very large companies.

(v) If your company is small but growing rapidly.

Step 2: Identifying the change method: Management may use one among numerous methods and techniques for organisational change and development. Some specific techniques are ***survey feedback***, ***team building***, ***sensitivity training***, ***management by objective***, ***job enrichment*** and the ***Managerial grid approach***.

Step 3: Unfreezing the status quo: If individuals are to change their present attitudes, their current beliefs need to be altered or unfrozen. Resistance to change needs to be eliminated or reduced if a change is to be effective. Resistance to change can be reduced by building trust and confidence, developing open communication and encouraging employee participation.

Unfreezing often generates self-doubt, but it also provides a means of overcoming it. Employees should be made to feel that ineffectiveness is undesirable but that it can be remedied. If organisation members are to be receptive to change, they should feel that they can change.

Step 4: Moving to a new condition: A change can be initiated through an order, a recommendation or a self-directed impetus. A manager with authority can command that a change be implemented and can enforce it by threats, punishment and close supervision. If a change is implemented by authority, its implementation has to be closely monitored. On the other hand, change is more permanent and substantial if people truly want and feel a need to change. Change may be effectively initiated by developing a two-way relationship between the person who is trying to implement the change and those who will be affected by the change. The person who implements the change should make suggestions and those who will be affected should be encouraged to contribute and participate in the implementation of change.

Steps 5: Refreezing to create a new Status Quo: Too often changes that are introduced do not stick. If persons who change to a set of new work habits for a short time and then revert back to the former practices, it means the change is not effective. If the change is to be permanent, people need to be convinced that the change is in their own interest and also in the interest of their organisation. One of the best ways to accomplish this is to collect objective evidence of the success of change.

People should feel competent about and take pleasure in using the new or changed behaviour. But the change will be completely accepted only if the reward system of the organisation is geared to the new form of behaviour (*i.e.*, changed behaviour). People tend to repeat behaviour that they find rewarding.

8.5 TYPES OF CHANGE

1. **Work change:** Work change is any alternation that occurs in the work environment. Its effect are as follows:
   (a) The whole organisation tends to be affected by change in any part of it.

(b) Change is a human as well as technical problem.

(c) Organisations tend to achieve an equilibrium in their social structure. The equilibrium is established when people develop a relatively stable set of relations with their environment.

The manager's role is to *introduce* continual organisational changes so as to bring about a better fit between the firm and its environment. The manager should be **proactive**–anticipating events, initiating change, and taking control of the organisation's destiny. Also the manager is **reactive**–responding to events adapting to change and tempering the consequence of change.

2. **Planned versus Reactive change:** Some changes are planned well in advance, while some other changes come about as a reaction to unexpected events.

   Planned change is a change that is designed and implemented in an orderly and timely fashion in anticipation of future events.

   Reactive change is a piecemeal response to events as they occur.

3. **Technological change:** High technology is one of the most important cause of organisational change today. As a result of technological advances, more than half of the existing jobs will be changed within the next decade and about 30 per cent of the jobs will be eliminated. In the manufacturing or production technology field, revolutionary changes have taken place. Robots and computer-controlled machines manufacture items while technicians stand by computer controls, monitoring activities.

- **Activity B**

Prepare a list of few planned as well as reactive changes you have observed in your organisation in last few months/years.

....

....

....

....

....

....

....

....

8.6 RESISTANCE TO CHANGE

Organisations and their members resist change. Resistance can be ***overt, implicit, immediate*** *or* ***deferred***. Overt and immediate resistance can be easily dealt with by managers as compared to the resistance to change which is implicit or deferred. Most organisational change efforts eventually run into some form of employee resistance. Change triggers rational and irrational emotional reaction because of the uncertainty involved.

Who do people resist change?

Four common reasons for resisting change are:

1. **Parochial Self-Interest:** One reason some people resist organisational change is the fear of losing something they value. Individuals fear the loss of power, resources, freedom to make decisions, friendships, and prestige.
2. **Misunderstanding and lack of trust:** When individuals do not fully understand why change is occurring and what its implications are, they resist change. Misunderstanding about the intent and consequence of organisational change is more likely to occur when trust is lacking between the individual and the person initiating the change.
3. **Different assessments:** Since individuals view change–its intent, potential consequence and personal impact–differently, there are often different assessments of the situation. Those initiating changes see more positive results because of the change, while those being affected and not initiating the changes see more costs involved with the change.
4. **Low tolerance for change:** People resist change because they fear they will not be able to develop the new skills necessary to perform well. Individuals may understand clearly that change is necessary, but they are emotionally unable to make the transition.

A low tolerance for change is also found in individuals who resist change to save face. Making the necessary adjustments and changes would be, they assume, an open admission that some of their previous behaviour, decision and attitude were wrong.

Resistance to change is a human response, and management needs to take necessary steps to minimise such resistance. Minimising resistance can reduce the time it takes for the change to be accepted or tolerated.

Sources of Resistance to Change

A change may cause some loss to the person or organisation affected by it. In major and unexpected changes, employees, groups and even departments or divisions often experience daze, shock, recoil or turmoil. *Exhibit 8.3* illustrate some of the many sources of resistance to change.

The sources of resistance to change are discussed in the following paragraphs:

1. **Insecurity:** For people working in a comfortable environment for quite sometime, a change of environment often brings about uncertainty and people no longer know exactly what to expect from the implementation of change. A sense of insecurity prevails in people who are subjected to change from one environment to another. *For example*, when a person moves from high school to college, or from one job in a city to another job in another city, a sense of insecurity may occur.

Exhibit 8.3 : Sources of Resistance to Change

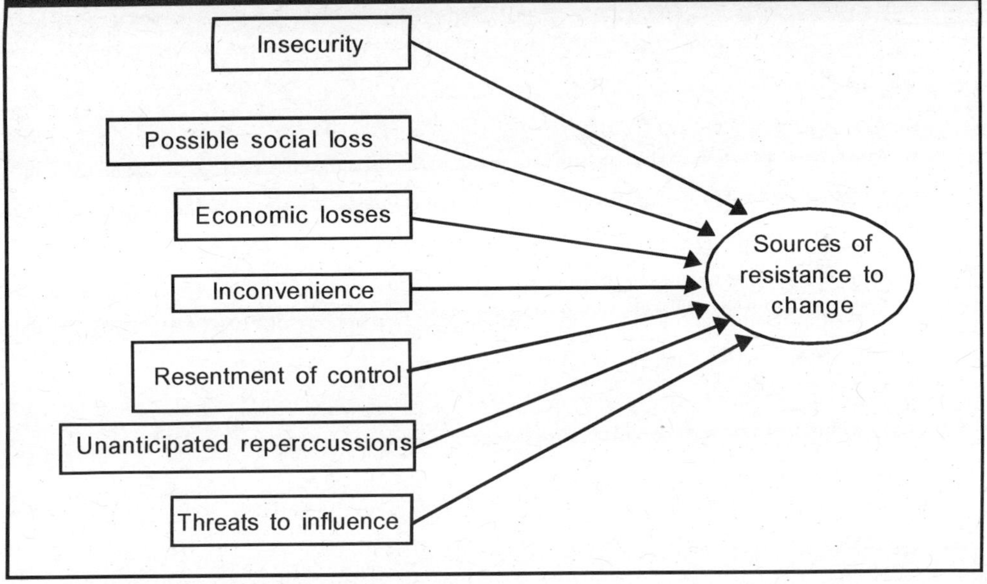

2. **Possible social loss:** Change has a potential to bring about social loss. The informal work group may be extremely strong. If a change causes an individual to be transferred, the power of the group is likely to be diminished. The individual who is transferred gets affected as he or she loses the association with the other members of the group. This loss is referred to as '**social loss**'.
3. **Economic losses:** New technology may enable a firm to produce the same amount with fewer employees. Even though some of the

employees rendered surplus in some department because of **automation,** may be redeployed and retained, some other workers may suffer an economic loss.

4. **Inconvenience:** Even when a change is not associated with a social or economic loss, new procedure and techniques may have to be learnt. Physical and mental energy need to be expended and some may not like the same.
5. **Resentment of control:** When employees are told that a change is to take place, they are made to realise that they do not have any other option other than implementing the change. This may create some resentment that employees may not have any control over their destiny. Even though the change may be for better, they are likely to resent the change. *For example*, if the management makes it compulsory for the employees to wear uniform, then such change may be resented because the employees feel that they do not have any other choice but to wear uniform.
6. **Unanticipated repercussions:** Because the organisation is a system, a change in one department or division is likely to have unforeseen repercussions in another. *For example*, a newly designed job may require a change in supervisory behaviour and supervisors may resist this change even if they initially supported the concept of *job enrichment* by redesigning the jobs.
7. **Threats to influence:** When a change is likely to reduce the power base of a group, department or division, even if it is good for the organisation as a whole, it is likely to meet resistance of employees concerned with the change.

8.7 APPROACHES FOR REDUCING RESISTANCE TO CHANGE

Change is often necessary despite the resistance that might arise. During downsizing, firms can minimise resistance by communicating the need for new strategies, treating people who are let go with respect and kindness, letting key people know that the firm and the people will be around for a long time.

Some of the approaches designed to reduce resistance to change are illustrated in *Exhibit 8.4* and discussed in the following sections:

1. **Provide information in advance:** Whenever possible managers should provide employee who will be affected by the proposed change, information in advance regarding the reasons for the upcoming change, its nature, its planned timing, and its possible effects on the organisation

and its personnel. Withholding information that could seriously affect the lives and future of particular individuals should be avoided if possible. However, competitive survival of a firm may require the information regarding future changes to be closely held until shortly before the change is to occur.

Exhibit 8.4 : Approaches for Reducing Resistance to Change

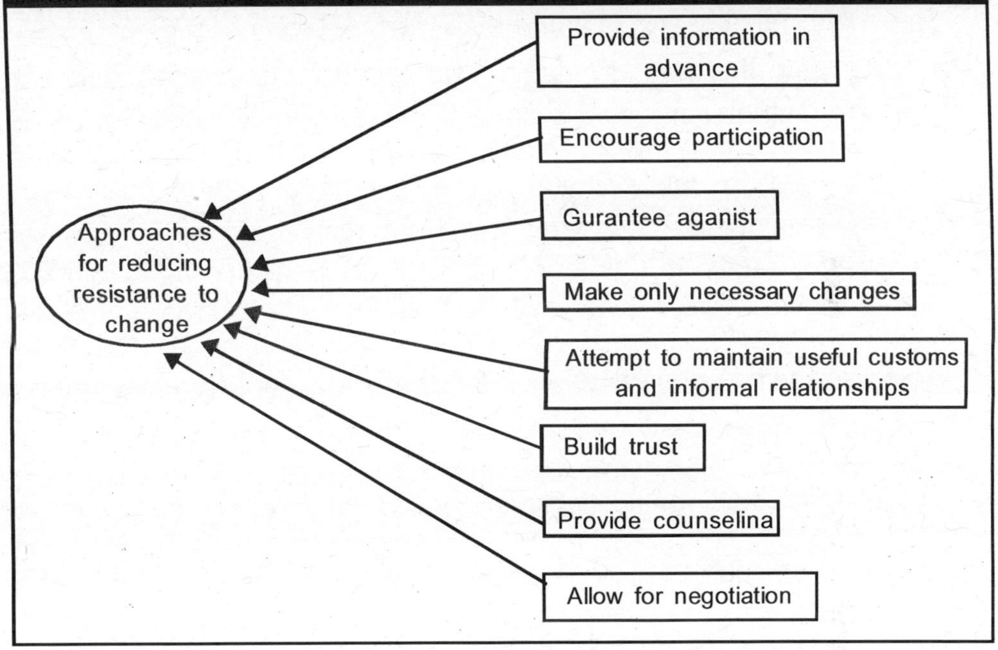

2. **Encourage participation:** When possible, employees should be encouraged to participate in establishing the change. A person who is involved in implementing change procedure will likely to be more supportive of the change.

3. **Guarantee against loss:** To promote acceptance of technological changes, some organisations guarantee that there will be no lay-offs as a result of such changes. In case of changes in methods and output standards, employees are often guaranteed retention of their present level of earnings during the learning period.

4. **Make only necessary changes:** Changes should be made only when the situation demands them, not because of the whims and fancies of managers. If a manager makes changes for the sake of change, he will soon discover that any changes proposed by him will receive only minimal acceptance irrespective of whether it is beneficial or not.

5. **Attempt to maintain useful customs and informal norms:** Whenever possible, changes should be made to coincide with the

cultural and informal norms of the organisation. This is important because of the real value of informal workgroup from the stand point of interpersonal relationships. For instance, when safety shoes were introduced, few would wear them willingly because of their unusual appearance. When they were redesigned to resemble normal shoes, the resistance faded. This implies that changes that go against established customs and informal norms will likely create resistance and have little chance of being readily accepted.

6. **Build trust:** If a manager has a reputation for providing reliable and timely information to employees, the explanation as to why a change is to be made will likely be believed. The change may still be resisted, but if the manager is trusted by the employees, problems will be minimised.
7. **Provide counselling:** Counselling or discussion with the employees who will be affected by the change may reduce the resistance and may stimulate them to voluntarily adopt a change. Nondirective counselling has been used effectively in many change situations.
8. **Allow for negotiation:** Resistance to change can be reduced by the process of negotiation. Negotiation is a primary method used by labour unions to effect modification of proposed managerial changes.

8.8 WHY CHANGE EFFORTS FAIL?

Not all change efforts are successful. Managers can not always bring about desired changes. Change efforts may fail because of the following reasons:

(i) **Faulty thinking:** Managers may fail to achieve desired change due to improper analysis of the situation. *For example*, an insurance company may try to increase the number of new clients without perceiving the need to promote a new culture that valued team work and internal cooperation rather than competition.

(ii) **Inadequate process:** Sometimes change efforts fail because of the process adopted to bring about the changes. The manager may not follow the steps properly or he may choose an inappropriate change agent (outside consultant)

(iii) **Lack of resources:** Some changes which require a significant expenditure of time and money may fail if adequate resources are not made available to the manager responsible to bring about the changes.

(iv) **Lack of acceptance and commitment:** If individuals, both managers and employees do not accept the need for change and commitment to

it, such a change will not occur. If managers are used to announce change but do not implement, then in such a situation, employees do not take change implementation seriously resulting in failure of change efforts.

(v) **Lack of time and poor timing:** Some situations do not allow enough time for people to think about the change, accept it and implement it. In some other instances, the timing is poor or not proper. *For example*, launching a new product during an economic downturn may not bring the desired sales and profits. Also if a company takes enormously more time to implement a change, the environment may drastically change and the plan devised for implementing the change may not be applicable.

(vi) **A resistant culture:** In some cases, the cultural climate of an organisation needs to be changed before any other change can be implemented. If employees resist change by culture, their attitudes must be changed first before anything else.

8.9 INNOVATION AND CHANGE

In considering more closely the concepts of change and innovation, it is useful to distinguish between these two terms. **Change** refers to any alteration of the status quo, whereas **innovation** is a more specialised kind of change. Innovation is a new idea applied to initiating or improving a process, product or service. ***All innovations imply change, but not all changes are innovations*** since changes may not involve new ideas or lead to significant improvements.

As long as an idea for bringing about an improvement is perceived as new by the individuals involved, it is generally considered as an innovation. But organisations must be careful in adapting ideas so as to ensure that they are not engaged in illegal copying, violating the copy right laws or infringing patents held by others.

Innovations in organisations can range from radical new breakthrough's (such as laser technology, Internet, fibre-optics and the like) to small incremental improvements (such as improved quality ribbon on a computer printer). Both radical and incremental improvements can be advantageous. Japanese companies have became known for their ability to enhance products and services through a series of small, incremental improvements referred to as "**continuous improvement**" (or **Kaizen** in Japanese language)

Innovation involves considerable amount of ***uncertainty,*** since progress and successful outcomes may be difficult to predict. Also, the process tends to be ***knowledge-intensive*** which means that those close to the development of innovation may possess most of the knowledge about the situation, during the development stages. This may result in high employee turnover.

Another characteristics is that the innovation process often is ***controversial*** because resources allotted to a particular innovation project could presumably be divided to pursue alternative courses of action.

Finally, the innovation process often crosses ***organisational boundaries;*** because development and implementation frequently involve more than one unit, increasing the complexity of effort for innovation. Hence, there is a need for managers not only to understand the major aspects of change but also the plan for the special needs of the innovation process.

Promoting Innovation: The processes of innovation and change are similar. Innovation is a special type of change which tends to be more difficult because it moves beyond traditional changes and relies on incorporating significant new ideas. Changes can be either **planned change** or **reactive change.** Planned change is change which involves actions based on a carefully thought out process for change that anticipates future difficulties, threats and opportunities.

Reactive change is the change which occurs when one takes action in response to perceived problems, threats or opportunities.

When managers operate in a reactive mode, they are more likely to make serious mistakes because they are continually making changes without planning. Hence, it is desirable that managers engage in planned or proactive changes and innovation rather than reactive changes.

A SIX STEP MODEL FOR PLANNED CHANGE OR INNOVATION

The process followed by managers when they engage in planned innovation and change are illustrated in *Exhibit 8.5*.

Step 1: Perceiving an Opportunity or a Problem: According to Peter Drucker, a noted management consultant, one reason why managers are not innovative is that they have a tendency to focus on immediate problems and to ignore opportunities. Progressive organisations which want to maintain *competitive* edge need to look ahead for opportunities as well as to solve current and anticipated problems. Drucker suggests holding periodic sessions at which senior managers would ask junior managers to indicate areas in which they see opportunities for or threats to the organisation and new things they think should be done.

Step 2: Diagnosing the Situation and Generating Ideas: Without diagnosing the situation and generating ideas it is very difficult to fix problems or take advantages of opportunities. In pursuing new ideas, it is important not to overlook the status of on-going activities relative to the competition.

Exhibit 8.5 : Model of Planned Innovation and Change Process

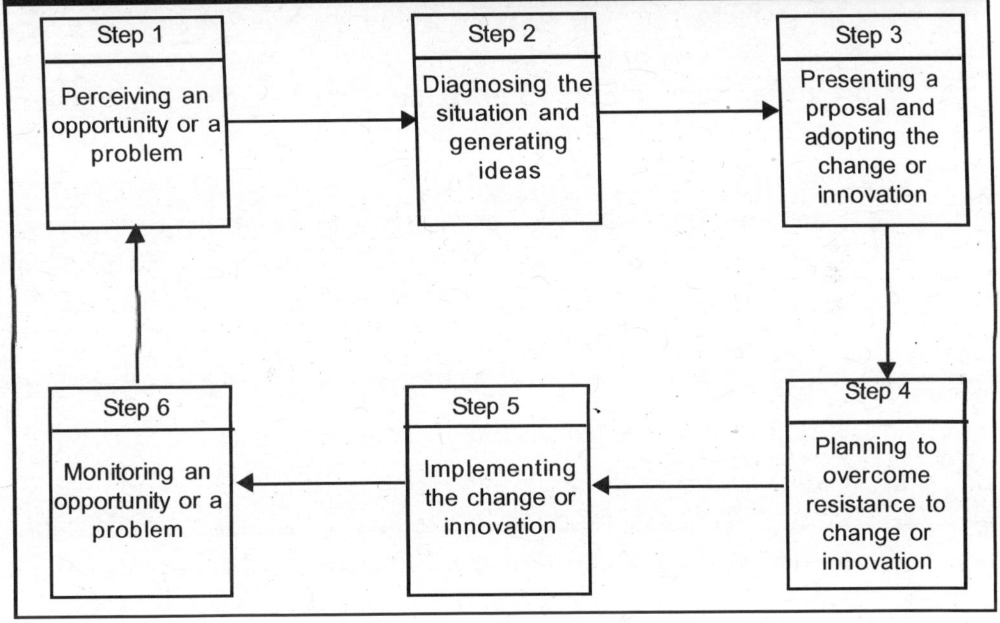

Step 3: Presenting a Proposal and Adopting the Change: Managers must work hard to establish the fact that innovation and change are important to the organisation. Otherwise, most good ideas will be rejected when they are proposed. Managers need to prepare a written business plan outlining how new ideas will be developed. Without this, they can not get their budget proposal approved for the new projects.

Step 4: Planning to Overcome Resistance: The fact that one group, even top management decide to adopt a change does not mean that others will readily go along with it. Managers must plan to overcome employee resistance to change and understand the reasons for such resistance to change. Such issues are critical to managing change and innovation effectively.

Step 5: Implementing the Change or Innovation: This is the **moment of truth** when the change is put into operation. If a change is thought out well to begin with and the planning step is carefully carried out, the implementation of the change or innovation will be smooth.

Step 6: Monitoring the Results: It is not advisable to implement a significant change without monitoring and evaluating what happens after the change has been implemented (Successful innovations and changes usually follow the six steps discussed above.)

8.10 MANAGING CHANGE

Managers are responsible to bring about organisational changes to accommodate the customer's changing needs. As **change agents,** managers must be committed to improve their organisation's performance. Initiating change involves identifying what organisational area might need to be changed and putting the change process into motion.

Managers are concerned with **planned change** and not merely any **change.** ***Change means making things different whereas planned change involves activities that are intentional and goal oriented.***

The goals of planned change are:

(i) It seeks to improve the ability of the organisation to adapt to changes in its **environment.**

(ii) It seeks to change **employee behaviour.** For its survival, an organisation must respond to changes in its environment. When competitors introduce new products, when government enacts new laws, and environmental change takes place, the organisation needs to adapt to the changes. Planned change activities directed at responding to changes in the environment include efforts to ***stimulate innovation, empower employees*** and ***introduce work-teams.***

Planned change is also concerned with changing the behaviour of employees (individuals and groups) within the organisation. Planned change can be viewed as **first order change** and **second order change** in terms of order of magnitude. First order change is linear and continuous whereas second order change is multi-dimensional, multilevel, discontinuous and radical.

The **change agents** are responsible for managing change activities. They can be managers or non-managers, employees of the organisation or even outside consultants. Senior executives and chief executive officers are typical change agents referred to as primary change agents, whereas outside consultants with specialised knowledge initiate second-order changes.

What can change agents do? The change agents can bring about changes which fall under four categories: *(i)* **Structure,** *(ii)* **Technology,** *(iii)* **Physical setting** and *(iv)* **People.**

Changing ***structure*** involves making changes in authority relationships, co-ordination mechanisms, job redesign and the like. *i.e.*, (structural variables) Changing ***technology*** encompasses changes or modifications in the processing of work and in the methods and equipments used.

Changing the physical setting includes altering the space and layout in the workplace.

Changing ***people*** refers to changes in employee attitudes, skills, expectations, perceptions and/or behaviours.

The above changes brought about by managers (change agents) are discussed in the following section:

Changing Structure: An organisation's structure encompasses structural issues such as ***work specialisation, span of control, departmentalisation, centralisation versus decentralisation, formalisation, job design*** etc. As the conditions change, the organisation needs to undergo structural changes to suit the changed conditions.

An organisation's structure determines how tasks are formally divided, grouped and co-ordinated. Managers as change agents can alter one or more of the key elements in an organisation's design. *For example*, departmental responsibilities can be combined, spans of control widened, vertical layers reduced etc., to make the organisation less bureaucratic. Decision making process can be speeded up by increasing decentralisation.

Also major modification in the structure can be brought about by changing the simple structure to a ***team-based structure*** **or** ***a matrix design.*** Jobs and work schedules may be redesigned. Job descriptions can be redefined, jobs enriched or flexible working hours introduced, organisation's compensation system may be modified, incentives may be introduced to increase motivation etc.

Changing Technology: Today, major technological changes involve introduction of new equipment, tools, or methods, automation and computerisation. Automation is a technological change that replaces people with machines which work automatically, without intervention from human beings. Computerisation has enabled introduction of management information systems which has totally changed the way in which business organisations operate.

Changing the Physical Setting: The layout of the workplace is done taking into consideration, work demands, formal interaction requirements, and social needs. It includes decisions regarding space configurations, interior design, equipments installation and the like. The layout of work place needs changes as products produced by the organisation changes, technology is changed etc.

Changing People: This involves changing the attitudes and behaviours of organisational members through processes of communication, decision-making and problem solving.

Organisational Development (OD): This concept encompasses an array of interventions designed to change people and the nature and quality of their working relationships.

8.11 IMPLEMENTING CHANGE SUCCESSFULLY

Today's business environment is very dynamic and changes are the order of the day. Some changes originate within the organisation, but many come form the external environment. For instance, new laws are legislated by the government which the organisations must comply, new developments in technology arise, competitors introduce new products / services, customer's likes and dislikes change, life styles change. There are pressures from customers, labour unions, communities and competitors which force change on organisations.

Several methods of implementing change in organisations are discussed in the following section:

(i) **By transformational leaderships:** Transformational leaders are managers who initiate bold **strategic changes** to position the organisation for its future. They articulate a **vision** and sell it vigorously. They stimulate employees to action and charismatically model the desired behaviours. They attempt to create ***learning individuals*** and ***learning organisations*** that will be better prepared for the unknown future challenges. Three important elements of transformational leadership are: *(a)* ***creating a vision***, *(b)* ***figuring charisma*** and *(c)* ***stimulating learning***.

Creating Vision: A **vision** is a crystallised long-range image or idea of what can be and should be accomplished. A vision may also integrate the shared beliefs and values that serve as a basis for changing an organisation's culture.

Communicating Charisma: Managers as leaders need to persuade employees that the vision is urgent and to motivate them to achieve it. **Charisma** is a leadership characteristic that can help influence employees to take early and sustained action. Charismatic leaders are dynamic risk takers, who show their depth of expertise and well deserved self-confidence, express high performance expectations, and use provocative language to inspire the followers. Charismatic leaders are respected and trusted by employees as they introduce change and tend to be emotionally committed to the vision of such leaders.

Stimulating Learning: Transformational leaders develop people's capacity to learn from the experience of change. This process is called **double-loop learning.** The employees, who are double-loop learners, develop the ability to anticipate problems, prevent many situations and to be more ready for the next change to be introduced in the future.

(ii) **By use of group forces:** The group is an instrument for bringing strong pressures on its members to change. Since behaviour is firmly grounded in the groups to which a person belongs, any changes in group forces will encourage changes in the individual behaviour. The idea is to help the group join with management to encourage desired change.

(iii) **By providing a rationale for change:** Capable leaderships reinforce a climate of psychological support for change. The effective leader presents change on the basis of the impersonal requirements of the situation, rather than on personal grounds. Change is more likely to be successful if the leaders introducing it have high expectations of success. Managerial and employee expectations of change may be as important as the technology of change.

(iv) **By participation:** Participation encourages employees to discuss, to communicate, to make suggestions and to become interested in change. Participation encourages commitment rather than mere compliance with change. Commitment implies motivation to support a change and to work to ensure that the change is effective.

Employees need to participate in a change before it occurs, not after. When they are involved in the planned change, right from the beginning, they feel committed to the implementation of such change.

(v) **By sharing rewards:** By ensuring that there are enough rewards for employees in the changed situation, managers can build employee support for change. Rewards also give employees a sense that progress accompanies a change. Both economic and psychic rewards are useful.

(vi) **By ensuring employee security:** Along with shared rewards, existing employee benefits need to be protected. Security during a change is

essential in the form of protection from reduced earnings when new technology and methods are introduced. Seniority rights, opportunities for advancement etc., are to be safeguarded when a change is made.

(vii) **By communication and education:** Support for change can be gained by communication and education. All individuals or groups that will be affected by change must be informed about the change in order to make them feel secure and to maintain group cooperation.

(viii) **By stimulating employee readiness:** Employers should be helped to become aware of the need for a change. Change is more likely to be accepted if the people affected by it recognise a need for it before it occurs.

Box 8.1 lists some guidelines for managing change.

It is also essential for managers to take a broader, systems-oriented perspective on change to identify the complex relationships involved. **Organisational development** can be a useful method for achieving this objective.

Box 8.1 : Guidelines for managing change

1. Make only necessary and useful change
2. Teach employees to expect continual change and the need to develop new skills.
3. Change by evolution, not by revolution.
4. Recognise the possibility of resistance to change and develop appropriate strategies for controlling each source of resistance to change.
5. Involve employees throughout the change process to diminish resistance.
6. Share the benefits of change with employees.
7. Diagnose the problems remaining after a change occurs and treat them.

8.12 CHANGE PROCESS ASSOCIATED WITH BPRE

Structure of Change

BPRE is viewed as a major change initiative. Employees of organisations that introduce changes as a part of BPRE, view these changes as ambiguous and threatening. They are not clear about their role in the change process and they fear about the consequences of change. They are afraid of losing their power and control, positions and even their jobs as a consequence of dramatic changes that will be brought about by introducing BPRE. Hence it is necessary for top management to clear this wrong perception of employees and allay their fear about the bad consequences of BPRE to their career.

Just like different persons have different perceptions of BPRE, different organisations may also have different views about BPRE. One organisation may view BPRE as a major challenge to be faced, internalised, institutionalised and exploited to keep pace with the changing demands of the market and also to provide opportunities for career growth of employees.

Another organisation may not be able to with-stand the pressure of change brought about by BPRE. It may not be able to change its traditional structure to an effective process-oriented, team based structure. What is needed for organisations is the ability to have resilience or flexibility to adapt to the changes which become necessary .

The organisational change process follows the following pattern:

1. Nature of change, 2. Process of change, 3. Rates of change, 4. Resistance to change, 5. Commitment to change, 6. Culture and change, 7. Synergy and change and 8. Resilience and change.

1. Nature of change : When an individual employee of an organisation has abilities and willingness to use his abilities to match with a change, he or she can predict the outcome of such a change and the change does not create any fear in the employee. On the contrary, an employee who does not have the abilities or willingness to meet the demands necessitated by the change, feels insecure and threatened by the change.

A person's attitude towards change depends on the nature of change as well as his or her perception of the extent to which his or her abilities can determine the result of change. A person develops a positive attitude toward change when he regards the change as positive and is able to control the outcome of such change. On the other hand, a person may have negative attitude toward change when he or she views the change as negative and not able to predict the outcome and does not have control over it.

Those who regard BPRE as an initiative to contribute their creative ideas to improve processes significantly and avail of opportunities for their career growth will develop a positive altitude towards BPRE and change. On the other hand those who view BPRE as a threat to their traditional ways of working and a road block to their career path will develop a negative attitude towards BPRE and change.

Different persons have different abilities, different perceptions and different altitudes.

Changes can occur at three levels namely *(a)* **Macro level,** *(b)* **Organisational level** and *(c)* **Micro level**.

Macro changes have global implications and have little impact on an individual's behavioural pattern. Organisational changes relate to the work place and the organisation in which an individual is employed. Micro changes are experienced by an individual at personal level.

Organisational changes caused by BPRE affect an individual's attitude and behaviour when he or she is required to make drastic changes in the way he or she is doing his or her work. Even though an employee's present way of doing work is not affected during the initial stages of introducing BPRE he or she may have to develop the ability to anticipate change in the future.

2. Process of change : BPRE is a major change initiative which should be regarded as a dynamic on-going process rather than an isolated, one-time event. The top management decides to introduce BPRE after examining

(a) the way the organisation is currently functioning.

(b) the price it is paying in terms of customer dissatisfaction and lost business opportunities as a consequence of maintaining status-quo and

(c) the benefits it may derive as a result of improvement to achieve the desired state.

The process of change involves there phases.

(i) Phase 1 – Present state, *(ii)* Phase 2 – Transition state and *(iii)* Phase-3 – Desired state.

Phase 1 or present state relates to status-quo in which an organisation is currently carrying out its activities. This status-quo is disrupted as a result of the introduction of BPRE due to external forces such as customer requirements, competitor's business practices etc.

Before introducing the process-oriented, team based approach envisaged in BPRE, the traditional, function-oriented organisation culture must pass through the transition state in which employees learn to change their ways of doing their job from functional orientation to process orientation.

To reach the desired state through the introduction of BPRE, two things must happen; *(i)* acceptance by the employees of the inevitable trauma of transition state with fortitude and flexibility and *(ii)* dissatisfaction with the present state.

Apart from the proper management of transition state, it is necessary to execute the change process at the right time with proper and economic utilisation of technical and human resources.

Since the impact of BPRE on existing organisational structure in disruptive, it is advisable not to take up too many BPRE projects at a time, particularly when BPRE in introduced for the first time in an organisation. This would reduce the disruptive impact of BPRE and enable the employees to undergo the transition state with less trauma and more flexibility.

3. Roles of change : In a change management the different individuals and groups play the following four distinct roles : *(i)* Sponsors of change, *(ii)* Agents of change, *(iii)* Targets of change and *(iv)* Advocates of change.

These roles are clearly visible in organisations implementing BPRE successfully.

Sponsors are those who are empowered to bring about change. In BPRE, the team leader who is the chief operating officer (coo) of the company is the sponsor.

Agent is an individual or group who is responsible for making the change. In BPRE, the process owners and the team members play the role of sponsors. They are appointed by the sponsor. The agents are required to understand the current process and evolve ways and means of improving the process significantly. They are also responsible for the implementation of BPRE projects.

Targets of change are the people who need to change their way of doing their work. They need to change their attitudes and behaviours to accept the change as a positive step. Their role is crucial for the successful implementation of BPRE.

Advocates of change represent individuals or groups who are keen to bring about change. They do not have the authority to implement the change. In BPRE the **"catalyst"** plays the role of advocate, who may be a middle or junior level manager and who has process orientation.

4. Resistance to change : The nature and source of resistance to change and its intensity are difficult to predict. The persons who are viewed as trouble makers in the traditional system do not resist change introduced by BPRE and rather welcome the change. At the same time, loyal employees who are happy with the traditional system resist change. They are not prepared to accept the challengers of reengineering.

5. Commitment to change : Commitment to reengineering at all levels of management is essential for the success of change brought about by BPRE. Commitment is required from not only leaders, process owners, BPRE team members, and catalysts but also from targets *i.e.,* those who are affected by the reengineered process and those who are supposed to implement the reengineered process. Lack of initiative will result in failure of major change initiatives including BPRE.

Various actions indicative of commitment are: *(i)* allotment of adequate resources, *(ii)* persistence in the face of covert and overt resistance, *(iii)* keeping away from the attraction of short-term benefits, *(iv)* constant focus on the ultimate goal, *(v)* encouragement and *(vi)* application of innovative ideas to achieve the desired goals etc.

6. Culture and change : Organisational culture is defined as a system of shared values and beliefs that interact with an organisation's people, structure and control systems to produce behavioural norms. It is a powerful force which determines individual and group behaviour in an organisation. It represents a key element of the work environment in which employees perform their jobs.

Successful introduction of a new culture tuned to the needs of a major change initiative such as BPRE requires the systematic development of a new set of values, beliefs and behaviours which are in tune with the change. It is the responsibility of top management to develop and nurture a new culture which is aligned to the change.

7. Synergy and change : Synergy is the cooperative action of two or more persons working together to accomplish more than what they could achieve working separately. The relationship between two individuals or two groups which interact may be positive, mixed or negative. In a positive or synergistic relationship, the participants demonstrate mutual trust, commitment, team spirit, confidence, clear understanding and acceptance of change and respect for the view of others. They are flexible to change and adapt themselves to change without much difficulty. An organisation characterised by positive relationship among its employees is likely to succeed in its efforts to implement and sustain in its efforts to implement and sustain the reengineering processes.

Two factors that determine synergistic behaviour are : willingness and ability. The employees should have willingness to accept the need for mutual dependence to achieve the common organisational goal. Also they must be able to put their best efforts to generate creative ideas for the success of their joint endeavour.

8. Resilience and change : Since BPRE involves major changes, it is essential that the employees develop resilience (or flexibility) and understand the need for change and also the consequence of change. This approach will enable them to confront change with confidence and fortitude. Once the employees understand the implications of change and their roles in the change process, they would be able to overcome their inherent resistance to change and welcome change. They are unlikely to have a feeling that they are victims of change.

APPROACHES TO RADICAL CHANGE

The organisation change that may have to be brought about in BPRE is radical or discontinuous in contrast to the other kind of change which is incremental or continuous.

The steps involved in successful implementation of radical change are:

(i) Establishing a sense of urgency.

(ii) Forming a powerful guiding coalition.

(iii) Creating a vision

(iv) Communicating the vision

(v) Empowering others to act on the vision.

(vi) Planning for and creating short-term successes.

(vii) Considering improvements and producing more changes.

(viii) Institutionalising new changes.

8.13 MANAGEMENT OF CHANGE IN BUSINESS PROCESS REENGINEERING

An organisation contemplating the introduction of BPRE should follow a seven step approach to manage change. These are:

(i) Assembling a change management team.

(ii) Establishing a new direction for the organisation.

(iii) Preparing the organisation for change.

(iv) Setting up change teams to implement change.

(v) Aligning structures, systems and resources to support change.

(vi) Identifying and removing road blocks to change.

(vii) Absorbing changes into the culture of the organisation.

These steps are briefly discussed in the following section.

(i) **Assembling a change management team :** The chief operating officer (COO) or the head of a strategic business unit (SBU) heads the BPRE team as its leader to initiate major changes in the business processes of the organisation. Since the BPRE team has other commitments, it is advisable to form a small team responsible for change management and to assist the team leader in reengineering efforts. In an organisation where the major change initiatives come from **catalysts** (those who are in middle or junior management level) instead of top management, the team formed to manage change is referred to as ***"transition management team"***.

(ii) **Establishing a new direction for the organisation :** In organisations where reengineering is introduced in earnestness, the mission statement should reflect the organisation's commitment to process-orientation and team work. This mission statement gives a new direction to the organisation.

(iii) **Preparing the organisation for change :** The message of change must be communicated to the employees at all levels of the organisation. The communication should emphasise the inevitability and the urgency of change and also the benefits of change and the adverse consequences if the organisation does not internalise change. Three aspects of effective communication in reengineering are

(a) Communicate only facts and not values

(b) Communicate directly (*i.e.,* face to face)

(c) Target front-line supervisors who take active part in introducing change.

Communication of facts relate to some of the critical business processes of the organisation in terms of costs, speed, quality, customer service etc., and the extent to which these are lagging behind those of competitors. The change management team should communicate face-to-face to small groups of front-line supervisors about the urgency of introducing major changes. Also the supervisors in turn keep the workers informed of the change initiatives taken up by the BPRE team. They should encourage employees to raise their concerns without hesitation and clear their doubts if any regarding the changes.

(iv) **Setting up teams to implement change :** The change teams referred to as reengineering teams are formed by the BPRE team leader. Each team is headed by a **"process owner"** and is responsible for implementing a reengineered business process.

Because reengineered processes are cross-functional, each reengineering team represents people from different departments. The team members should be knowledgable, creative and enthusiastic. They should be willing to face and handle employee resistance during the implementation of reengineered processes. Also the team members must be willing to work as members of teams. They should subordinate their individual interests to group interest and organisational interest.

(v) **Aligning structures, systems and resources to support change :** The change management team should examine the existing organisational structure, systems and procedures to ensure that these

are aligned properly with the change process. Reengineering teams assist the change management teams in these tasks. In BPRE, the emphasis is on process orientation and team work which will reduce insular functional activities. As a result the organisation structure will become flatter. (*i.e.*, with less number of hierachical levels). The BPRE teams must be provided with adequate resources and authority to implement the changes required to achieve drastic improvements. The team members must be empowered to take decisions and must be given enough autonomy to work on their own. The change management team should support the reengineering team members to put their ideas into practice.

(vi) **Identifying and removing road blocks to change :** Since reengineering involves major changes, resistance to such changes is inevitable. Many drastic modifications of many existing systems may have to be incorporated as per the recommendation of reengineering teams. Since the resistance to change creates a road block to the implementation of the recommendations of the reengineering team, the change management team should help to remove these road blocks. It may be necessary to counsel and train those who resist change to convince them about the need for change and give them a clear picture of the things that are going to be changed. Resistance to change and BPRE may be expressed overtly or covertly by executives at any level of management. Hence it is necessary that top management act as role models to implement change and motivate others to follow suit.

(vii) **Absorbing changes into the culture of the organisation :** As a fall out of BPRE, change should be institutionalised and internalised. This will lead to more and more employees identifying themselves with process and not functions or departments. They are held responsible for the whole process and not for specific discrete functions or jobs they perform as a part of the process. This calls for radical changes in the performance appraisal and reward systems. Also, the organisation needs to invest substantially in training to impart new skills, values and attitudes to employees. The new system must focus on team work, process-orientation and customer satisfaction.

Further to above changes, BPRE also brings about major changes in organisational communication. BPRE emphasises more face-to-face communication and front-line supervisors act as a major link in the communication chain.

8.14 SUMMARY

Since BPRE is a major break-through initiative, it calls for drastic changes or innovation improvements in the ways business processes are carried out and organisations function. For any organisation that desires to keep up with its competitors, change is inevitable.

Eventhough managing change is not easy, it can be done well by following change management process systematically. BPRE deviates from traditional function-oriented vertical organisational structure. Implementation of reengineered processes requires managers and employees forget their old ways of doing things and learn new ways of doing things.

BPRE team faces the greatest challenge of managing the human resources in dramatically changing work environment. Hence there is a need for organisations to continuously adapt to new situations for their survival and prosperity. The current trend in organisational change is toward development of learning organisations.

In the 21st century, organisations are encountering a wide variety of dramatic changes. Hence managers must be able to understand the nature of change, reasons for resistance to change and ways to introduce change more successfully.

Change is defined as any alteration in the current work environment. The sources of change are classified as external sources and internal sources. The types of change are: strategic, structural, process oriented and people oriented changes.

Change can be viewed as evolutionary or revolutionary based on the pace or rate of change. The forces of change are: nature of workforce, technology, economic shocks, competition, social trends and world politics.

The steps in the change sequence are:

(i) recognising the need for change, *(ii)* identifying the change method, *(iii)* unfreezing the status-guo, *(iv)* moving to a new condition and *(v)* refreezing to create a new status-quo.

Resistance to change is inevitable. Resistance can be overt, implicit, immediate or deferred. The reasons for people to resist to change are:

(i) parochial self-interest, *(ii)* misunderstanding and lack of trust, *(iii)* different assessments, *(iv)* low tolerance for change.

The sources of resistance to change are:

(i) insecurity, *(ii)* possible social loss, *(iii)* economic losses, *(iv)* inconvenience, *(v)* resentment of control, *(vi)* unanticipated repercussions and *(vii)* threats to influence.

Approaches to reduce resistance to change are:

(i) provide information about change in advance to those who will be affected by change.

(ii) encourage participation of those affected by change in implementing the change.

(iii) guarantee against loss

(iv) make only necessary changes

(v) attempt to maintain useful customs and informal norms

(vi) build trust

(vii) provide counselling and

(viii) allow for negotiation.

Change efforts fail because of *(i)* faulty thinking, *(ii)* inadequate process, *(iii)* lack of resources, *(iv)* lack of acceptance and commitment, *(v)* lack of time and poor timing, *(vi)* a resistant culture.

Innovation and change are not the same. Change refers to any alteration of the status-quo whereas innovation is a more specialised kind of change. Innovation is a new idea to improve a process, product or service. It is also known as a planned change.

The steps involved in planned change or innovation are:

(i) perceiving an opportunity or a problem.

(ii) diagnosing the situation and generating ideas

(iii) presenting a proposal and adopting the change

(iv) planning to overcome resistance

(v) implementing the change or innovation and

(vi) monitoring the results

Managers act as change agents. They are committed to improve their organisation's performance by initiating changes and incorporating them. Managers can bring about changes in the organisational structure, technology, physical setting and people.

Several methods of implementing change in organisations are:

(i) By transformational leadership, *(ii)* By use of group forces, *(iii)* By providing a rationale for change, *(iv)* By participation, *(v)* By sharing rewards, *(vi)* By ensuring employee security, *(vii)* By communication and education and *(viii)* By stimulating employee readiness.

The change process associated with BPRE is mainly concerned with the change in the organisational structure. It follows the following pattern:

(i) Nature of change, *(ii)* Process of change, *(iii)* Rates of change, *(iv)* Resistance to change, *(v)* Commitment to change, *(vi)* Culture and change, *(vii)* Synergy and change and *(viii)* Resilience and change.

The steps involved in successful implementation of radical changes are

(i) Establishing a sense of urgency.

(ii) Forming a powerful guiding coalition.

(iii) Creating a vision

(iv) Communicating the vision

(v) Empowering others to act on the vision.

(vi) Planning for and creating short-term successes.

(vii) Considering improvements and producing more changes.

(viii) Institutionalising new changes.

The steps to be followed in managing change due to introduction of BPRE are:

(i) Assembling a change management team.

(ii) Establishing a new direction for organisation.

(iii) Preparing the organisation for change.

(iv) Setting up change teams to implement change.

(v) Aligning structures, systems and resources to support change.

(vi) Identifying and removing road blocks to change.

(vii) Absorbing changes into the culture of the organisation.

8.15 SELF ASSESSMENT QUESTIONS

1. What is change management?
2. What is the relevance of change management to BPRE?
3. Discuss the forces of change.
4. Describe the steps involved in the change sequence.
5. Discuss the various types of change.
6. What is "resistance to change"?
7. Discuss the various sources of resistance to change.
8. Discuss the various approaches for reducing resistance to change.
9. What is innovation? What is planned change?
10. Discuss the six step model for planned change or innovation.
11. What is meant by managing changes?
12. What are change agents? What can change agents do?
13. Describe how would you implement change successfully.
14. Describe the pattern of the organisational change process.
15. State the steps involved in successful implementation of radical change.
16. Discuss the seven step approach for managing change while introducing BPRE in an organisation.

♦ ♦ ♦ ♦ ♦

Chapter

9 REINVENTING THE ORGANISATION

Objectives

After going through this chapter, you would be able to :

- Understand the importance and need for restructuring or reinventing the organisation.
- Learn about various objectives to be kept in mind while doing organisation design.
- Get knowledge about various factors which affects organisational design.
- Learn about various organisational theory.
- Get knowledge about various types of organisation structures and their advantages as well as limitations.
- Understand the role of Human Resource Management function in organisation design for bringing in improvements.
- Get insight into what after BPRE? i.e. the concept of Holonic Business System, which allows businesses to continually to de-invent and re-invent themselves as they face increasingly ambiguous markets.

Structure

9.6 Contingency Factors Affecting Organisational Design

9.7 Organisational Theory

9.8 Major Approaches to Organisational Theory

9.9 Types of Organisational Structures

9.10 Reorganising the Firm Without Destroying it

9.11 The Role of Human Resource Management in Organisational Improvements

9.12 Beyond Business Process Reengineering

9.13 The Holonic Concept

9.14 The Virtual Corporation

9.15 Reengineering the Corporation

9.16 Reinventing the Corporation

9.17 Summary

9.18 Self Assessment Questions

9.1 INTRODUCTION

Today, the Indian Economy is changing very fast because of the entry of multinational companies. The domestic firms need to compete with multinational firms for their very survival and growth. They must export and exploit global opportunities. For this they have to match the MNCs in terms of quality, speed (time to deliver), cost innovations and governance advantages. The domestic firms must become world-class, whether they would like to go for global business or to remain contended with domestic business. Since the introduction of Exim Policy-1992 (Liberalisation, Privatisation and Globalisation) companies in the corporate sector in India face a jungle like situation (with the philosophy of the survival of the fittest) with fierce competition for survival. This has resulted in mergers, acquisitions and restructuring of many companies in their quest for survival or in their strategies for growth.

Integrating two or more business entities with different processes, redundancies and disparate cultures is difficult and it requires change of system and procedures, adapting new technologies and new work cultures and the like. It may be even necessary to go for **restructuring the organisation** or **reinventing the organisation.** This is also referred to as **corporate reengineering** or **corporate restructuring.**

RESTRUCTURING THE ORGANISATION

In order to cope with the changes they now face, companies are being advised to redesign their business processes, restructure or reinvent their organisations and recreate their corporations. Various terms are used in this context, *viz.*, *reassessing, repositioning, reconfiguring, restructuring* and *revitalising the business*. This can be done by adopting new approaches, applying new methodologies or processes, and using new technologies and techniques already developed or in the process of development. The global approach to business process reengineering involves examination of all aspects of the total quality concept – *i.e.*, the needs of the shareholders, customers and organisation's members – then identify the mainstream process operations and the management of these activities as well as the support processes; such as finance and human resource management. The examination of each facet of the business process for the purpose of improvement and the implementation of changes contribute to the achievement of the global objectives of the organisation and to the well being of its people.

The major feature of this global approach is its shift from a ***microvision*** to a ***macrovision*** of the organisation, its systems, its structures and its work methods. Macrovision encompasses the microvision within its longer scope. In this approach, instead of assigning individual departmental or sector-based objectives, all departments and sectors in the organisation have the common, explicit (rather than traditionally implicit) objective of contributing to the company's shareholders and customer-driven global objectives. Integrating all activities within an organisation, in addition to taking into account the external upstream and downstream partner's activities presents a serious challenge.

Before we discuss the topics such as reorganising, restructuring or reinventing the organisation, we need to know the various types of organisations. The following section gives an account of organisational structure, organisational design, organisational theory and types of organisational structures. The readers must be familiar with these topics before reading topics such as reorganizing, restructuring or reinventing the organisation or reengineering the corporation.

One of the major ingredients in managing any business is the **creation of structure** to link the various elements that comprise the organisation. Organising is defined as the process of creating the organisational structure. The challenge for managers is to design an organisational structure that allows employees to do their work effectively. We will discuss how the elements of organizing can be combined to create an overall design of the organisation in the following section.

9.2 WHAT IS AN ORGANISATIONAL STRUCTURE?

An organisational structure is the formal network by which jobs/tasks are divided, grouped and coordinated. It reflects the formal relationships among groups and individuals in the organisation. The structure provides guide lines for effective employee performances and overall organisational success. It should clarify and communicate the lines of responsibility and authority within the firm and assist management in coordinating the overall operation.

Organisational structures of some kind are required for every firm, large or small which may or may not have an organisational chart. Small businesses may have structures which are simple and easy to understand, may be informal and highly changeable. Whereas large, diverse and complex organisations usually have a highly formalized structure which may not be rigid and may need to be changed quite frequently.

Determining the most appropriate organisational structure is not a simple matter and many firms often experience major restructuring or reorganisation. Also many variations of organisational structures are used. The most common types of structures developed are **line, line and staff, functional authority, divisional, project, matrix and hybrid** organisational structures which are discussed in detail later in this chapter.

9.3 WHAT IS ORGANISATIONAL DESIGN?

Organisational design is the overall set of structural elements and the relationships among those elements used to manage the total organisation. It is a means to implement strategies and plans to achieve organisational goals. It involves designing an organisational structure by developing or changing an organisation's structure.

Organisational design is the process by which managers select and manage aspects of structure so that an organisation can control the activities necessary to achieve its goals. It is about **how** and **why** various **means** are chosen. Organisational design enables managers to strike a balance between external pressures from the organisational environment and the internal pressures from its internal environment (say *for example*, choice of technology).

Relationship Between Organisational Design and Organisational Structure

Organisations in the computer software industry which operate in the high-tech computer industry, need to be flexible and capable of quick responses to their competitor's strategies and need to be innovative in developing and using a new technology. At the same time such organisations must have stable task relationships that allow their member to work together to create value, solve problems and achieve organisational objectives. On the other hand, companies manufacturing metals such as steel and aluminum, face relatively stable environment in which customer needs are more predictable and technology changes more slowly. Hence, the organisational design choices of such companies are likely to reflect the need for a structure that reduces production costs rather than promotes flexibility.

9.4 OBJECTIVES OF ORGANISATIONAL DESIGN

The four objectives of organisational design are briefly discussed in the following paragraphs:

Responding to change: "Nothing lasts for ever", "Change is inevitable", "Either change or perish", "Change is the only thing that is permanent" – these could be the slogans of organisational designers. For a firm to remain competitive, it must respond to changes in the environment – competition, technology, global economy and consumer needs – as well as the changes that emerge from the company's evolutionary development and proactive initiatives.

Integrating new elements: As organisations grow, evolve, expand and respond to changes, many new positions and departments will have to be added to deal with factors in the external environment or with new strategic needs. These new elements will have to be integrated into the overall structure of the organisation which means virtually restructuring the organisation. For instance, the strategic need to enhance quality of customer service may need dismantling of functional departments, creating teams and redelegating authority.

Coordinating the components: After creating new departments, managers need to find a way to tie all the departments together to ensure coordination and collaboration across the departments. The departments have to work together either through reporting relationships, cross-functional teams or task forces in order to avoid conflicts and problems and to meet customer needs.

Encouraging flexibility: Organisational designers want to build into the organisation – with all its authority, chains of command, bases of departmentalisation – flexibility for decision making, for responding and redirecting resources and for focusing employee's talents. This objective differs from that of responding to changes.

9.5 THE IMPORTANCE OF ORGANISATIONAL DESIGN

Increased global competitiveness and increasing use of advanced information technology has made organisational design as one of management's top priorities in the present business environment. Managers of today are under pressure to search for new and better ways to coordinate and motivate their employees to increase the value created by their organisations. Organisational design has major implications for an organisation's ability to deal with contingencies, achieve competitive advantage, effectively manage diversity and increase its efficiency and ability to innovate new goods and services.

The design of an organisation determines how effectively an organisation responds to various factors in its environment and obtains and makes use of the scarce resources it has. An organisation can design its structure to increase control over its environment. More effective types of structures are developed to respond to the increasing pressures from competition, consumers and the government which will make the environment more complex and difficult to respond to. Organisational design becomes more important in a global context because to become a global competitor, a company often needs to create a new structure. Changing technology also puts pressure on organisations to respond. *For example*, today the emergence of **Internet** as an important new medium through which organisation manage relationships with their employees, customers and supplies is fundamentally changing the design of organisational structure (*for example* call centers and back offices).

9.6 CONTINGENCY FACTORS AFFECTING ORGANISATIONAL DESIGN

Managers having the responsibility for organisational design, study the contingency factors that affect organisational design and then design a structure to fit these contingency factors. The contingency factors to be studied are briefly discussed in the following paragraphs.

(i) **Strategy:** Logically structure follows strategy because organisational structures are built to achieve objectives by implementing the strategies. When strategy changes, structures must change. At the corporate level, strategies are formulated based on the company's mission and strategic goals or objectives.

(ii) **Environment:** Environment has an impact on decision making – specifically the difficulty of making decisions in an uncertain or unpredictable environment. Similarly, the stability and predictability of the environment have a direct bearing on the ability of the organisation to function effectively. An unstable environment that changes rapidly and is less predictable has two requirements:

- The organisation must be able to adapt to change, for which it needs to be flexible and responsive.
- The organisation needs greater coordination among departments.

(iii) **Size of the organisation:** The number of employers working in an organisation indicates its size. It is observed that large organisations differ structurally from small ones in terms of division of labour, rules and regulations, performance appraisal and budgeting procedures.

(iv) **Age of the organisation:** With age, an organisation incorporates standardised systems, procedures and regulations. Like people, organisations evolve through stage of life cycle – ***birth***, ***youth***, ***midlife*** and ***maturity***. In the birth stage, the organisation created by the

entrepreneur is informal, with no rules and regulations. Decision making is centralised with the owner and tasks are not specialised.

In the youth stage, the organisation is growing – it expands and hires more employees. It incorporates division of labour and formal rules and policies. Decision making is still with the owner although it is shared by few persons close to the owner.

In the midlife stage, the company has become quite large. It now has extensive sets of rules, regulations, policies and systems to guide the employees. Control systems are used, professionals are hired, tasks are decentralised and authority is delegated to functional departments. In the maturity stage, rules, regulations, specialised staffs, budgets, a refined division of labour and control systems are in place.

(v) **Technology:** Some kind of technology is used to convert the resources into outputs in every organisation. Technology includes the knowledge, machinery, work procedures, and materials that convert the inputs into outputs. The technology used to manufacture the products decides the kind of the organisation for the production system.

- **Activity A**

Analyse the organisation design of your firm and list a few factors which has affected in formation of present structure.

....

....

....

....

....

....

....

....

9.7 ORGANISATIONAL THEORY

Organisational theory is the study of how organisations function and how they affect and are affected by the environment in which they operate.

The knowledge of organisational theory enables managers to analyse the structure and culture of their organisation, diagnose problems and utilize the process of organisational design, make changes in the structure and culture that help the organisation to achieve its goals.

Exhibit 9.1 illustrates the relationship among organisational theory, structure, design and culture.

Exhibit 9.1 : The relationship among organisational theory, design, and culture

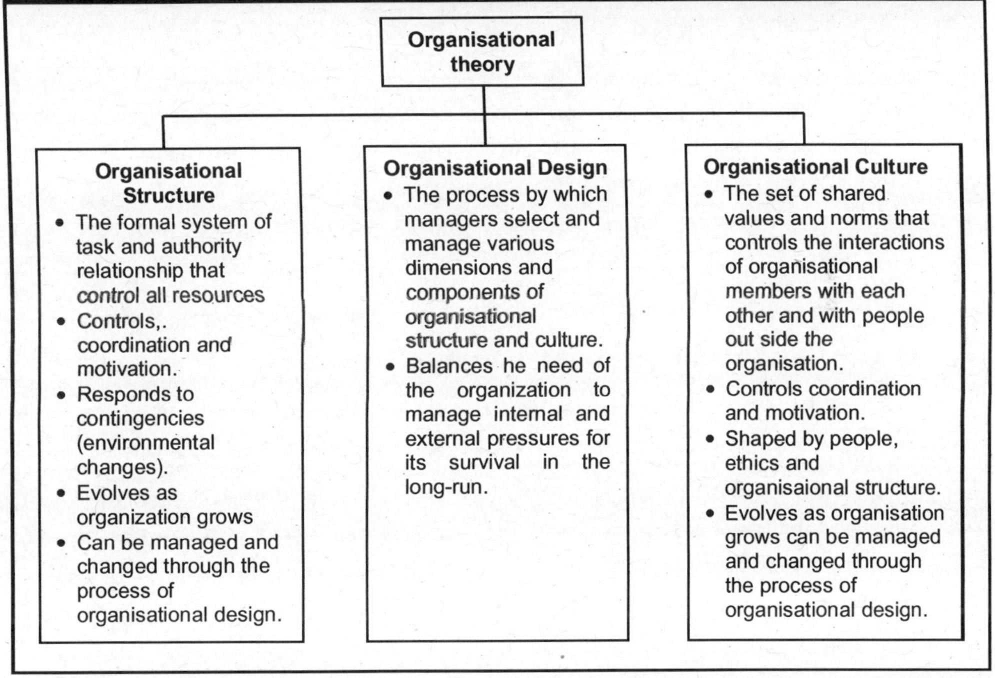

The organisational theory and major approaches in organisational theory are discussed in the following paragraphs.

Organisational Theory Defined

Organisational theory is concerned with the organisational structure *i.e.,* how to design an organisational structure that ensures a firm's effectiveness.

Organisational theory can be defined as the subject concerned with understanding, explaining and predicting how best to design the best structure for an organisation to fulfill its objectives/goals.

Organisational theory is a set of rules developed by organisational experts to help managers re-organize their companies effectively.

Organisations are systems *i.e.,* purposeful social units and consist of people who carryout differentiated tasks which are coordinated to contribute to the organisational objectives/goals.

Two basic aspects of organisation are:

(a) Their Structure and *(b)* How compliance is assured.

Organisational structure and design is concerned with how to distribute specific tasks and responsibilities among the members of the organisation.

Structural dimensions include span of control, departmentation, centralisation and decentralisation, delegation and co-ordination and how context affects each dimension.

Compliance: It is not enough to simply assign tasks to individuals. We have to ensure that those tasks are in fact carried out *i.e.,* compliance takes place. Tasks are assigned to people who are directed to comply with orders and carryout the tasks assigned to them.

Context: The organisations context is its environment, technology and size which influence how it is organized and managed. Context has a major influence on how the organisation is structured and managed.

Organisation as a process has three issues :

1. Provision of an organisational climate so that people are motivated to give off their best in achieving organisational objectives.
2. Design of communication systems for effective decision making, control and co-ordination *i.e.,* adequate information flow at each decision center.
3. An overall organisation that is innovative and responsive to relevant environmental changes.

9.8 MAJOR APPROACHES TO ORGANISATIONAL THEORY

1. Classical Approach (Theory X)

Emphasis is on structural factors and functions or activities to achieve the objectives. Stress on specialisation and co-ordination, and chain of command facilitates co-ordination and communication.

Four key pillars of classical theory are :

(a) Division of labour

(b) Scalar and functional processes such as unity of command, chain of command, delegation of authority, defining responsibility and accountability.

(c) Structure-line and staff.

(d) Span of control.

The classical theory has relevant insight into the nature of the organisation. The theory concentrates on the structure of formal organisation neglecting the interplay of individual personality, informal or social groups and intra-organisational conflicts. The classical theory (Theory X) views organisation as a structure which centers around work and not around people. Theory X views man as an economic being, results in carrot and stick approach to motivation.

The classical approach believed in authoritarian and autocratic managerial style.

Disadvantages of Classical Theory

1. Ignores human behaviour and human relation.
2. Absence of rapid and free channels of communication.
3. Discounting innovation, initiative and change.
4. Lack of flexibility and adaptability.
5. Tight control through force and coercion.
6. Absence of intrinsic rewards.

2. The Neo-classical Approach (Theory-Y)

This approach reflects human relations movement as well as behavioural science approach. It studies motives, supervision, group and intergroup behaviours. It points out that effective co-ordination of activities is impossible without the willing co-operation of people.

This theory propagates **people-oriented** organisational structure which will integrate informal and formal organisations (democratic/participative management style). Two concepts of Theory-Y approach are individual and work group. *i.e.,* inter personal relations and need for two way communication in the organisation demanded special attention in developing humanised organisational structure

Contributions

1. Emphasised role of informal organisations as agencies of social change (Informal Leadership)
2. Division of labour-Neo classical theory developed motivational theory and theory of co-ordination and leadership. Human problems are caused by lack of understanding of human behaviour in organisations.

- **Activity B**

Make a comparative statement between theory X and theory Y. According to you, which theory should be preferred and why?

....

....

....

....

....

....

....

....

3. Behavioral science approach : This approach utilises methods and techniques of social sciences such as psychology, sociology, social-psychology and anthropology for the study of human behaviour. This approach advocates that managing an organisation involves getting things done with and through people and the study of management must be centred around people and their interpersonal relations. It emphasizes motivation, individual drives, group relations, leadership, group-dynamics etc.

4. Modern organisational theory : This approach defines organisation as a system and also considers the impact of environment on the effectiveness of the organisation. This theory has three approaches namely.

   ***(a)* Systems approach *(b)* Contingency approach and *(c)* Multi-variate approach.**

(a) **Systems approach :** This approach is based on the view that an organisation is an open system composed of inter-related and inter-dependent elements. The organisation is an open-adaptive system interacting with its own environment. The salient features are: *(a)* Environmental influences on structure, *(b)* Adaptability (*i.e.*, responding to change), *(c)* Efficiency and effectiveness, *(d)* Emphasis on human values, *(e)* Emphasis on inter-relationship and inter-dependency of sub-systems, *(f)* Integration and co-ordination of all sub systems into the total system, *(g)* Attention is paid towards the over-all effectiveness of the system rather than the effectiveness of the sub-systems.

(b) **Contingency approach :** This is concerned with the analysis of specific organisations with their external environments and the adoption of a suitable structure to meet the requirements of the situation. The emphasis is on the need to adapt the organisation to the demand of changing technology, need for innovation generating from environmental and decision making uncertainty. This approach suggests that "There is no one best way to handle any of the managerial problems and there is no one best organisational structure to suit all situations."

The salient features are:

(i) Situational factors play an important role in the design of organisational structure and a suitable management style

(ii) The determinants are *(i)* Size of the organisation: Bigger the size, higher the complexity, *(ii)* Interaction need : free flow of communication needed.

(c) **Multivariate approach :** This approach is a modification of the contingency approach. It views the organisation as consisting of four interacting variables namely: *(i)* **Task**, *(ii)* **Structure**, *(iii)* **Technology** and *(iv)* **People**-Interactive means a change in any one variable automatically produces a change in other variables. The interacting variables are:

(i) Task–Basic business

(ii) Structure–System of authority, workflow and communication

(iii) Technology–Tools and equipments

(iv) People–(Actors)-People and their behaviours.

Change can effectively begin in any one variable as people are re-oriented, structure, task and technology can be changed. *Exhibit 9.2* illustrates the multi-variate approach to organisational theory.

Exhibit 9.2 : Multivariate Approach to Organisational Theory

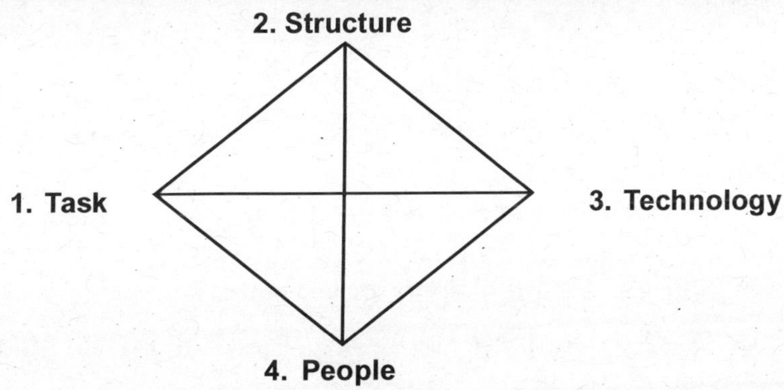

If technology improves (*i.e.,* computer numerically controlled machines, robotics, automation) there is a need to change people skills and organisational structure and task will also change.

If people are re-oriented (new labour force), structure, task and technology will also change.

9.9 TYPES OF ORGANISATIONAL STRUCTURES

Formal and Informal Organisations

All managers must bear that there are two organisations they must deal with-one **formal** and the other **informal.**

The formal organisation in usually delineated by an **organisational chart** and job descriptions. The official reporting relationships are clearly known to every manager.

Along side the formal organisation exists are informal organisation which is a set of evolving relationships and patterns of human interaction within an organisation that are not officially prescribed.

Formal organisational structures are categorised as:

(i) Line organisational structure.

(ii) Staff or functional authority organisational structure.

(iii) Line and staff organisational structure.

(iv) Committee organisational structure.

(v) Divisional organisational structure.

(vi) Project organisational structure.

(vii) Matrix organisational structure and

(viii) Hybrid organisational structure.

These organisational structures are briefly described in the following paragraphs:

1. Line Organisational Structure

A line organisation has only direct, vertical relationships between different levels in the firm. There are only line departments-departments directly involved in accomplishing the primary goal of the organisation. *For example*, in a typical firm, line departments include production and marketing. In a line organisation authority follows the chain of command.

Exhibit 9.3 illustrates a single line organisational structure.

Exhibit 9.3 : Line Organisational Structure

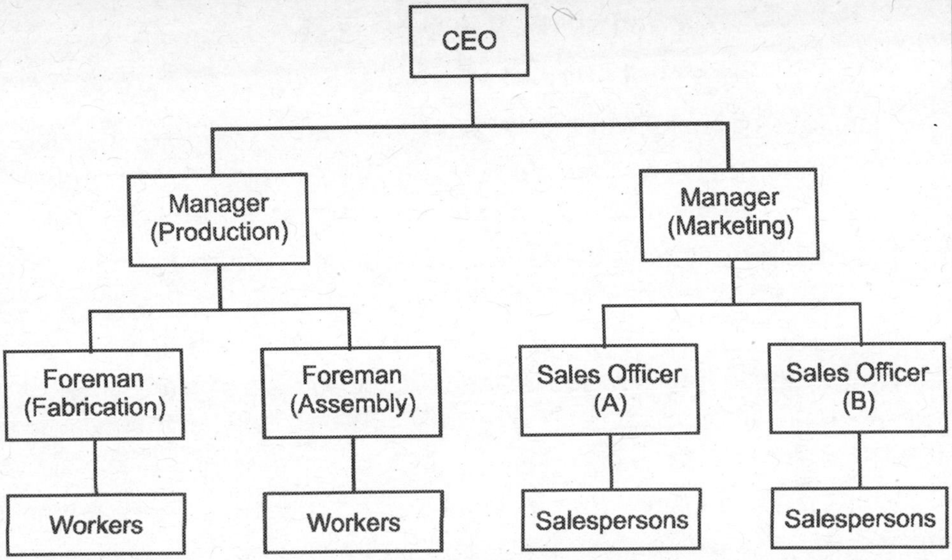

Features : Has only direct vertical relationships between different levels in the firm.

Advantages :

1. Tends to simplify and clarify authority, responsibility and accountability relationships
2. Promotes fast decision making
3. Simple to understand.

Disadvantages :

1. Neglects specialists in planning
2. Overloads key persons.

Some of the advantages of a pure line organisation are:

(i) A line structure tends to simplify and clarify responsibility, authority and accountability relationships. The levels of responsibility and authority are likely to be precise and understandable.

(ii) A line structure promotes fast decision making and flexibility.

(iii) Because line organisations are usually small, managements and employees have greater closeness.

However, there are some disadvantages also. They are :

(i) As the firm grows larger, line organisation becomes more ineffective.

(ii) Improved speed and flexibility may not off set the lack of specialized knowledge.

(iii) Managers may have to become experts in too many fields.

(iv) There is a tendency to become overly dependent on the few key people who an perform numerous jobs.

2. Staff or Functional Authority Organisational Structure

The jobs or positions in an organisation can be categorized as:

(i) **Line position** – a position in the direct chain of command that is responsible for the achievement of an organisation's goals and

(ii) **Staff position** – a position intended to provide expertise, advice and support for the line positions.

The line officers or managers have the direct authority (known as **line authority**) to be exercised by them to achieve the organisational goals. The staff officers or managers have **staff authority** (*i.e.,* authority to advice the line) over the line. This is also known as **functional authority.**

An organisation where staff departments have authority over line personnel in narrow areas of specialization is known as functional authority organisation. *Exhibit 9.4* illustrates a staff or functional authority organisational structure.

Exhibit 9.4 : Staff or Functional Authority Organisational Structure

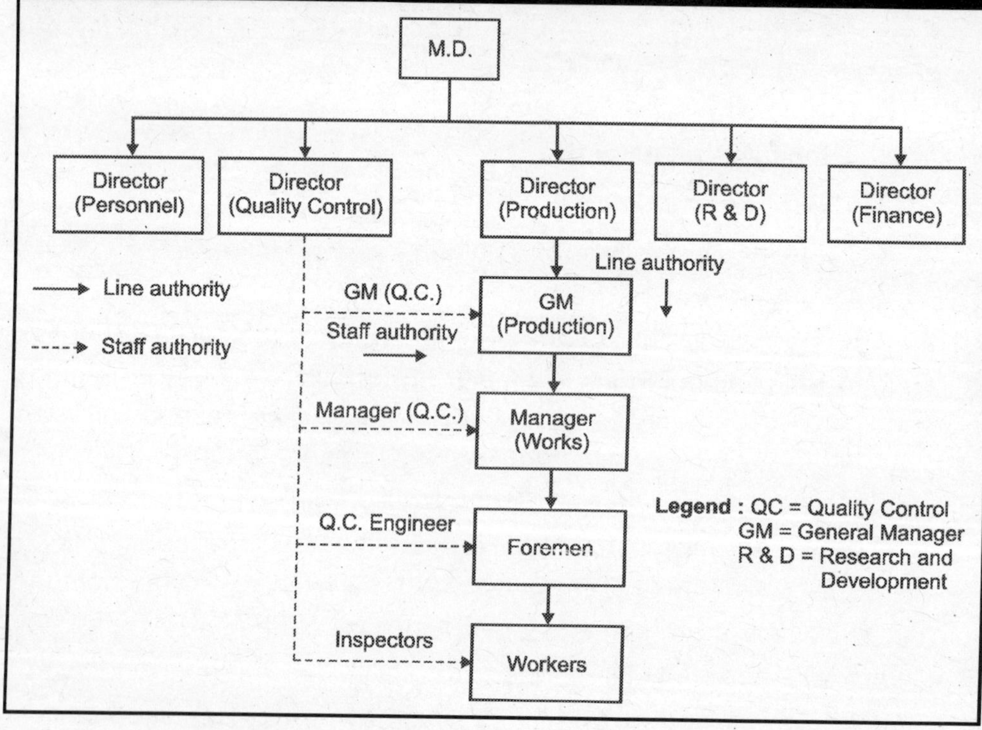

In the line organisation, the line managers cannot be experts in all the functions they are required to perform. But in the functional authority organisation, staff personnel who are specialists in some fields are given **functional authority** (The right of staff specialists to issue orders in their own names in designated areas).

The principle of **unity of command** is violated when functional authority exists *i.e.*, a worker or a group of workers may have to receive instructions or orders from the line supervisor as well as the staff specialist which may result in confusion and the conflicting orders from multiple sources may lead to increased ineffectiveness. Some staff specialists may exert **direct authority** over the line personnel, rather than exert **advice authority** (*for example*, quality control inspector may direct the worker as well as advise in matters related to quality).

While this type of organisational structure overcomes the disadvantages of a pure line organisational structure, it has some major disadvantages : They are: *(i)* the potential conflicts resulting from violation of principle of unity of command and *(ii)* the tendency to keep authority centralized at higher levels in the organisation.

3. Line and Staff Organisational Structure

Most large organisations belong to this type of organisational structure. These organisations have direct, vertical relationships between different levels and also specialists responsible for advising and assisting line managers. Such organisations have both line and staff departments. Staff departments provide line people with advice and assistance in specialized areas (*for example*, quality control advising production department).

Exhibit 9.5 illustrates the line and staff organisational chart. The line functions are production and marketing whereas the staff functions include personnel, quality control, research and development, finance, accounting etc. The **staff authority** of functional authority organisational structure is replaced by **staff responsibility** so that the principle of unity of command is not violated.

Three types of specialized staffs can be identified: *(i)* advising, *(ii)* service and *(iii)* control. Some staffs perform only one of these functions but some may perform two or all the three functions. The primary advantage is the use of expertise of staff specialists by the line personnel. The span of control of line managers can be increased because they are relieved of many functions which the staff people perform to assist the line.

Exhibit 9.5 : Line and Staff Organisational Structure

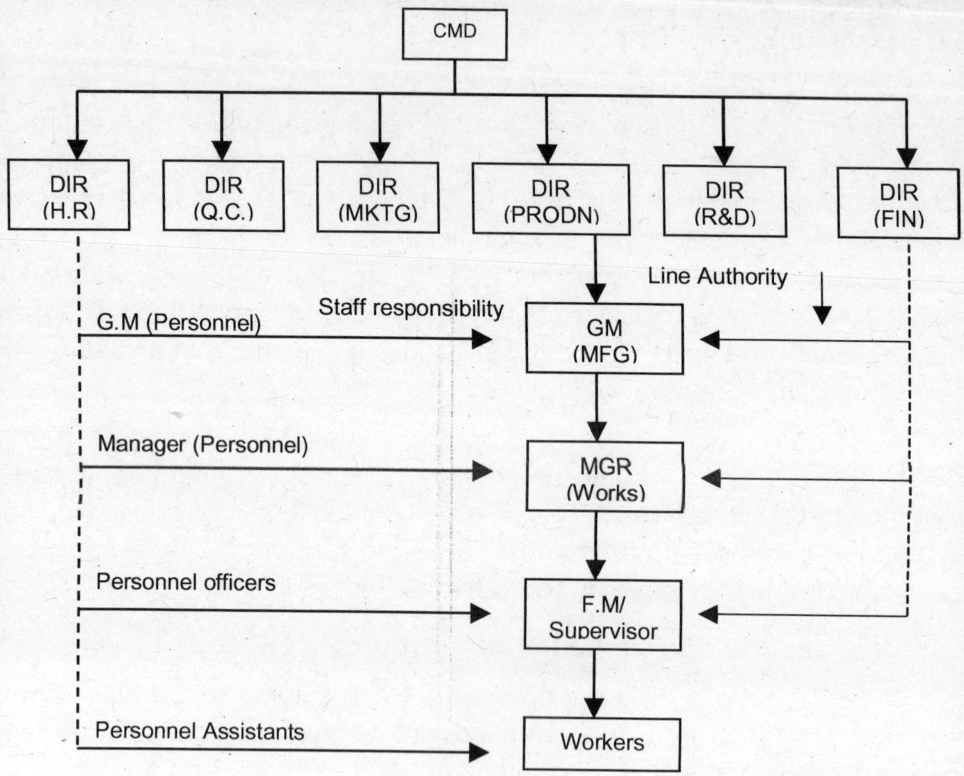

Legend:

HR – Human Resources
DIR – Director
MKTG – Marketing
QC – Quality Control
R & D – Research and Development
PRODN – Production
MFG – Manufacturing
FIN – Finance
MGR – Manager
GM – General Manager
FM - Foreman

Some advantages are :

(i) Even through a line and staff structure allows higher flexibility and specialization it may create conflict between line and staff personnel.

(ii) Line managers may not like staff personnel telling them what to do and how to do it even through they recognize the specialists' knowledge and expertise.

(iii) Some staff people have difficulty adjusting to the role, especially when line managers are reluctant to accept advice.

(iv) Staff people may resent their lack of authority and this may cause line and staff conflict.

Features :

1. Line and staff have direct vertical relationship between different levels.
2. Staff specialists are responsible for advising and assisting line managers/officers in specialized areas.
3. These types of specialized staff are *(a)* Advisory, *(b)* Service, *(c)* Control *e.g.*,

   ***(a)* Advisory :** Management information system, Operation Research and Quantitative Techniques, Industrial Engineering, Planning etc.

   ***(b)* Service :** Maintenance, Purchase, Stores, Finance, Marketing.

   ***(c)* Control :** Quality control, Cost control, Auditing etc.

   Advantages:

   (i) Use of expertise of staff specialists.

   (ii) Span of control can be increased

   (iii) Relieves line authorities of routine and specialized decisions.

   (iv) No need for all round executives.

   Disadvantages:

   (i) Conflict between line and staff may still arise.

   (ii) Staff officers may resent their lack of authority.

   (iii) Co-ordination between line and staff may become difficult.

4. Committee Organisational Structure

Features:

(a) Formed for managing certain problems/situations

(b) Are temporary decisions.

Advantages:

1. Committee decisions are better than individual decisions
2. Better interaction between committee members leads to better co-ordination of activities
3. Committee members can be motivated to participate in group decision making.
4. Group discussion may lead to creative thinking.

Disadvantages:

1. Committees may delay decisions, consume more time and hence more expensive.
2. Group action may lead to compromise and indecision.
3. 'Buck passing' may result.

5. Divisional Organisational Structure

In this type of structure, the organisation can have different basis on which departments are formed. They are: *(i)* function, *(ii)* product, *(iii)* geographic territory, *(iv)* project and *(iv)* combination approach.

Exhibit 9.6 illustrates organisational structures formed based on the above basis of departmentation.

6. Project Organisational Structure

The line, line and staff and functional authority organisational structures facilitate establishment and distribution of authority for vertical coordination and control rather than horizontal relationships. In some projects (complex activity consisting of a number of interdependent and independent activities) work process may flow horizontally, diagonally, upwards and downwards. The direction of work flow depends on the distribution of talents and abilities in the organisation and the need to apply them to the problem that exists. The cope up with such situations, **project** organisations and **matrix** organisations have emerged.

A *project organisation is a temporary organisation designed to achieve specific results by using teams of specialists from different functional areas in the organisation.* The project team focuses all its energies, resources and results on the assigned project. Once the project has been completed, the team members from various cross functional departments may go back to their previous positions or may be assigned to a new project. Some of the examples of projects are : research and development projects, product development, construction of a new plant, housing complex, shopping complex, bridge etc.

Exhibit 9.7 illustrates a project organisational structure.

Exhibit 9.6 : Divisional Organisational Structure (Departmentation)

Features : Structure based on division of work based on a functional activity such as finance, marketing etc., or based on type of products manufactured or based on geographic location of the units or based on projects undertaken.

(a) Departmentation by Function

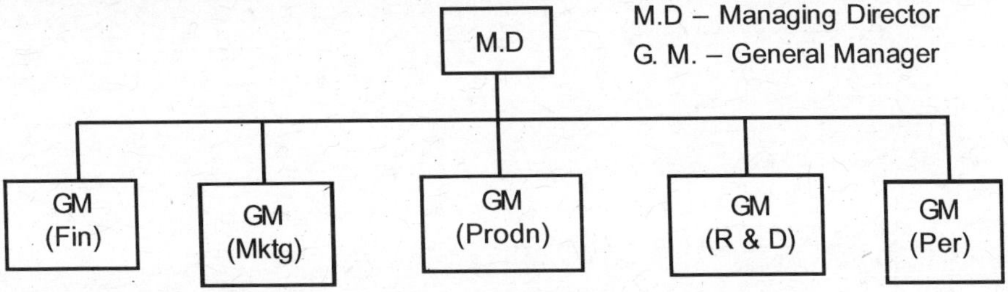

(b) Departmentation by Product

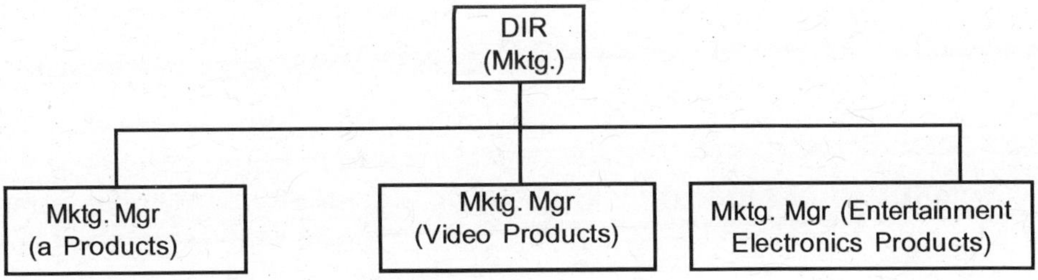

(c) Departmentation by Geographic territory

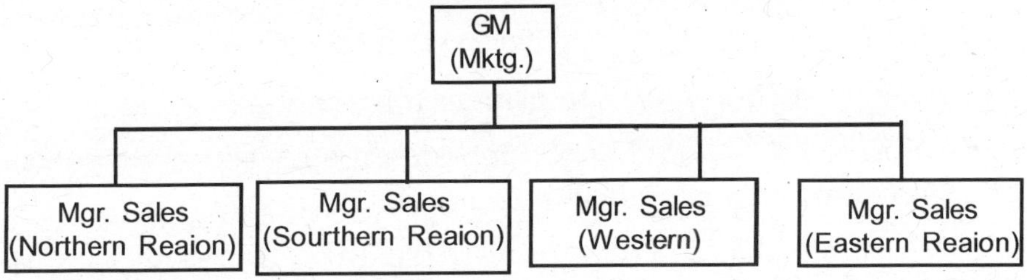

(d) Departmentation by Project

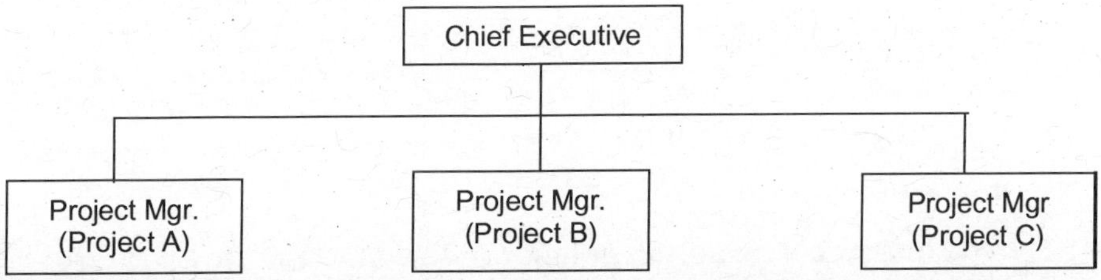

(e) Departmentation by combination approach (Combination of any two or more bases discussed above).

Exhibit 9.7 : Project Organisational Structure

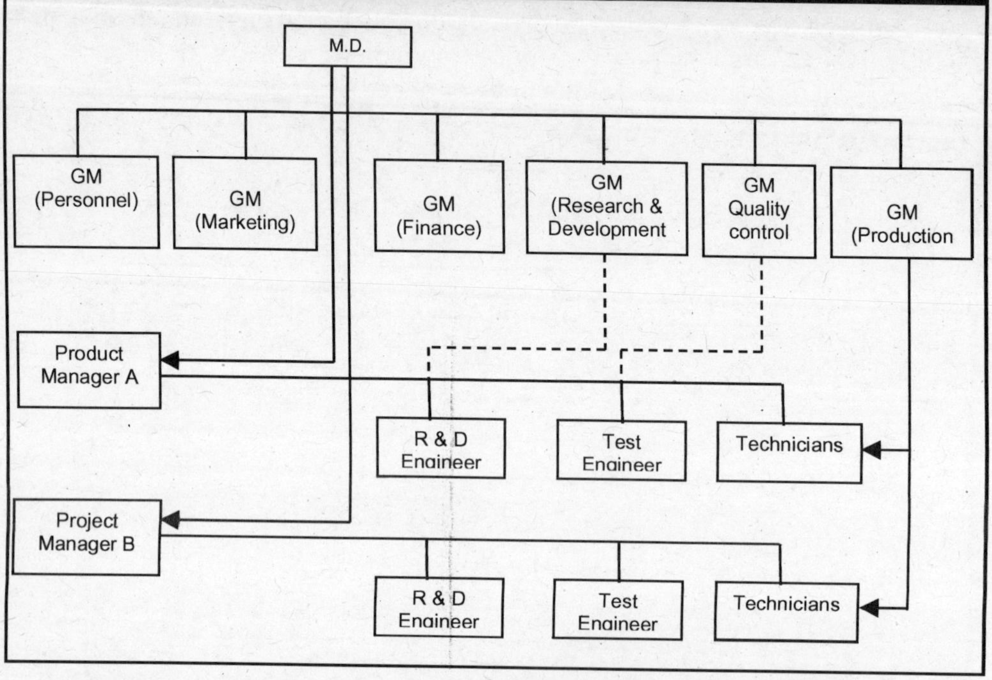

Feature : **Temporary** organisation designed to achieve specific results by using teams of specialists from different functional areas in the organisation.

Importance of Project Organisational Structure : Project organisational structure is most valuable when :

(i) Work is defined by a specific goal and target date for completion.

(ii) Work is unique and unfamiliar to the organisation.

(iii) Work is complex having independent activities and specialized skills are necessary for accomplishment.

(iv) Work is critical in terms of possible gains or losses.

(v) Work is not repetitive in nature.

Characteristics of Project Organisation

1. Personnel are assigned to a project from the existing permanent organisation and are under the direction and control of the project manager.
2. The project manager specifies what effort is needed and when work will be performed whereas the concerned department manager executes the work using his resources.

3. The project manager gets the needed support from production, quality control, engineering etc. for completion of the project.
4. The authority over the project team members is shared by project manager and the respective functional managers in the permanent organisation.
5. The services of the specialists (project team members) are temporarily loaned to the project manager till the completion of the project.
6. There may be conflict between the project manager and the departmental manager on the issue of exercising authority over team members.
7. Since authority relationships are overlapping with possibilities of conflicts, informal relationships between project manager and departmental managers (functional managers) become more important than formal prescription of authority.
8. Full and free communication is essential among those working on the project.

7. Matrix Organisational Structure

It is a permanent organisation designed to achieve specific results by using teams of specialists from different functional areas in the organisation. The matrix organisation is illustrated in *Exhibit 9.8*.

Exhibit 9.8 : Matrix Organisational Structure

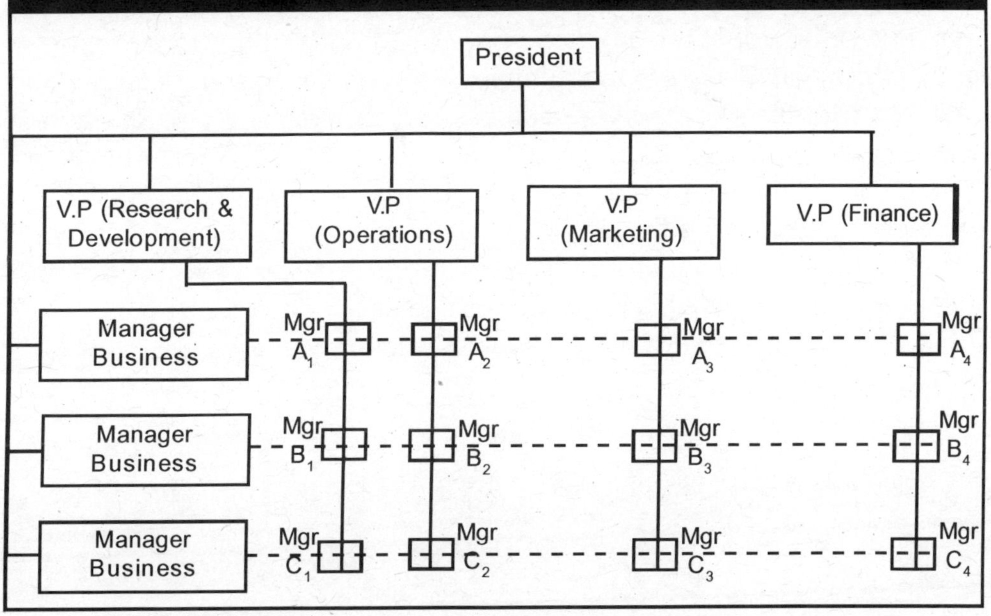

Feature : Superimposes a horizontal set of divisions and reporting relationships onto a hierarchical functional structure.

Advantages:

1. Decentralised decision making.
2. Strong product/project co-ordination.
3. Improved environmental monitoring.
4. Fast response to change.
5. Flexible use of resources.
6. Efficient use of support systems.

Disadvantages :

1. High administration cost.
2. Potential confusion over authority and responsibility.
3. High prospects of conflict.
4. Overemphasis on group decision making.
5. Excessive focus on internal relations.

This type of organisation is often used when the firm has to be highly responsive to a rapidly changing external environment.

In matrix structures, there are functional managers and product (or project or business group) managers. Functional manager are in charge of specialized resources such as production, quality control, inventories, scheduling and marketing. Product or business group managers are incharge of one or more products and are authorized to prepare product strategies or business group strategies and call on the various functional managers for the necessary resources. The problem with this structure is the negative effects of dual authority similar to that of project organisation. The functional managers may lose some of their authority because product managers are given the budgets to purchase internal resources. In a matrix organisation, the product or business group managers and functional managers have somewhat equal power. There is possibility of conflict and frustration but the opportunity for prompt and efficient accomplishment is quite high.

10. Hybrid Organisational Structure

Exhibit 9.9 (a) illustrates the hybrid organisational structure.

Exhibit 9.9 *(a)* : Hybrid Organisational Structure (IBM Structure)

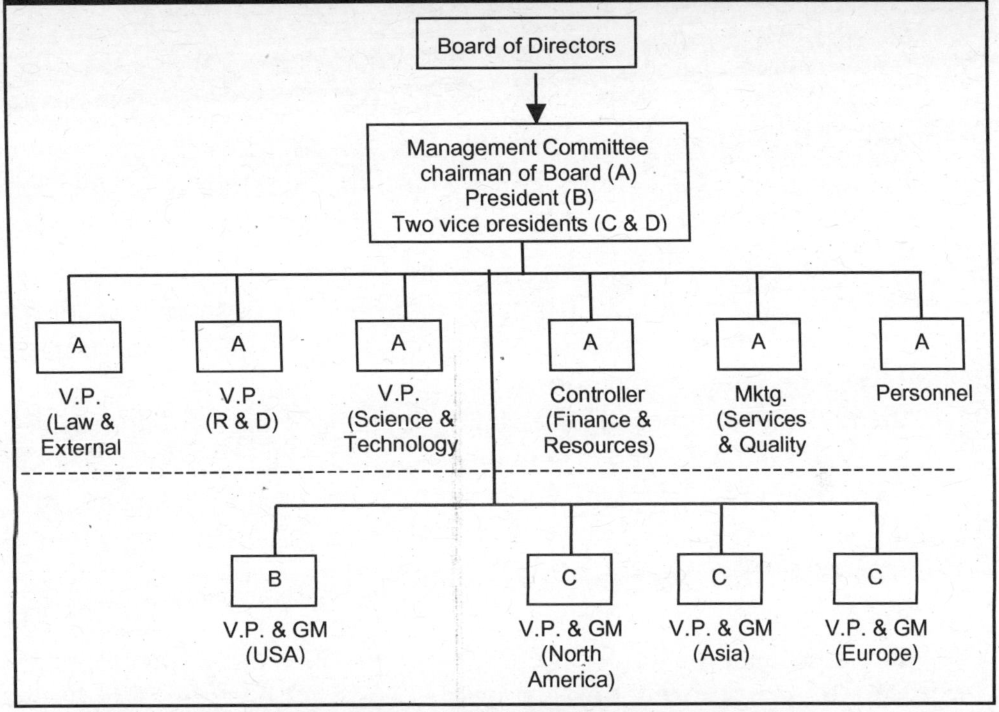

Exhibit 9.9 (b) illustrates a combination structure.

Exhibit 9.9 *(b)* : Combination Structure (Functional and geographic divisions)

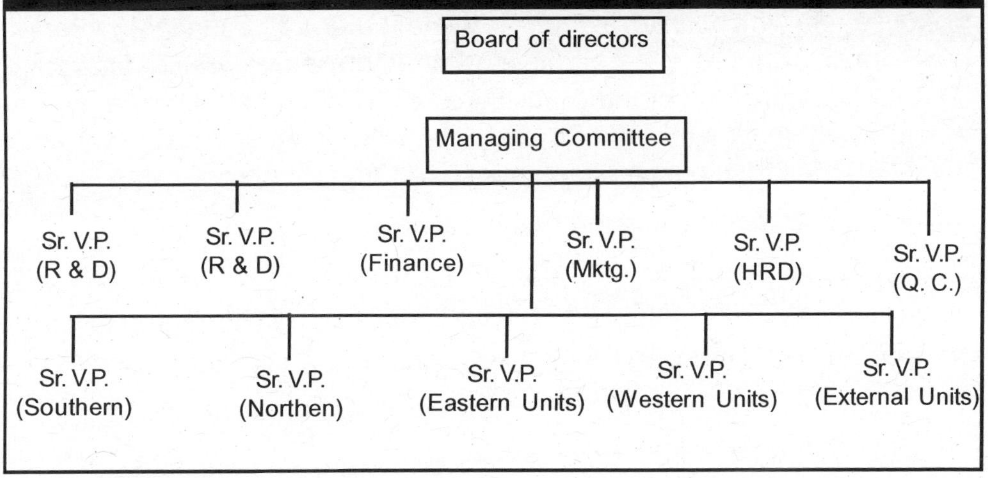

Advantages :

1. Alignment of corporate and divisional goals.
2. Functional expertise and efficiency.
3. Adaptability and flexibility in divisions.

Disadvantages :

1. Conflicts between corporate departments and units.
2. Excessive administration overhead.
3. Slow response to exceptional situations.

Uses : Used in organisations that face considerable environmental uncertainty that can be met through a divisional structure and that also required functional expertise or efficiency.

This type of structure is used by multinational companies operating in the global environment, *for example,* International Business Machines USA. This kind of structure depends on factors such as degree of international orientation and commitment. Multinational corporations may have their corporate offices in the country of origin and their international divisions established in various countries reporting to the CEO or president at the headquarters. The international divisions or foreign subsidiaries may be grouped into regions such as North America, Asia, Europe etc. and again each region may be subdivided into countries within each region.

While the focus is on international geographic structures, companies may also choose functional or process or product departmentation in addition to geographic pattern while at the head quarter's the departmentation may be based on function.

The Informal Organisation : An informal organisation is the set of evolving relationships and patterns of human interaction within an organisation which are not officially presented. Alongside the formal organisation, an informal organisation structure exists which consists of informal relationships created not by officially designated managers but by organisational members at every level. Since managers can not avoid these informal relationships, they must be trained to cope with it

The informal organisation has the following characteristics

(i) Its members are joined together to satisfy their personal needs (needs for affiliation, friendship etc.)

(ii) It is continuously changing : The informal organisation is dynamic.

(iii) It involves members from various organisational levels.

(iv) It is affected by relationship outside the firm.

(v) It has a pecking order : certain people are assigned greater importance than others by the informal group.

Even though an informal organisational structure does not have its own formal organisational chart, it has its own chain of command :

Benefits of Informal Organisation

(i) Assists in accomplishing the work faster.
(ii) Helps to remove weakness in the formal structure.
(iii) Lengthens the effective span of control.
(iv) Compensation for violations of formal organisational principles.
(v) Provides an additional channel of communication.
(vi) Provides emotional support for employees.
(vii) Encourages better management.

Disadvantages of informal organisation

(i) May work against the purpose of formal organisation.
(ii) Reduces the degree of predictability and control.
(iii) Reduces the number of practical alternatives.
(iv) Increases the time required to complete activities.

Other Types of Organisations

1. Tall Versus Flat Organisational Structure

Tall organisations have narrow span of management and hence many hierarchical levels. Flat organisations have wide span of management and hence few hierarchical levels. *Box 9.1* gives a comparison between the two.

Box 9.1 : Comparison of tall and flat organisational structures

Tall Structure	Flat Structure
Advantages *(i)* Closer control because of narrow span of control. *(ii)* Helps managers to develop their subordinates *(iii)* Better coordination of work. *(iv)* In crisis situations closer supervision is possible. *(v)* Good for subordinates who like closer supervision **Disadvantages :** *(i)* Slowed decision making because of more levels involved. *(ii)* Communication may get distorted.	**Advantages** *(i)* Managers are forced to deligate to junior levels. *(ii)* Reduces the number of supervisors required. *(iii)* Faster and better communication because of few levels. *(iv)* Encourages individuals who desire challenge, higher responsibility, autonomy etc. **Disadvantages :** *(i)* Managers are overloaded due to bigger span of control. *(ii)* Competent supervisors and managers may be difficult to hire. *(iii)* Difficulty in controlling and coordinating.

2. Mechanistic versus Organic Organisations

Mechanistic or **classical** organisations are traditional, pyramid shaped structures having centralization of authority at the top management level, departmentalization of jobs, hierarchy of command, narrow span of management and extensive division of labour.

Organic or Behavioural organisations have wide span of management, flat organizational structure, general supervision and decentralization of authority.

3. Craft Organisation

In this type of organisation the chief executive engages in technical matters rather than administrative duties, with little planning and change in operations and minimum use of supervisory or indirect labour. Examples are a tool room or an automobile service station.

4. Promotion Organisation

In this type of organisation, the chief executive is the promoter, figures charismatic personality to the subordinates, has fluid policies which change at the discretion of promoter, middle management is often by-passed, indirect labour provides technical support to the promoter, has limited life span, needs to change or perish (example: private banks, chit funds, hotels etc.)

5. Administrative Organisation

In this type of organisation, the chief executive manages professionally, directs a planned structure towards clearly defined goods, adjusts to changes in its marketing environment.

6. Team-based Organisation

In this type, the entire organisation is made up of work groups or teams that perform the organization's work. In this structure, employee empowerment is crucial because of absence of line of managerial authority from top to bottom. Employee teams are given freedom to design work in the way they think is best. But the teams are held responsible for the work activities and the results achieved in their respective areas. In large organisations, team-based structures complement a typical functional or divisional structure to improve efficiency and flexibility.

7. Boundaryless Organisation

It is an organisation whose design is not defined by, or limited to, the horizontal, vertical or external boundaries imposed by a predefined structure. Boundaries can be "horizontal" vertical and external boundaries. Horizontal boundaries are imposed by work specialization and departmentation; the vertical boundaries separate employees into organizational levels and hierarchies and external boundaries separate organisation from its customers, suppliers and stakeholders. The boundary less organisation helps organizations to operate in today's environment by remaining flexible and unstructured; the ideal structure for them is not having a rigid, predefined structure. Boundaryless organisation seeks to eliminate the chain of command, to have appropriate spans of control and to replace departments with empowered teams. Vertical boundaries can be removed through cross-hierarchical teams and participative decision making, horizontal boundaries can be removed by using cross-functional teams, and external boundaries can be minimized or eliminated by using strategic alliances with supplies.

8. Learning Organisation

A learning organisation is an organisation that has developed the capacity to continuously adapt and change because all members take an active role in identifying and resolving work-related issues. In such organisation, employees practice **knowledge management** by continually acquiring and sharing new knowledge and are willing to apply that knowledge for decision making and performing their work.

Exhibit 9.10 illustrates characteristics of a learning organisation.

Exhibit 9.10 : Characteristics of a learning organisation

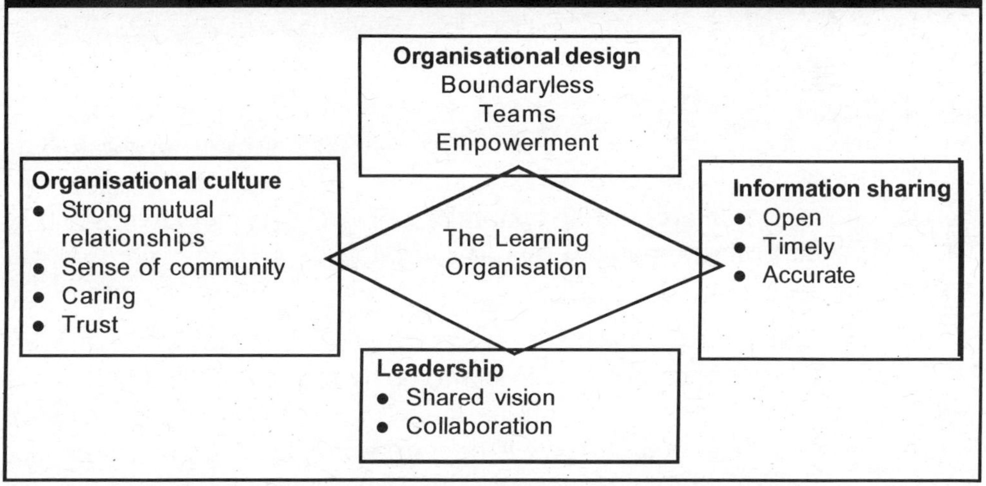

9.10 REORGANISING THE FIRM WITHOUT DESTROYING IT

Past studies on reorganising the business have revealed that more than 50% of the firms reported stagnant or reduced productivity after downsizing. While many firms had actually cut expenses after downsizing, only a few had increased profits or productivity.

Despite these failures of downsizing, change is still unavoidable. Simply stopping change is not acceptable, but neither a 50% failure rate is acceptable. We need to transform the firm without losing the things that made it work. The goal of reorganising is to achieve a transformation which fundamentally shifts an organisation's strategy, business system and culture to deliver measurable and sustainable improvements.

The ***law of unintended consequences*** states that any change will be accompanied by a set of consequences that cannot be predicted accurately. The problem stems from two sources: *(i) the objective of the change* and *(ii) the process.* Major programmes of change are taken up for unpopular reasons such as downsizing, business process reengineering and take-overs–all seem unattractive and threatening to employees. The result is low employee morale, low productivity, loss of employee trust on management and loss of the value of change.

To avoid these problems, we need to understand the underlying causes and design our own processes so that we can reorganise the firm without destroying its soul. For this we need to avoid some mental traps and need to follow some rules to avoid effects of the awful law of unintended consequences.

Mental traps: The four mental traps to be avoided are: *(i)* People vs Performance, *(ii)* Structure vs System, *(iii)* Us vs Them and *(iv)* Concurrent vs Consecutive.

These are briefly discussed below:

(i) People vs Performance: Successful companies recognise that they can improve only through people. *For example*, in a service economy and with the growth of the value of intangible assets, the **"human capital"** of a firm or its employees are treated synonymously with the identity of the firm. One can't change the firm without changing its people. People and performance are not the issues that can be separated in creating effective change.

(ii) Structure vs System: Many change programs are overly focused on the formal organisational structure and on its rearrangement by shifting the positions and changing the chain of command. But this is only partial solution to the problem. Change will only be effective if the structure is a part of a broader systemic transformation. Structure is only one of several levers that lead to dramatic performance improvement. The other levers are ***strategy, execution, culture, talent management, leadership, innovation***, and ***growth*** through successfully managed mergers and acquisitions.

(iii) Us vs Them: The role of a leader in creating a transformational process is to create an environment in which people can take leadership of the changes wherever they are. Talented people (*i.e.*, employees) are motivated by autonomy, and the opportunity to rise to challenges.

(iv) Concurrent vs Consecutive: Because the elements of the transformation programme are complementary to one another, successful change can not be achieved by tackling them one at a time. Improvements to leadership, culture and management process should be made concurrently with changes to customer management, operational processes and organisational designs. Effective transformation work simultaneously on more than one element of the change. The ten golden rules to be followed to avoid unintended consequences of change are:

1. Confront the facts continuously: Make sure you understand the reasons for your current situation – good or bad. Analyse the organisation's current performance with an open mind.

2. Build a coherent and compelling transformation story: Employees, customers, analysts and investors need to see for themselves why the organisation needs to change; where it is going and how you plan to get there.

3. Use the collective wisdom of the organisation: Transformation is more effective when people discover a new reality for themselves and adopt new ways of working. But the transformation will take place only if it taps into the organisation's collective energies and insights.

4. You can hold a few elements of your transformation sacrosanct but be flexible about the rest: Be clear about the few elements of the business process that are non-negotiable and ensure that they are not compromised by any element of the transformation.

5. Work through leaders at all levels: The transformation needs leaders throughout the organisation to build commitment to the new possibilities that will emerge and to engage people in the transformation.

6. Get the right balance between action and reflection: Without sufficient action, the transformation process will lose momentum and will fail. Reflection is also needed to furnish renewal, check that the change continues to respond to the reality of the situation.

7. Demonstrate early success: Demonstrate early progress in micro-levels that deliver visible improvements in operating and financial performance, and customer satisfaction to motivate the employees participating in the transformation.

8. Make the change process unique: Follow a tailored, dynamic change process that meets your needs and responds to events as they unfold. Because your organisation is unique, your people are unique and you need a unique transformation process.

9. Expect resistance – listen constantly, but be clear about the boundaries: Transformation is not easy. People, including some members of the leadership team may resist the change either through active opposition or through passive, but visible lack of support. Top management must listen to those people who oppose the change process limiting the degree of resistance that is acceptable.

10. Measure progress at every stage: To be effective in the role as leader for change, one needs access to real information about how things are going. Progress must be measured constantly against specific milestones such as operational performance and financial performance.

ORGANISATIONAL RESTRUCTURING

The past two decades have witnessed a dramatic transformation in how firms are structured. Tall organisations are becoming flatter as the number of hierarchical levels is reduced in order to become more effective.

Mergers and acquisitions have reached a new peak but often mergers fail because the cultures and HR systems of the firms which are merged do not coalesce. A new form of inter-organisational bonding comes in the form of **joint ventures, strategic alliances** and **collaborations** among firms which remain independent, yet work together on specific products to spread costs and risks.

To be successful, organisational restructuring requires effective management of human resources. For instance, **downsizing** or flattening of organisation requires careful examination of some issues related to the human resource of the organisation. Downsizing involves a reduction in a company's workforce to improve its bottom line. In the practice of downsizing, companies lay-off workers. This will foster a lack of emotional commitment. It will also cause social problems associated with employment insecurity. Flattening of organisations needs the careful consideration of staffing demands, workflows, communication channels, training needs and so on. Likewise, mergers and other forms of inter-organisational relations require the successful blending of dissimilar organisational structures, management practices, technical expertise etc.

The other issues to be handled by Human Resource Managers are *(i)* **Self-managed work teams,** *(ii)* **Organisational culture**.

***(i)* Self-managed work teams:** Another sweeping organisational change has been in the relationship between the supervisor and worker. The traditional system in which individual employees report to a single boss is being replaced by the self-managed team system in some organisations. In this system, employees are assigned to a group of peers and collectively, they are responsible for a particular area or task. Self-managed teams are found to be more successful in today's business environment which demands intense improvement in productivity, quality and response time.

***(ii)* Organisational culture:** Organisational culture refers to the basic assumptions and beliefs shared by members of an organisation. The key elements of organisational culture are:

(i) *Observed behavioural regularities* when people interact, such as the language used.

(ii) The *norms* that evolve in working groups such as the norm of a fair day's work for a fair day's pay.

(iii) The *dominant values exposed* by an organisation such as product quality or low prices.

(iv) The *philosophy* that guides an organisation's policy toward employees and/or customers.

(v) The *rules of the game* for getting along in the organisation.

(vi) The *feeling* or *climate* that is conveyed in the organisation by the physical layout and the way the members of the organisation interact with one another, customers and outsiders.

9.11 THE ROLE OF HUMAN RESOURCE MANAGEMENT IN ORGANISATIONAL IMPROVEMENTS

According to the criteria for Baldrige award, human resource management and development is considered as one of the most important issues for firms to emphasise. This includes specific training programs in quality, training and development programs, communication systems, suggestion systems, performance appraisal systems and opinion surveys.

HR professionals are familiar with the various personnel systems in the organisation *For example*, training, compensation, motivation etc. They can ensure that new programs are designed to fit the existing systems. HR department should be actively involved in organisational efforts to improve quality and productivity. HR managers in many firms are actively involved in designing, implementing and evaluating improvement interventions called **organisational development interventions** (O.D. interventions). *For example*, HR staff members may be required to work closely with top managers in the organisation-wide TQM initiative.

HR professionals need to involve employees, managers and the labour union when designing improvement programs. This can be facilitated by training managers and employees in human relations skills and encouraging participatory management and employee involvement and employee empowerment. Task forces or teams are established comprising of representatives from every group who work together to define the problems and offer recommendations to solve the problems.

When the programs are being implemented, HR professionals are responsible for training managers and employees in the new systems. They have to deal with any potential resistance to change and convince the employees about the benefits of the proposed changes.

A Model of Organisational Transformation and Reengineering

Reengineering involves four primary systems for bringing organisational transformation. These systems are: *(i)* The management system, *(ii)* **The social system**, *(iii)* **The technical system** and *(iv)* **The behavioural system**.

The ***management system*** provides the vision and strategies, the ***social system*** provides the cultural support to implement new ideas, the ***technical system*** provides the tools to achieve outstanding service or products and the ***behavioural system*** provides the human side of the reengineering process. *Exhibit 9.11* illustrates a model of organisational transformation and reengineering.

Exhibit 9.11 : A model of organisational transformation and reengineering

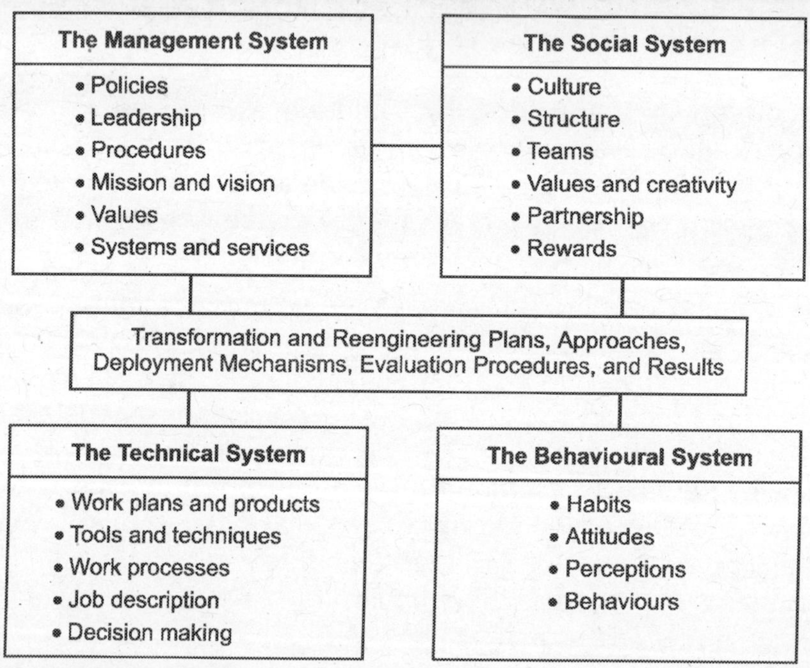

(*Source:* H. John Bernardin, Joyce E.A. Russell, *Human Resource Management*, 2nd Edition, Irwin McGraw-Hill, p.354)

Another way of conceptualising the approach is given with the six R's in *Exhibit 9.12*. The 6 R's of transformation and reengineering are: *(i)* **Realisation**, *(ii)* **Requirements**, *(iii)* **Rethink**, *(iv)* **Redesign**, (*v*) **Retool** and (*vi*) **Reevaluate**.

It starts with ***realising*** the extent of the problem, identifying the ***requirements*** of the internal and external customers, ***rethinking*** the current practices, ***redesigning*** the processes, ***retooling*** or adopting new technologies and tools and ***reevaluating*** the entire process.

Exhibit 9.12 : The Six R's of Transformation and Reengineering

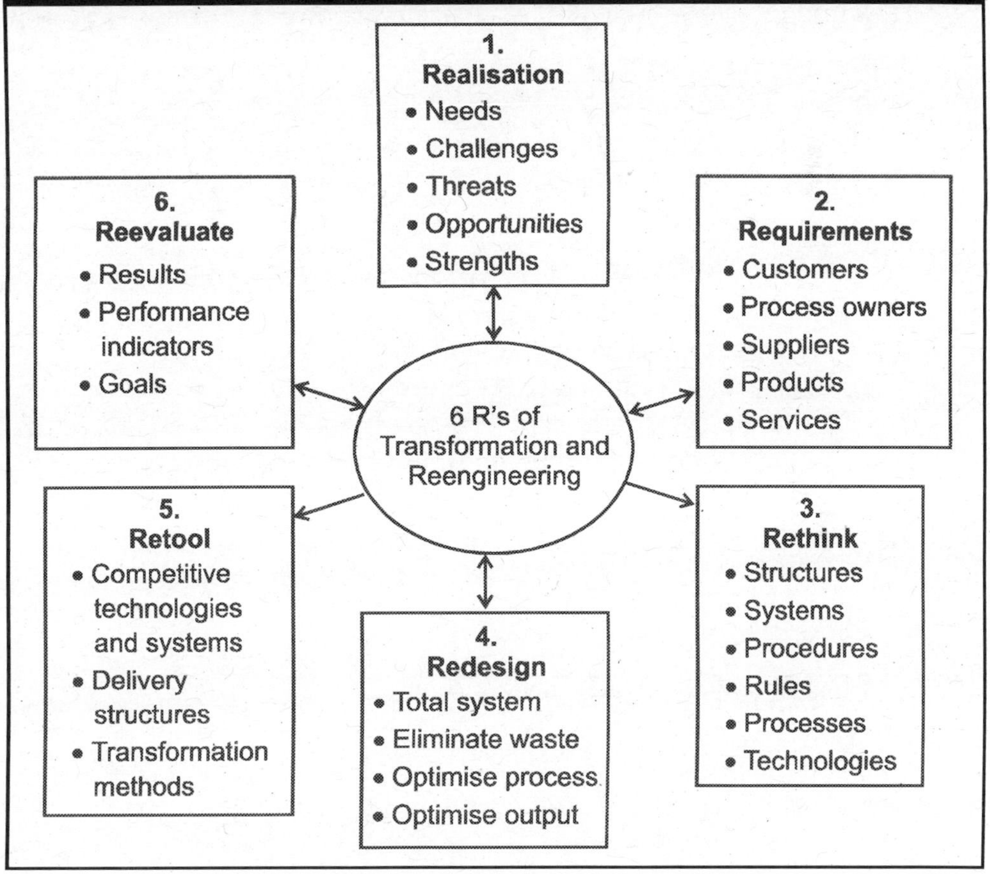

Source: H. John Bernardin, *et al., op. cit.,* page 355

9.12 BEYOND BUSINESS PROCESS REENGINEERING

Business Process Reengineering (BPRE) has become hardwired in individual companies. The core-business processes are designed to satisfy in the *"one best way"* a particular customer need. Many Business Process Reengineering efforts do not seem to consider what will happen if that need changes. The ***"holonic business system"*** allows businesses continually to de-invent and re-invent themselves as they face increasingly ambiguous markets.

BPRE experience is now being established. The leaders of reengineering efforts must turn their attention beyond the analysis of complex process maps and information systems towards two new challenges. They are :

(i) How can the reengineered core business processes contribute to a strategic re-positioning of the business and

(ii) How to effectively direct and accelerate major organisational change.

There are three kinds of BPRE efforts and these define the scope and ambition of a company's BPRE efforts. They are :

(i) **To achieve improvement** – usually through cutting costs and aims at support or management processes. It is often accompanied by such efforts as divestment, delayering and downsizing.

(ii) **To achieve a "Break-Point"** – A Break-point is a new level of process innovation – as measured by the value set of cost, quality, lead time, delivery reliability and product functionality – that provides a significant and positive market impact. Break-Point Process Reengineering is concerned therefore to go beyond traditional efforts to improve performance. It has the focus on re-inventing the industry.

The **"holonic business system"** extends this idea. For any core business process, a set of nodes within the *holonic network* can be found that can carry out a core business process in the most effective and efficient manner possible.

9.13 THE HOLONIC CONCEPT

A ***"holonic network"*** is a set of companies that acts integratedly and organically, it is constantly reconfigured to manage each business opportunity a customer presents. Each company in the network provides a different process capability and is called a *"holon"*.

Each configuration of process capabilities within the holonic network is called a ***"virtual company"***. By combining the core competencies of many individual companies within the network, each virtual company is more powerful and flexible than the participating members alone could be. Each company in a virtual company is chosen because of its process excellence.

BPRE is market and opportunity driven; and customer focussed. So is the holonic business system. The customer focusses on the holonic network. Each customer can move from being a *consumer* to a *prosumer*. Prosumers contribute by various degrees to the design of the product they request. They are *proactive consumers* that work with sellers to define the products and services they are buying. Through the design process, the consumer forces the network to configure itself to provide the optimum processes to meet his needs. In this way, holonic networks go beyond Business Process Reengineering in that they define for the first time how to sell customer specific products while realising economies of scale.

Exhibit 9.13 : MEGA – PC's Holonic Network

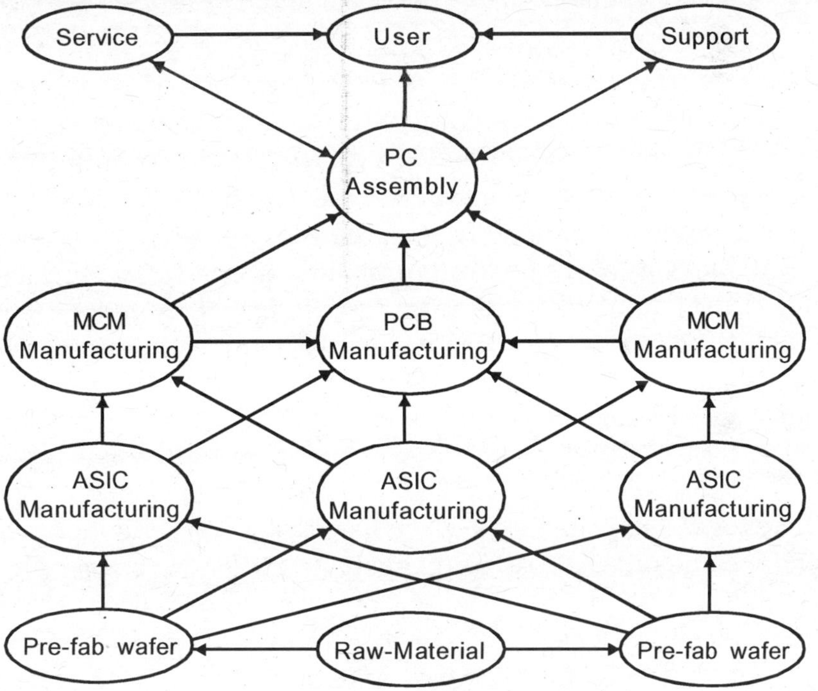

Legend :

PC	–	Personal Computers
PCB	–	Printed Circuit Board
ASIC	–	Application Specific Integrated Circuit
MCM	–	Multi Chip Module
Pre-fab wafer	–	Pre-fabrication of wafer used for ASIC manufacturing.

Source : Patrick McHugh, Giorgio Merli and William A. Wheeler III, *"Beyond Business Process Reengineering,"* John Wiley and Sons, p. 6.

In a holonic network, continuous improvement occurs at the network level because the network is constantly improving co-ordination and communication between nodes. And at the individual node level, each node is constantly improving its core competencies. But within any one virtual company, only nodes that operate the "best practices" level participate. The only way to improve a virtual company is to remove one or more of the nodes and replace them with better nodes. This is tantamount to creating a new virtual company. This is what is meant by the network constantly configuring itself to present the best core business processes in virtual companies.

Within a holonic network, each holon is unique and is unable by itself to create a Break-Point in the market. Only the power of the virtual company formed of nodes within a holonic network can create a Break-Point.

In a single company BPRE model, the market place does not "know what it wants". It is only through a design of experiments that a company can decide what is most important to the market place. In this, a company asks the market "If we could provide you, *for example,* with three of the following eight characteristics, which three would you like?" In the holonic business system, by contrast, each prosumer knows what he wants and therefore the virtual company knows the Break-Point needed by its customers. Going beyond Business Process Reengineering, it is possible to see how with the holonic business system, small companies can compete with large companies. Also, large companies can become cost competitive with small businesses.

How the Holonic-network Works?

Take *for example*, the nine-day house built by the Japanese Company Sikisui. The customers, a wife and husband, enter the sales office to buy a house. There they find several computer terminals, each linked to company's design office. First, the couple design the basic layout of the house, restricted only by building codes and the size of the plot on which the house will be built. Then they begin to personalise it.

They discuss options, with or without the help of the salesperson. They try out "what ifs" on the screen. Eventually they devise a plan that meets their exact specifications. The sales agent offers them tea while they wait for their quotation to be ready, including the cost of building the house. The couple agree to the quotation and come to terms on a payment schedule. The contract is signed.

Within minutes, the company has sent orders to all of its suppliers to prepare the materials for this customer-designed house. If a supplier of one item cannot fulfil its order within three days, it is responsible for finding another vendor in the network of suppliers who can.

Two days before the house is to be built on the customer's site, the components of the house are at the building company's factory. Here, they are assembled into modules.

Sikisui, with its sales staff and design centres, acts as the integrator in this holonic network that includes dozens of suppliers. Each home-designed by the prosumer – is supplied by a different group of suppliers – in effect a different virtual company for each product. Fifty percent of the parts in the typical home are ordered on a *kanban* system (*i.e.* they are repetitive orders) while the other 50 percent are special orders for each home.

This kind of process can only take place within a network of companies that work with real time communication tools. The user interface software enables the customer to design his or her own product.

That the holonic network is effective can be attested by the fact that annual revenues per Sikisui employee are almost $ one million each.

Advantages of Holonic Business System

(i) **Leverage :** There is true synergy achieved by combining the best capabilities of many operations. Small companies can develop the competitive clout of large companies at a fraction of the cost.

(ii) **Speed :** Decision making is streamlined and hence fast. There are no "layers of management", so no need to sell ideas up the management ladder. Information moves through all forms of telecommunication (Electronic Data Interchange). Businesses as that are able to act as nodes in a virtual company have had their core competence that they alone manage. Thus, decisions are as rapid as saying "yes" or "no" to the questions. This speed shows up as *"time to market"* because one company does not have to "invent" an entire new product. It can call on a host of partners with their own core competencies to create a virtual company and to design the new product. It can also show up as "speed to customer" since the virtual company establishes the most effective production core business process.

(iii) **Flexibility :** Coupled with speed is the ability to change the service or product capabilities to match rapidly changing market requirements.

(iv) **Shared risk :** Because several nodes form a holonic network, there is a shared risk and reward. There is also a reduction in the fear of change, since each *holon* is confident in its capabilities.

(v) **Independence :** Each holon is independent, free to come and go as it pleases and to compete and cooperate as it wants, but the holonic system requires a great deal of cooperation.

(vi) **Faster growth and increased profits :** It was observed that companies that are one-third more responsive to their customers had a growth rate of three or more times their competition and were two to five times more profitable.

(vii) **Sustainable customers :** Once customers have become used to the flexibility and responsiveness of a holonic system as their supplier, it will be tough for competitors to wean them away.

(viii) **Less capital required :** A holonic system significantly requires less capital because each node only uses equipment that is specific to its core business processes. This in turn results in requirement for less working capital, lower maintenance costs, higher return on assets and considerably fewer fixed assets.

(ix) **Quick failure recognition :** Since the network operates in real time it should recognise failure quickly. A well-designed network will have an exit strategy that can be put into effect quickly. The network should be capable of getting dismantled without damaging the reputation or image of any node.

(x) **Increased ability to deal with inevitable change :** This can be explained with an example of a joint venture of Digital Equipment Company (DEC) of US with Tandy, the low cost manufacturer of radio shank products to participate in the personal computer (PC) market in the mid 1980s. Along came Compaq which offered higher performance to the market. DEC forced to compete on the performance plans, reconfigured its alliance, adding Intel as a partner in the development of its next generation of PCs. Then came Dell into the market, which offered both low cost and good performance. DEC dropped the alliance with Tandy and began manufacturing on its own. This was a mistake as it turned out and in practice was also directly contrary to the PC industry's trend towards holonic network.

Types of Holonic Networks

The various types of holonic networks are :

- Vertical networks
- Horizontal networks
- Regional networks
- Out-of-necessity networks and
- Self-promoted networks.

Vertical networks : These most closely resemble what we think of as the traditional supply chain. Usually one node adds some value to an object and passes it off to another node, which in turn adds value and so on down the value chain.

But within the virtual company, there are differences from the traditional model. Automotive Original Equipment Manufacturers (OEMs) used to be vertically integrated. *For example,* General Motors still makes almost every sub-assembly in GM shops and those it cannot make are made by suppliers quasi-dedicated to them. In this way, GM maintains control, GM's leverage over the supplier is the fear of losing GM as a customer.

Horizontal Networks : These are networks in which all nodes have the *same core competence* and share capacity back and forth. This type of network exists to a large extent in the textile and clothing industry. Here, large retail companies order large blocks of items – more than any supplier who receives the contract can deliver in the short period given. To meet demand, the supplier lays off parts of the order into preselected competitors, creating a system of cooperation. The relationships are usually reciprocal within a small group of companies.

Regional Networks : These networks are created by large groups of small companies, each having about 45 employees on an average. To handle orders of any size, these companies form tight partnerships with other entrepreneurs. Over time, they have come to specialise in small, discrete parts of the value chain. Such networks are common in clothing, jewellery manufacturing industries and in agriculture.

Out-of-necessity Networks : These networks consist of small companies that do not have the capital to develop a market or product. *For example,* a group of seven small cabinet making companies pooled their collective expertise to develop a computer numerical control (CNC) router that has become their core technology. Their collective goal was to produce a machine that would cost in the range of $ 30,000 to $ 70,000, bringing down the cost of the machine from $ 200,000. Not only can the seven companies manufacture finished products more effectively, but by pooling their capital they can expand into new product lines. Moreover by acting as holonic partners, they can specialise more closely in the components they are best at making and work for each other.

Self-Promoted Networks : These are usually single nodes that have core competence and seek partnerships with other nodes. In each case, the company has defined a strategic direction that sets the company's mission to be a node in as many holonic networks as possible irrespective of the ultimate consumer product being made. These companies survive on their ability to be a node.

- **Activity C**

Collect information about any organisation which has adapted principles of Holonic Network and describe the same.

....

....

....

....

....

....

....

....

9.14 THE VIRTUAL CORPORATION

The virtual corporation which began as a vision of futurists, became a possibility for business theorists and is now an economic necessity for corporate executives. It has become an inevitable new business model.

In 1980, Alvin Toffler first made a mention of **"prosumers"** (consumers who produced what they consumed) and **"de-massified"** production. Also, Toyota's Taiichi Ohno introduced the lean production technique with the ability to combine the benefits of mass production with quick market response. The 21st century is the age of the **virtual products and services**. These products and services can deliver instant customer gratification in a cost-effective way. They frequently can be produced in diverse locations and offered in a great number of models. The ideal virtual product or service is one that is produced instantaneously and customised in response to customer demand.

What will a virtual corporation look like?

To the outside observer, it will appear almost edgeless, with permeable and continuously changing interfaces between company, suppliers and customers. From inside the firm, it will look like a traditional corporation with traditional offices, departments and operating divisions constantly reforming according to need. Job responsibilities will regularly shift as will lines of authority in virtual corporations.

In the words of manufacturing expert Earl Hall *"The complex product markets of the 21st century will demand the ability to quickly and globally deliver a high variety of customised products. These products will be differentiated not only by form and function, but also by the services provided with the product, including the ability for the customer to be involved in the design of the product. A manufacturing company will not be an isolated facility of production, but rather a node in the complex network of suppliers, customers, engineering and other service functions."*

Building virtual products will require taking a sophisticated information network that gathers data on markets and customer needs, combining it with the latest design methods and computer-integrated production processes and then operating that includes highly skilled employees of the company together with suppliers, distributors, retailers and even consumers.

There will be profound changes in the company's distribution system and its internal organisation as they evolve to become more customer-driven and customer managed. Supplier networks will have to be integrated with those of customers. Suppliers will become very much dependent on their downstream customers and the customers will be equally trapped by their suppliers.

For many firms the challenge of all this change will prove too great. For some employees, the experience will be more traumatic than that of the changes demanded by the past transformations. The change will be unpredictability, lack of comfortable structure and too much of responsibility. All companies which are contented to maintain status-quo indefinitely may not only encounter change but be forced to endure continuous, unremitting, almost unendurable transmutation.

Meaningful Restructuring: Corporations that expect to remain competitive must quickly achieve mastery of both information and relationships. The process of corporate revision must be both rapid and complete. The only way to build virtual product is to revise R & D, manufacturing, marketing, sales, service, distribution, information systems and even finance – all must metamorphose.

The employees of the virtual corporation must change as well. Virtual corporations will require large numbers of highly skilled, reliable and educated workers – people who can understand and use the new forms of information, who can adapt to change, and who can work efficiently with others. An environment of team work, one in which employees, management, customers, suppliers and government – all work together to achieve common goals, will be necessary for virtual corporation to thrive. A meaningful corporate restructuring is required instead of blindly installed computer and robotic systems. The virtual corporation which was a matter of speculation just a few years ago, has now become an economic necessity. It will be central to the new business revolution. It is a vision of the future. The modern manufacturing organisations have adopted techniques such as just-in-time supply, work teams, flexible manufacturing, worker-empowerment, computer-aided design, total quality, mass customisation etc. But the virtual corporation will tie all these diverse innovations together into a single cohesive version of the corporation in the twenty-first century.

9.15 REENGINEERING THE CORPORATION

The book **"*Reengineering the corporation*"** authored by Champy, James and Michael Hammer is seen as the key book in the reengineering revolution. It encourages organisations to take a fresh look at inefficient and out-dated processes, and to focus on dramatic improvements in *cost, quality, service* and *speed*. Even today reengineering remains a powerful management tool for change.

Reengineering must focus on the fundamental rethinking and radical redesign of key business processes. With the objective of dramatic improvements in cost, quality, service and speed, the organisations must make key processes as lean and profitable as possible, discarding peripheral processes and people if necessary.

Reengineering should go far beyond altering and refining the processes. Reengineering puts a premium on the skills and potential of the people at the centre of the organisation. It should also tackle three key areas of management – managerial *roles, styles* and *systems*. The book **"Reengineering the corporation"** emphasises the following approach to reengineering.

1. Focus on improving core processes: In the context of fiercely competitive environment and the ability of information technology to transform business processes, organisations should take a fresh look at their inefficient and outdated processes.

2. Create a lean organisation: According to Champy, James and Michael Hammer, organisations need to identify their key processes and make them as lean and profitable as possible, discarding the peripheral processes and people if necessary. However it does not mean deliberate downsizing.

3. Achieve a complete corporate revolution: Simple process reengineering is not enough. True reengineering is a recipe for a corporate revolution and should go beyond altering and refining processes. Reengineering is concerned with rejecting conventional wisdom, and ignoring the experience of the past.

4. Transform the future: Organisation should start with a blank piece of paper (or a clean slate) and map their processes to identify how their business should operate. They should then attempt to translate the paper into concrete reality.

5. Reengineering management as well: Managers fail to impose change on themselves. They concentrate on tearing down processes, but they leave their own jobs and management styles intact. The old ways of management could eventually undermine the very structure of their rebuilt enterprise. Therefore, the reengineering process should tackle three key areas of management – ***managerial roles, styles*** and ***systems***.

6. Reengineering should be built on trust, respect and people: Reengineering actually puts a premium on the people at the centre of the organisation. Once the peripheral activities are discarded, the new environment puts a premium on skills of the existing people. Downsizing should not create a difficult environment in which trust is absent.

9.16 REINVENTING THE CORPORATION

Nowadays, people are reinventing education, health-care, politics and virtually all social structures. But the corporation is often the quickest and most responsive to change. Each day the corporation must confront the changes taking place in the market place. People have the opportunity to transform not only their jobs but also their company for the new information society.

In the present day, two crucial elements for social change exist – ***new values*** and ***economic necessity***. To produce social change, there must be a confluence of both – changing values and economic necessity. New humanistic values and global economic imperatives which are present now, produce social change. Even though people-oriented values changed a lot of individuals, social institutions like the corporation do not readily respond to changes instituted by individuals. *For example*, sensitivity training has changed managerial personnel but centralised hierarchies remained intact in organisations.

Corporate changes in the 1970s were in response to the economic necessity. *For example*, to compete with the US–the global leader of the 70s, Japanese firms experimented with decentralised new models such as small teams and quality control circles.

Beyond the 1980s, both the elements *viz.*, changing values and economic necessity are present in the business environment. The economic imperative for a more competitive, more productive work force is leading people back to the kind of humanistic values expressed earlier in terms of trust, freedom and respect for the individual.

In the coming decade, business enterprises will synthesise values and economics into the new corporate, social and economic model of the 1990s. Many corporates are reinventing themselves and have become ideally suited to today's social, demographic and economic environment. Such an environment is compelling even well-established companies to reinvent the corporation.

The ten considerations to be borne in mind as we reinvent the corporation are:

1. The shift in strategic resources from an individual to an information society. In the industrial society, capital was the strategic resource. But in the new information society, the key resource has shifted to *information, knowledge* and *creativity*. This key resource can be mined from a place: *employees*, which means the new emphasis will be on *human resources* (*i.e.*, human capital).

2. The coming seller's market and the new competition for the best employees. The average age of potential employees is becoming lesser and lesser in developing countries like India and China.

3. The whittling away of middle management. The computer technology is automating the kinds of jobs that middle managers used to do earlier. Cuts in middle management staff have gone up from 10 percent to 40 percent in the US. As a result, corporations are experimenting with flatter structures with reduced number of middle managers.

4. The continuing entrepreneurial revolution. Corporate planners are introducing programs to promote inside entrepreneurism (intrapreneurship) and attempts to transform employees into capitalists and stock holders through new incentive plans, stock option plans etc.

5. The emergence of the new variegated work force. The work force is no longer dominated by the male bread winner. Today's work force is younger, better educated and the number of female employees is on the rise.

6. The demographic revolution of working women. The coming days will witness virtually all women working except for a few months or years when they are raising children full-time. Todays women workers are reinventing both career patterns and motherhood and etching their new life styles on corporate policy.

7. The growing use of intuition and vision. Intuition is now being recognized as a powerful management tool. Leaders of today's newly reinvented corporations are drawing on their vision to guide the creation of new structures and rally support to build them.

8. The mismatch between the education system and the needs of the new information society. The need for new basic skills in the information society in forcing the education to be reinvented. The corporation need for skilled and will educated graduates is bringing alliance between business and the educational institutions.

9. The rising importance of corporate health issues. Concern over the high cost of health and the need to invest in and maintain the company's most valuable resource–its people–is fueling a corporate health boom designed to cut costs while encouraging fitness and well being of employees.

10. The value of the new generation. The best educated, affluent, independent, entrepreneurial, self-reliant, socially liberal and health-conscious young adults of today will be the future corporate managers. The corporate policies they enact as managers, entrepreneurs and corporate leaders will reflect their values.

Each day we grow more fully entrenched in the new information society. Hence, many of us must change our corporations – we just do not know how.

You will have to reinvent the corporation on your own. You have to create a workforce where both people and profits can flourish. And you are living among a generation of contemporaries who share your vision. The success of corporations depends on that vision.

The emerging trends in the changing corporation world where companies are reinventing themselves to be more competitive and growth oriented are presented to the readers in the following section.

1. The companies that create the most nourishing environment for personal growth of their employees will attract the most talented people. In the best companies, the employee's growth and the companies' growth are compatible and mutually nourishing. The human capital of an enterprise brings it the biggest return on investment. The corporates should be committed to the personal growth of its people and provide a dynamic environment for the work and learning. Some of the measures companies need to take in this direction are:

(a) instituting flexible hours by creating an intellectually stimulating environment.

(b) structuring jobs holistically to stretch, develop and integrate new skills.

(c) moving people laterally to develop well-roundedness.

(d) making employees experience growth.

2. The manager's new role is that of coach, teacher and mentor. The manager's role is to create a nourishing environment for personal growth in addition to the opportunity to contribute to the growth of the organisation. The managers should develop and cultivate human potential. The corporates face the challenges of not retraining the workers, but retraining the managers.

3. Compensation systems that reward performance and innovations are transforming employees into stockholders (owners). In new companies, people get paid not for their position on the organisation chart, but for their productivity. Pay for performance is replacing pay for just attending the work.

4. Companies will increasingly turn to third-party contractors, shifting from hired labour to contract labour. There is an increase in the number of "leased" employees. Employee leasing may be the best way for small businesses to attract best people.

5. Authoritarian management is yielding to a networking, people style of management. The top-down authoritarian management style is yielding to a networking style of management, where people learn from one another horizontally. In such environments, everyone is a resource for everyone else and each person gets support and assistance from many different directions.

6. Entrepreneurship within the corporations – intrapreneurship – is creating new products and new markets and revitalising companies inside out. Many companies are reinventing themselves as confederations of entrepreneurs, operating under the main tent of the corporation. By allowing the creative, intuitive entrepreneur to maintain control and responsibility for a venture, the corporation produces both a deeply satisfied employee and a healthier bottom line.

7. In the reinvented corporation, quality will be paramount. Today, people are very much concerned about quality. To the consumer, value equals the sum of quality products, quality service, a quality environment, quality employee relations and quality community involvement. Consumers perceive quality in terms of the whole, not just the parts, a company must offer quality in the totality of its dealings with the public.

8. Intuition and creativity are challenging the "it is all in the numbers" business school philosophy. Intuition becomes increasingly valuable in the new information society precisely because there is so much data or information about such complex issues that it is often impossible to take it all in. hence one has to learn to rely on intuition. The most successful CEOs of corporate use intuition regularly in planning and decision making. In the words of Professor Henry Mintzberg of McGill University, the top CEO is a ***"holistic, intuitive thinker who is constantly relying on hunches to cope with problems far too complex for rational analysis"***.

9. Large corporations are emulating the positive and productive qualities of small business. Large companies are discovering that to compete in a changing market place, they must adopt many of the values of small business.

In large corporations, whenever an operations grows too large, divisions which get too big, lose vitality, family atmosphere and easy, informal communication. Hence when there are more than a couple hundred people, a new unit breaks away to form an autonomous profit centre run by a small team. The philosophy underlying small units is that ***"freedom and respect for the individual are the best motivators, especially when innovation and growth are the objectives"***.

10. The dawn of the information economy has fostered a massive shift from infrastructure to quality of life. During the long industrial era, the focus while locating a plant was on infrastructure, transportation, natural resources, water, proximity to market etc. In the new information/ electronics economy, a facility can be located anywhere without having concern for infrastructure. The focus will be on the quality of life: good climate, good schools, cultural opportunities, recreational opportunities and increasingly opportunities for two-career couple. Today's economy is an entrepreneurally driven economy.

The new strategy in the competition for economic development is to create an environment that is nourishing to entrepreneurs.

9.17 SUMMARY

In the fast changing Indian economy, the domestic firms need to compete with MNCs in terms of quality, speed, cost innovations and governance advantages in order to survive and grow. The LPG (Liberalisation, Privatisation and Globalisation) policy of the government of India created a situation of fierce competition which has further resulted in mergers, acquisitions and restructuring of many companies.

Since integrating two or more businesses with different processes and cultures is quite difficult, restructuring or reinventing the organisation has become inevitable. Restructuring involves adopting new approaches, new technologies or processes. It also involves examination of each facet of the business process for the purpose of improvement and the implementation of changes contribute to the achievement of the global objectives of the organisation and to the well being of its people.

To have a clear understanding of the concept of organisational restructuring or reinventing, some basic concepts such as organisational structure and organisational design, and the topics such as organisational theory and types of organisational structures are briefly discussed:

An **organisational structure** is the formal network by which jobs/tasks are divided, grouped and coordinated. It reflects the formal relationships among groups and individuals in the organisation.

Organisational design is the overall set of structural elements and the relationships among those elements used to manage the total organisation. It is the process by which managers select and manage aspects of structure, so that the organisation can control the activities necessary to achieve its goals.

Organisational theory is the study of how organisations function and how they affect and are affected by the environment in which they operate. The various major approaches to organisational theory are *(i)* Classical approach (Theory X), *(ii)* The Neo-classical approach (Theory Y), namely *(a)* systems approach, *(b)* contingency approach and (c) multi-variate approach.

The various types of organisational structures are: *(i)* Line organisation, *(ii)* Staff or functional authority organisation, *(iii)* Line and staff organisation, *(iv)* Committee organisation, *(v)* Divisional organisation, *(vi)* Project organisation, *(vii)* Matrix organisation and *(viii)* Hybrid organisation.

Reorganising or restructuring the firm may result in downsizing (lay off of employees), the effect of which may be reduction in expenses and increase in profits but sometimes it may result in stagnant or reduced productivity. The goal of reorganizing is to achieve a transformation which shifts an organisation's strategy, business system and culture to deliver measurable and sustainable improvements.

Major programs of change such as downsizing, business process reengineering and take overs may result in low employee morale, low productivity, loss of employee trust in management and loss of the value of change. To avoid these problems, it is advisable to reorganise a firm without destroying its soul. For this we need to avoid four mental traps *viz.*, *(i)* People vs Performance, *(ii)* Structure vs System, *(iii)* Us vs Them and *(iv)* Concurrent vs Consecutive.

The ten golden rules to be followed to avoid unintended consequences of change are: *(i)* Confront the facts continuously, *(ii)* Build a coherent and compelling transformation story, *(iii)* Use the collective wisdom of the organisation, *(iv)* Hold a few elements of your transformation sacrosanct but be flexible with the rest, *(v)* Work through leaders at all levels, *(vi)* Get the right balance between action and reflection, *(vii)* Demonstrate early success, *(viii)* Make the change process unique, *(ix)* Expect resistance – listen constantly, but be clear about the boundaries, *(x)* Measure progress at every stage.

Organisational restructuring becomes necessary because of the problems of bonding the organisations which come together as a result of mergers, acquisitions, joint ventures, strategic alliances or collaborations. To be successful, organisational restructuring requires effective human resource management. The HR managers need to handle effectively issues such as downsizing, self-managed work teams, organisational culture, organisational development interventions etc.

A model of organisational transformation and reengineering involves four systems for bringing organisational transformation. They are: *(i)* the management system, *(ii)* the social system, *(iii)* the technical system and *(iv)* the behavioural system.

The 6 R's of organisational transformation and reengineering are: *(i)* Realisation, *(ii)* Requirements, *(iii)* Rethink, *(iv)* Redesign, *(v)* Retool and *(vi)* Reevaluate.

Business process reengineering redesigns the core processes of an organisation to satisfy in the "one best way" a particular customer need. If that customer need changes, BPRE does not have an immediate answer. In such cases one can look beyond BPRE to the **"holonic business system"** which allows businesses continually to deinvent and reinvent themselves as they face increasingly ambiguous markets.

The **"virtual corporation"** is a modern concept of an organisation developed in the 21st century and it has become an economic necessity for corporate executives. Virtual products and services can deliver instant customer satisfaction in a cost-effective way. A virtual corporation is an almost edgeless organisation with permeable and continuously changing interface between company, suppliers and customers. It may look like a traditional corporation with offices, departments and operating divisions constantly reforming according to need. Job responsibilities will regularly shift as will lines of authority in virtual corporation.

Reengineering the corporation is the key to reengineering revolution. It is a powerful management tool for change. But reengineering should not be limited to just altering or refining the processes, but should go beyond that. It should tackle three key areas of management – managerial roles, styles and systems.

In reengineering the corporation, the following approach is adopted:

(i) Focus on improving core processes, *(ii)* Create a lean organisation, *(iii)* Achieve a complete corporate revolution, *(iv)* Transform the future, *(v)* Reengineer management as well and *(vi)* Reengineering should be built on trust, respect and people.

Reinventing the corporation involves changing the corporation to confront the changes taking place in the market place. Two crucial elements of social change are *(i)* **new values** and *(ii)* **economic necessity**.

Beyond 1990s, many corporates have reinvented themselves and have become ideally suited to today's social, demographic and economic environment.

The ten considerations to be borne in mind as we reinvent the corporation are:

(i) The shift in strategic resource from an individual to an information society.
(ii) The coming seller's market and the new competition for the best employees.
(iii) The whittling away of middle management.
(iv) The continuing entrepreneurial revolution.
(v) The emergence of the new varietgated workforce.
(vi) The demographic revolution of working women.
(vii) The growing use of instuition and vision.
(viii) The mismatch between the education system and the needs of the new information society.
(ix) The rising importance of corporate health issues and
(x) The value of the new generation.

The emerging trends due to reinventing of corporations are:

(i) The companies that create the most nourishing environments for personal growth of their employees will attract the most talented people.
(ii) The manager's new role is that of coach, teacher and mentor.
(iii) Compensation systems that reward performance and innovations are transforming employees into stockholders.
(iv) Companies will increasingly turn to third-party contractors, shifting from hired labour to contract labour.
(v) Authoritarian management is yielding to a networking, people style of management.

(vi) Entrepreneurship within the corporations – intrapreneurship – is creating new products and new markets and revitalising companies inside out.

(vii) In the reinvented corporation, quality will be paramount.

(viii) Intuition and creativity are challenging the "it is all in the numbers" business school philosophy.

(ix) Large corporations are emulating the positive and productive qualities of small business.

(x) The dawn of the information economy has fostered a massive shift from infrastructure to quality of life.

9.18 SELF ASSESSMENT QUESTIONS

1. What is meant by restructuring the organisation?
2. Explain what is meant by reorganising the firm without destroying it.
3. What is meant by reinventing the corporation?
4. What is meant by the "law of unintended consequences of change" in organisations?
5. Discuss the four mental traps that should be avoided in order to avoid the effects of awful law of unintended consequences.
6. Discuss the ten golden rules to be followed to avoid unintended consequences of change.
7. Discuss the role of human resource management in organisational improvements.
8. Explain the model of organisational transformation and reengineering with a block diagram.
9. Discuss the 6 R's of transformation and reengineering with a diagram.
10. Describe the features of the virtual corporation.
11. What is meant by "meaningful restructuring?"
12. Discuss the approach to reengineering the corporation.
13. What is meant by holonic concept?
14. What is meant by "Beyond Business Process Reengineering?"
15. Describe the working of a "holonic business system" with an illustration.
16. Discuss the advantages of "holonic business system."
17. Discuss the various types of "holonic networks."
18. Discuss the ten considerations to be borne in mind as we reinvent the corporation.
19. Discuss the emerging trends in the changing corporate world where companies are reinventing themselves.

20. Write short notes on
    - *(a)* Organisational structure
    - *(b)* Organisational design
    - *(c)* Organisational theories
    - *(d)* Types of organisations
    - *(e)* Learning organisation
    - *(f)* Boundaryless organisation
    - *(g)* Organisational culture
    - *(h)* Self-managed teams.

♦ ♦ ♦ ♦ ♦

PROCESS REENGINEERING IN ACTION

1. REENGINEERING A SUCCESS AT WESTING HOUSE

Westing house was clear about its problems :

(i) Increasing competition worldwide, *(ii)* the company was forced to reduce its prices eventhough the cost of materials, labour and overhead kept increasing and *(iii)* higher customer expectations demanded shorter production cycle times, superior quality and greater customer satisfaction.

Reengineering was the answer for all these problems. Reengineering embraces such techniques as: *(i)* work teams, *(ii)* training employees in multiple skills so that they can do more on the job and *(iii)* employee empowerment which means giving decision making authority to employees as far down in the organisation as possible.

It also entails reengineering processes in both assembly lines and offices, to simplify and increase the speed of flow of work. The company developed a technology to improve process, named WESTIP. Cross-functional employees used WESTIP to perform process analysis, redesign and implementation, quickly and easily.

As a result, Westinghouse won a Baldrige National Quality Award. Other benefits gained by the company were

(i) 22 million in savings in one year.

(ii) Two-thirds reduction in material costs.

(iii) Reduced manufacturing costs by 30% through improved cellular layout.

(iv) A drop in time it takes to handle purchase orders from 14 days to 6 hours.

(v) Reduced ordering costs from $ 86 to $ 12.

(*Source :* Jay Heizer and Barry Render, *'Operations Management'*, 5th edition, Prentice Hall Inc. p 238)

2. IBM FIXES CREDIT APPLICATION PROCESS

The traditional IBM credit application process took many steps. The first step consisted of the people answering phones and logging calls from field sales personnel requesting credit for customers. After receiving calls from field sales personnel, phone personnel made paper notations which they sent upstairs to credit personnel for credit checks. Then the paper went down the hall to the business practice group where the data were entered into a computer for determination of terms and interest rates. From there the packet of data went to a clerical group. A week or two after the request, the results of the requests were available.

IBM tried to fix the process by keeping a log of each step of every request. Although logging allowed credit personnel to know where in the process the application was, it added a day to the turnaround. Finally two managers tried a radical approach. They walked a loan request through each step from office to office and found that it took only 90 minutes of actual work. The additional week was spent shuttling paper work among departments. This meant that the work along the way was not the problem. Instead the process was at fault. Reengineering resulted in IBM replacing all the its specialists with generalists, called "case workers" who process applications from start to finish. The firm also developed software that uses the expertise of specialists to support case workers. The reengineered process reduced the number of employees and achieved better results. The weak plus turnaround time for a credit request came down to 4 hours. The company now handles 100 times the number of credit requests that it did under the old system.

(*Source :* Jay Heizer, *et, al, op cit.*, p. 239)

3. REENGINEERING ACCOUNTS PAYABLE AT FORD

The accounts payable department at Ford, which processes bills and pays suppliers, had over 500 employees. Executives visited the Japanese auto manufacturer Mazda (in which Ford owns 25% interest) and found only five people in its accounts payable department. Eventhough Mazda is a smaller company, no way could that alone can account for the hundred fold difference in personnel. The reality was that Ford's procurement process was bloated and wasteful. *For example,* whenever a purchase order was issued, a copy was sent to accounts payable, when the supplier sent a shipment, the invoice was sent to bills payable and when the shipment was received at Ford, a copy of the receiving documents were sent to accounts payable.

The receiving documents had to be matched against the invoice and purchase order. If everything matched, a cheque was sent to the supplier, if not, the source of mismatch had to be determined, which took a lot of time, held up payment to suppliers and generated much paper work.

The new, reengineered process eliminates invoices and mismatched documentation. When a purchase order is being completed, information is simultaneously entered into a database. Upon arrival of the shipment at the receiving dock, a clerk retrieves the purchase order on a computer terminal. If the shipment and the purchase order match, the clerk enters acceptance into the system, which automatically issues a payment cheque to the vendor. If the shipment and purchase order do not match, the shipment is sent back to the vendor. The accounts payable department now has 125 people, one fourth of the earlier 500 people!.

(*Source :* John M. Nicholas, *"Competitive Manufacturing Management"*,
Tata Mc Graw Hill Edition, 2001,
Tata Mc Graw Hill Publishing Company Limited, p,52).

4. CHANGING LAYOUT AT HAMILTON STANDARD

Hamilton standard's Windsor Locks plant used a paper doll layout approach for planning facility layout changes. Since many of the machines are huge in size and weight, moving them on trial-and-error fashion is impossible and work flow analysis on paper is in-accurate. So to analyse alternate layouts, cardboard pieces were cut out with the same floor dimensions as the machines. The pieces were then arranged and rearranged in an empty area of the parking lot until people were satisfied with the layout and walk patterns. The machines were then located within the plant according to the new pattern. Consequently, required floor space was reduced by 75% and required travel distance between machines was reduced by 85 percent.

(*Source :* John M. Nicholas, *op.cit*, p 327)

5. PROCESS MANAGEMENT AT AT & T

AT & T believes strongly in process management. Its employees are known as *process managers*, not workers, supervisors or associates. All work is considered part of a process. Therefore, every one manages a process at some level and is simultaneously a customer of and a supplier to other processes.

For example, there are management processes (such as business planning), information processes. (such as measuring customer satisfaction), product and service processes (such as product development) and support processes (such as education and training) that cut across departmental lines. Employees work roles in this type of environment are familiar to those of self-employed professionals.

Process owners, previously known as managers, are ultimately responsible for an entire process from end to end, rather than people or departments. Process owners have the authority to change a process, but they do not normally perform the process or manage its day-to-day activities. They enlist the aid of a **process management team** (PMT) to manage the day-to-day activities and suggest improvement initiatives. The PMT performs regular analysis and planning to establish process control, evaluate process performance measures, manages ongoing process improvement and ensures that the process creates value for its customers. When necessary, the PMT may charter a reengineering team to completely redesign a process. Reengineering projects are much easier and quicker when they begin with a PMT that already understands the process, can provide in-depth knowledge of customer requirements and gathers benchmarking information on a regular basis.

For example, when new product introductions got bogged down in a software division, the ORION team was formed to examine the problem. The team documented 50 steps in their development process, only 40 of which added value. Taking this as a starting point, they redesigned the process so that the same amount of work could get done with 40 percent of the efforts. As a result, the business unit was able to introduce products to the market 9 months earlier than before. This meant they could also introduce about 50 per cent more new products and services to the market, for millions of dollars a year in additional profits.

In this way, process focus at AT & T is an enabler of change.

(*Source :* Roberta. S. Russel, Bernard W. Taylor III, *"Operations Management"* 4th Edition, Pearson Education, P141)

6. REENGINEERING AT BANCA DI AMERICA EDI ITALIA (BAI)

Senior executives at Banca di America edi Italia (BAI) reengineered its processes to become a "paperless bank" and again become competitive with other European banks. They created two cross-functional teams to diagnose and redesign the bank's processes without considering the constraint of the current organisation. The best people were assigned to the design teams. The executives made significant investments in information technology and skill training. The team divided the transactions that customers make, into 10 categories such as deposits, credit cards, money orders and the like. They carefully documented the flow of activities needed to complete each process. Once a detailed picture emerged, they redesigned each process from scratch. *For example,* the check-deposit transaction previously has 64 operations and required 9 forms. It now involves only 25 operations and 2 forms. The redesigned process were then given to the technology team, which focused on strong data and creating the necessary software. As a result of the redesigned processes, BAI was able to add 50 new banks without any new personnel. The number of employees per branch dropped from 8 to 4. The two hours formerly needed to close the cashier positions have been reduced to 10 minutes. Revenues have doubled and BAI executives attribute 24 percent of the increase to the reengineered process.

(*Source :* Lee. J. Krajewski and Larry P. Ritzman, *"Operations Management".* 5th Edition, Addison - Wesley, 'p'. 88)

7. PROCESS IMPROVEMENT AT MUTUAL BENEFIT ASSURANCE COMPANY LIMITED (MBACL)

In the old days, mutual benefit assurance company limited processed its applications like every other insurance company. An application went through five departments, 20 people and 30 steps. Under this system, the hour or so of work associated with an application took between 5 to 25 days to be completed!

MBACL's CEO believed that customer service had to be improved and ordered a 60 percent improvement in productivity. The team assigned to produce this improvement realised that this goal could not be achieved by minor changes, but a complete process redesign would be necessary.

The new arrangement abolished the existing system of departments and job descriptions and created the new role of **"case manager"**. Case managers have complete responsibility for applications-from receipt to completion and work autonomously. They can operate in this manner due to the support of computer work stations that run an expert system and other programs.

The benefits of the new process are impressive. Application processing time has come down to as few as four hours and on an average take only 2 to 5 days. Case managers can now process twice as many applications as the previous system, despite the fact that the number of field office positions has been reduced by 100.

(*Source :* James R. Evans, James W Dean, Jr. *'Total Quality'*, 2nd Edition, South Western - Thomson Learning, p 214)

8. REENGINEERING THE TRAVEL SYSTEM AT U.S DEPARTMENT OF DEFENCE

Moving hundreds of thousands of troupes or tons of humanitarian aid materials quickly is no problem for the Pentagon, but sending employees on routine travel has been a different story. The pentagon travellers had to secure numerous approvals and fill out reams of paper work before they could even board a bus. After the trip, the average traveller spent six hours preparing vouchers for reimbursement.

The department of defense set up a task force to reengineer the cumbersome travel system, with the objective of making it cheaper, more efficient and more customer friendly. The reengineered system reduces the steps in the pretravel process from an astounding 13 to only 4. Travel budgets and authority to approve travel requests and vouchers, which have traditionally rested in the budget channels of the various service commands will be transferred to local supervisors. Travellers will make all their arrangements through a commercial travel office, which will prepare a "should cost" estimate for each trip.

This document will be all a traveller needs before, during and after a trip. With a supervisor's signature, it becomes a travel authorization, during travel, it serves as an itinerary, after amendments to reflect variations from travel plans, it becomes an expense report. Other travel expenses and needed cash or traveller's cheque will be charged to a government-issued travel card, with payment made directly to the travel card company through electronic fund transfer.

A second task force has been created to implement the reengineering recommendations. "Tiger teams" bringing together employees from across previously isolated functional departments, have been set up to tackle specific issues such as how to simplify the defence department's travel regulations. Within three months, 230 pages of regulations had been reduced to a 16 page pamphlet.

In reengineering travel, says Gerry Kauvar, deputy director of the defence performance review, the defence department "is linking authority, responsibility and accountability at the local level". If the reengineered system is successful, it could serve as a management model that can be duplicated in other areas.

(*Source :* Richard L. Daft, *'Management'*, 5th Edition, Thomson - South-Western, p 340)

9. SOUTH KOREA'S BRIGHT STAR

In 1990, Gold star company was in deep trouble. The largest South Korean manufacturer of electrical appliances and consumer electronics has seen its market share slip as product quality plummeted, losses piled up, margins fell and costs rose.

However, the healthy and vibrant company has regained its sales position in south Korea for colour televisions, refrigerators and washing machines. The chairman Leen Hun-Jo is responsible for this transformation, he has shifted Gold Star from a family-managed business to one enjoying the skills and training of professional managers.

To initiate the change, Hun-Jo focused on people first. "You have to transform human beings. If you can't change your people, you can't change your organisation too". He won workers' confidence by closing the communication gap. He revealed as much financial information about the company as he could. He opened his doors to visits by employees at any time (open door policy).

Having won employee support, Hun-Jo began to restructure. He organised Gold Star into nine SBUs that include twentynine operational groups, each with a multi disciplinary team of designers, engineers, factory workers and marketing people. The plan called for decentralising management as far down as possible, thereby encouraging line managers, workers and sales people to open up the lines of communication among themselves.

Hun-Jo then changed the product development process. In the past Gold Star concentrated on bringing in a foreign product and reverse-engineering it. Although it allowed for some technology gains, it also kept the company permanently behind the cutting edge. Hun-Jo changed the focus. He sent engineers out to see for themselves what customers wanted. It resulted in the development of refrigerator that helped Gold Star regain the number one position in its domestic market.

(*Source :* Warren R. Plunkett and Raymond F. Attner, *"Management"*, 6th Edition, South - Western College Publishing, p 295)

10. RUBBERMAID'S APPROACH TO REENGINEERING

Outsourcing, downsizing, wholesale layoffs and overburdened workers are all too often connected with reengineering and great leaps forward. However as Rubbermaid proves, they do not have to be.

Thinking out-of-the box is a hall mark of Wolf Schmitt's and Rubbermaid's approaches to everything. He gets great ideas by observing his kids at play, commuting with nature, trusting his intuition, and looking for unfavourable trends. Schmitt leads Rubbermaid, a company known for introducing a vast array of new low-tech products each year. If you think Honda, Toyota or Ford makes America's best-selling car, you are wrong. It is Rubbermaid's Cozy Coupe, selling over one-half million cars per year.

Rubbermaid's profitability depends on the unleashing of the creativity of all its employees. Twenty-one product teams have the responsibility for creating a large quantity of new ideas, rapid processing of them to obtain a nucleus of the best, and then turning them into product. Rubbermaid overwhelms its competitors by putting so many products and each year that only a few can be copied. To avoid run away costs, Schmitt keeps his company continuously focused on increasing productivity, but not by decreasing people. "Sure we could take out a lot of our people. But we would give up our future" Schmitt knows that wholesale layoffs lead to disloyal, demotivated, job seeking left over employees. "Instead, Schmitt is hiring. Rubbermaid in the next three or four years will hire 300 "culturally diverse" young managers, mostly from foreign countries". Rubbermaid keeps its competitive edge by carefully nurturing and continually hiring creative people, the product ideas key flowing in, along with the dollars they generate.

(*Source :* Warren R. Plunkett and Raymond F. Attner, *'Management'*, 6th Edition, South-Western Publishing, page 75)

11. REENGINEERING AT SUNDARAM FASTENERS

When Sundaram Fasteners, the Chennai based fasteners-manufacturer realised the necessity to upgrade its quality to global levels – in order to export large enough volumes to offset imports – it reengineered ruthlessly. Identifying manufacturing as its core process, the firm discovered that manufacturing was clustered more around operations – forging, heat treatment and tooling – than around products. Each worker was concentrating only on his area and the efficiency of the entire process for producing a product was not being maximised.

With the help of reengineering consultants – Lucas Engineering System, Sundaram Fasteners transformed the process from being ***task-centric*** to ***product-centric***. Machines was regrouped into two **zones of autonomous production** (ZAP): ZAP 1 to handle products between 6 mm and 16 mm diameter and ZAP 2 to handle parts upwards of 16 mm diameter.

Reengineering shifted the responsibility for meeting customer requirements from the marketing department to the manager of each of the two ZAP modules. The module manager was empowered to order components from the in-house raw material module according to requirements and even outsourcing if necessary. The module manager has become the single reference point for the customer and the owner of the process. The gains were significant 50 percent improvement in adherence to delivery schedule, increase in inventory turnover from 4 times to 20 times at its Chennai factory and a 25 percent increase in productivity.

(*Source:* Business Today: December 7–21. 1995)

12. REENGINEERING AT INDFOS INDUSTRIES

The Objective: To drastically cut the time taken by raw material to be transported from the factory gate (inwards goods store) to the assembly line. This time is referred to as the ***"Production Order Release Time"*** (PORT).

The Old Process: The process had two components: Port 1 – from the gate to the holding stores and Port 2 – from the holding stores to the assembly line. Port 1 involved 16 people and took 540 minutes. First the material was despatched from the gate to the transit store for counting (inspection) and the transit manager prepared a document (consignment receiving report) to offer the goods received for inspection by quality department. The quality department checked the goods and returned the document to the store where it was correlated with the material and a final document (goods inspection note) was prepared. This was sent to the holding (or inventory) store from where the activities of port 2 begins.

According to the general manager of Indfos Industries, "the main problem was the waiting time between each stage. Every time the quantity mentioned in the initial document (consignment receiving report) did not match with the bill raised at the transit store, the issue was referred to the planning department."

Reengineered Process: In the modified process, all cross-referrals have been eliminated. A computer terminal has been installed at the gate, with the security guard being trained to use it. As the incoming material (raw material) is logged in at the gate, the final document is created on the spot in the computer. The material is then sent to the transit store, where it is checked by the quality control staff, with problems being cleared by a cross-functional team, led by the manager in charge of production planning and stores. The new time for clearance of goods was 31 minutes. Most of the time spent was to go on chasing the material. Reengineering has eliminated that.

(*Source:* Business Today. December 7–21, 1995)

13. REENGINEERING AT HINDUSTAN MOTORS

The Objective: To create a manufacturing process for the 10 product earth moving machinery division that allows the different methodologies required for different products to co-exist while permitting prioritisation of orders according to customer needs. Additional targets: adhere to delivery schedule, and streamline the flow of materials and machinery on the shop floor.

The Old Process: The old manufacturing process was designed for only one kind of machinery. However, it continued to be used for every category of product, leading to less than optimum usage of resources. The same assembly line was used for all products, resulting in confusion and making the adjustment of production schedules for different products impossible. The work flow allowed no clear points of transit between one stage and the next.

Reengineered Process: Three mini plants have been formed – one each for dumper equipment, holder equipment and tract vehicles – in order to create separate processes for separate product groups. With the help of the engineering consultants CSC Manufacturing, the plant has been divided into cells, each staffed with multi-skilled workers.

Each cell is responsible for fabricating and assembling the entire product, cutting out delays that resulted from hand-offs that used to occur when jobs were passed from one worker to another and from one part of the factory to another. The cells were categorised as either **repeater cells** – handling several products whose demand is sporadic and low – or **consumer cells** – handling the few products needed around the year – work-in-progress has already been reduced by 20 percent and is expected to be cut by another 30 percent.

14. REENGINEERING AT SIEMENS

The Objective: To improve installation time and service quality of hi-tech medical diagnostics equipment.

The Old Process: The installation of a new machine and post-installation service were concentrated in the same department. When an order came to a regional sales office, copies of it would be forwarded to the commercial department, the despatch departments passed it to the service department, which would check with the customer about the readiness of the site for installation.

The response would then return to first, the commercial department, then the despatch department and finally to the factory. And a similar process would ensue for providing post-installation service to the customer.

According to the general manager, Siemens, – "there were too many interferers, and far too many people involved in the old way of doing things."

Reengineered Process: A proposal to create computer links between different service offices was discarded. Instead, the installation of the machine has been delinked from the service department. A separate project management team and a commercial and technical assistance centre (C–TAC) have been created for the purpose. The sales order is sent directly to the project management team, which handles all pre-installation work.

The C-TAC manages documentation, on-site technical assistance, – all of which earlier needed coordination with other departments. Relieved of the responsibility of installation, service engineers focus on the primary function: providing post-installation service. Which installation time has come down from 10 to 3 days, the service engineers have improved their response time to complaints and quality to a great extent.

(*Source:* Business Week. Dec. 7–21, 1995).

15. REENGINEERING AT HEWLETT-PACKARD

The Objective: *(i)* To cut the time to design a new product to three months. *(ii)* To cut the new product launching time to six months. *(iii)* To launch replacement for a product over the next three months.

The Old Process: The steps were strictly sequential. The marketing team analysed market forces and recommended a selling price for a new product. The research and development team scanned the technologies available and chose one which is appropriate. Design objectives were created and the CAD/CAM lab was commissioned to design the new product.

The design was forwarded to marketing for approval; in case of any problems, it went back to the drawing boards. The procurement department was alerted about components, the software team loaded the software, and manufacturing release tests were conducted to check how well the product could be manufactured in the company's plants. The bill of materials was needed by the marketing department and the product forwarded to the sales and service team.

Reengineered Process: At weekly meeting of cross-functional teams from the marketing, manufacturing and research departments, the marketing team's suggestions are married on the spot to available technologies, which are tracked by a special team. Problems with product designs initiated earlier are thrashed out by the cross-functional team. As work begins on designing one product, the next weekly meeting sees the birth of another idea and another product. At any point, several product designs are in various stages of completion, ensuring a continuous stream into the market. New products are being introduced at intervals of four months.

♦ ♦ ♦ ♦ ♦

CASE ILLUSTRATIONS

CASE 1. COLGATE RETHINKS A SUPPLY CHAIN

When it comes to tooth paste in China, Colgate is the market leader, according to a recent AC Nielsen Media International survey on China's emerging consumer society. But in the shampoo category, a Colgate-Palmolive rival tops the list.

Driving sales through brand building and smart marketing is as necessary for fast-moving consumer products companies in China and the rest of Asia as it is in the mature markets of North America and Europe. But in Asia, with its fickle tastes, falling prices and unpredictable competitors, the pressure to keep ahead of the pack and make a proper return on investment is relentless.

The trick is to control tightly what can be controlled. The one area a consumer products company can be firmly in charge of is its own internal business processes. Eliminating waste and wringing out costs can have a dramatic effect, especially with products like shampoo, toothpaste and soap, where volumes are large but margins are thin and tight.

In the past two years Colgate-Palmolive has rolled out an ambitions program to do just that in the Asia Pacific region. The company's entire supply chain was reengineered, and new back-office systems were put in place with stunning speed-all the more remarkable considering that the undertaking involved 57 sites across 11 different markets including China. As a result, these far-flung operations were transformed into a single, closely integrated organisation.

Colgate-Palmolive's entire business-process reengineering effort-code named "Project Dragon" - was accomplished without missing a single self-imposed deadline. All the while the company had to battle in a furiously competitive market place - that was being rocked by regional economic turmoil.

Well positioned

Today Colgate-Palmolive is following a new model. Subsidiaries throughout Asia use the same automated systems, whether they are handling orders or managing credit. Sourcing has become more economical, with selected countries being the primary suppliers of products for the region. Supporting each market is a shared service organisation providing region-wide information technology and financial functions.

The upshot is that one of the global leaders in consumer products is strongly positioned to win profitable market share as Asia's economies shake off the malaise of the past three years.

Project Dragon was conceived and driven by both wider corporate goals and specific Asian issues. The former included Colgate Palmolive's strategy to allocate 60 percent of capital expenditures to cost savings programs. Among the latter was the realisation that there was no guarantee that the company could sustain its double-digit growth rates of the past few years, which, in past, had been due to the region's rising prosperity.

Many operational anomalies had also arisen in Asia over the years, with Colgate-Palmolive units in various countries conducting businesses in different ways. The result was a series of separate systems and procedures often unique to individual markets. This made it more difficult to obtain a more complete picture of the company's global finances - a crucial task, given the fact that 70 percent of Colgate-Palmolive's revenues come from outside the U.S, a figure that is expected to grow.

To Simpson (the general manager of Asia Pacific Information Technology for Colgate-Palmolive) who led a similar reengineering effort in the US, the goal was to streamline the production and distribution cycles. "To do this meant matching information flows" he explains "so that the right products were made at the right time and unwanted inventory did not sit on the shelf".

This goal translated into three specifics:

(i) reengineer the entire supply chain

(ii) standardise business processes and

(iii) build regional hubs for information technology and finance

The first step was to decide where to base "project dragon". Given the region's cultural diversity and operational quirks, the question was crucial. Australia was too far away. Hongkong and Singapore were convenient, but their markets were too small.

Malaysia was finally chosen because Colgate-Palmolive produced all categories of goods there and the market was large enough to provide a valid test bed. The Malaysian government was also actively seeking IT investments in that country.

The strategy was to develop the overall plan from Kaula Lampur and then roll out in Malaysia-Simpson assembled a core team in Asia to run the project. The company brought together Colgate-Palmolive people from Philippines, Thailand, India and Malaysia and teamed with a multinational Accenture team from Australia and Asia. They quickly embarked on an intense five-month design phase.

From the beginning the idea was to avoid the notion of imposing a solution from "on high" and instead to encourage involvement from the subsidiaries. Simpson brought people from local subsidiaries to Kaula Lampur for training and to be involved in the Malaysian roll out. Having enthusiastic staff from one market support their colleagues in another became a feature of the entire program.

According to Brian Strange, the Accenture client partner on the project, it was necessary to have a "quick win" to boost the project's credibility within Colgate-Palmolive's Asia Pacific operations. A decision was made up front to standardise the processes. Because of time pressures, specific features were added later.

The Malaysian roll out started in early 1997. A flurry of new finance, procurement, sales and distribution systems was introduced. Staff members-including warehouse men, production managers, shift supervisors, accounts clerks and sales teams - had to understand the new processes. The final weeks before the "big bang" implementation, set for July 1977 were characterised by workshops, coaching sessions with practice databases and a final full **"day in the life"** simulation.

Firm Dead lines

As soon as Malaysia was up and running, attention moved to other markets. The unfolding regional economic crisis in mid 1997 encouraged Colgate-Palmolive to drive the project faster, instead of doing one market after another, markets were rolled out simultaneously.

To Simpson, the key to successful implementation is **"to copy, copy, copy"** rather than **reinvent**. He estimates that 85 percent of Colgate experiences in the US and Europe fit Asia. But he advocated accepting the **"80 percent rule"**. It was better to achieve 80 percent of the design requirement now than to wait for 100 percent and miss dead lines.

And dead lines were set in store. "As part of the change-management process, we set up clear communications with country managers" says Simpson. "They were told what was expected of them and were given a set of dates two years out".

The roll out was aggressive. The final two markets, China and Hongkong, went live in May 1999.

Each market offered its own challenges, although many had been identified in advance in Kaula Lumpur during visits by staff from the local markets. And in every market, systems had to be adapted to take account of local taxes and other official requirements.

Capturing orders, credit management and accounts receivables are among a host of functions that have improved. More crucially, better information flows make it easier to predict demand and therefore create better manufacturing schedules and working back down the supply chain, the source materials more effectively.

In the wider picture, project dragon will allow Colgate-Palmolive to take advantage of the revival of Asia's economies. The economist poll of forecasters has predicted that GDP growth in 2000 for the likes of India, Singapores, Taiwan and Malaysia should top rates achieved in 1999. With confidence returning, the battle for consumers' wallets will intensity. Colgate-Palmolive will be ready.

(*Source: "Out look"* Journal : case study)

CASE 2. "REBUILDING MAHINDRA"

It is remaking itself. Exactly half of a century after it was born, the Rs. 1700 crore Mahindra and Mahindra (M & M) - the Bombay based producer of automobiles and tractors, which was incorporated on October 2, 1945 - is trying to manufacture a future for itself.

In what is the biggest exercise in the history of manufacturing in India - not in terms of **men, materials** or **machines**, but in terms of **methods** - MM is going back to the basics : **manufacturing**. And for the first time, an Indian engineering giant seems to be implicating Peter Drucker's rule for managing manufacturing: "Production is not the application of tools to materials, but the application of logic to work".

By rapidly revamping the production systems at its factories in Bombay, Nashik and Igatpuri - which together employ over 15,000 workers - M & M is trying to instil sense into its systems. On the drawing boards, therefore, is a blue print that could well create a **"factory of the future"**. Keshub Mahindra, M & M's 73 year old chairman declares "We are working towards a new goal. We have to be the leaders in the automotive business".

Over the past 50 years. M & M had constantly regeared itself for growth, forging **alliances** with global automobile giants on three continents: with Willys and Chrysler of the US for utility vehicles, with Automobile Peugeot of France for engines and now with Ford Motor company of the US to produce its Fiesta and Escort cars in India.

With a 26 percent share of the Rs. 2500 crore tractors market and a 70 percent share of the Rs. 1600-crore utility vehicles market, M & M has not only secured market leadership, but has also succeeded in consolidating its bottom line over the years.

M & M is not trying to fix anything that isn't broke. It is merely cementing the cracks in its shop floor that could become the chasms into which it could tumble tomorrow. Despite its prime position, the M & M - mobile is actually a bureaucratic, flabby and inefficient manufacturer that guzzles costs and throttles margins. But until the early 1990s, M & M didn't care because **it didn't know what competition was**.

Raw materials costs at M & M have risen from 45 percent of its operating costs in 1993-94 to 57 percent in 1994-95. Labour costs account for almost 12 percent of the total, and at **eight vehicles per worker per annum**." M & M has one of the lowest productivity ratios in the automobile industry in the world" according to its managing director R.K. Pitamber who is 63. In contrast to M & M, Maruti Udyog's productivity was 60 vehicles per employee per year.

The low labour productivity is dangerous to M & M because of competition from their archrival Telco (the Sierra, the Estate and the Sumo) and Bajaj (Tempo Trax) who are muscling into the utility vehicles market. And M & M's market share has actually fallen from 76 percent in 1992-93 to 70 percent in 1994-95.

Anand Mahindra, deputy managing director admits "we were aware that there was growing vulnerability within M & M, especially in manufacturing". According to K.J. Devasia (president and executive director of tractors division) of M & M "we are following expensive and inefficient ways of production. We figured that to stop or we wouldn't be able to survive".

Suspecting the need for outside help to solve its problem, M & M went scouting for a consultant. By late 1993, M & M had found the driver and the vehicle for change: the UK based Lucas Engineering and Systems was brought in to implement what is code named as **"Mahindra Top Gear Programme"**, with the aim to boost productivity by 50 percent in a year.

For starters, M & M's twin-factory complex at Kandivli, a suburb of Bombay, is being **retooled** while its other factories at Nashik and Igatpuri in Maharastra will soon follow. The first thing of course, has been **retraining**, in India and abroad, starting with Pitamber and going down to every worker. "I feel that our people are most enthusiastic about what we are going through" says Keshub Mahindra.

Change has slowly started sweeping across M & M's shop floors, where the writing is literally on the wall. Placards and signs loudly hector the virtues of M & M's new manufacturing systems every where and the employee morale is high. Alan Durante, 55, president and executive director (automotive division) M & M says "This is only the beginning, we have a long way to go".

There are several lessons that corporate India can learn from M & M today as it tries to rebuild its factories. Especially since M & M's new production systems are a synthesis of the best practices on three continents.

What, then, are the **six principles of manufacturing management** that can be learnt from the shop floors - and the board rooms - of M & M?

These are:

1. Build Product Units
2. Create Cellular Systems
3. Deploy Flexible Processes
4. Try to Cut Cycle Times
5. Customerise Your Shop Floors
6. Let Your Workers Own the Factory.

These six principles are briefly presented in the following sections:

1. Build product units

Take a walk between the yellow lines on your shop floor and ask yourself the following three questions:

(i) Does the factory flow **linearly** or do your men, materials and methods keep doubling up?

(ii) Does the structure encourage or hamper work flows?

(iii) Do you see cohesion, confusion or chaos around you?

If the answer to even one of these is not clear, your shop floor is a doodle. This was exactly the situation at M & M.

When the top management team at M & M looked down at the bays of M & M's tractors and automotives factory at Kandivli, it realised that even they were actually laid out with all the subtlety of a snarled piece of knitting, over the decades the various segments had been scattered over 40 acres of land with **little rationality in the linkages**. For instance, the transmissions machining unit and the engine machining unit had been clubbed together while the transmissions gear assembly and subassemblies were on the other side of a field. And every bit of spare space was being haphazardly used as a dump for tractors, tyres and components. "It was a classic **functional layout**, which had itself gone awry" says Ashok Pai, 35, module manager (engine product unit) M & M.

The situation was no better in the automobiles plant as well. The machine shop where automobile components were manufactured and the assembly shop where these components were assembled into subunits were separated by a 20 feet wide road. According to HB Deasi, 50, general manager (reengineering) M & M. "The lack of a structural design had led to long lead times, poor material flows, inefficient space utilisation and low productivity." "The quality was poor. Since similar operations were clubbed together, there was little focus on the products that each shop floor produced" says Vijay Dhongde, 41, manager (manufacturing systems design) M & M.

So M & M decided to evolve a **new layout** for its production units, based on the **product unit structure**: each facility would be relaid in a fashion that allowed it to manufacture a single, homogeneous group of components that went straight into the final assembly line.

The fresh blue print for the tractors factory streamlined its operations into three product units: *(i)* **the transmissions,** *(ii)* **engine** and *(iii)* **final assembly**.

Likewise at the automotives plant, M & M has broken its operations into six product units: *(i)* **chassis**, *(ii)* **axle**, *(iii)* **engine**, *(iv)* **transmission**, *(v)* **body** and *(vi)* **final product**.

Desai explains "If we classify our main components as products, there is bound to be a focus on the quality".

Within each unit, production modules have been created for sequential work patterns. Two or more cells form a module and within each module, cells are grouped in such a way that they are aligned with the logical work process sequence. *For example,* the transmission case cell, the transmission case cover cell, and the gear lever forks and shafts cell form one module. And three or four such modules constitute a product unit.

One immediate benefit is that the movement of materials is far more disciplined. Vinay Devrath, 41, a senior consultant at process engineering, the Pune-based manufacturing consultancy, says “once you focus on products and not parts or components - your production system will immediately spring to life”. At M & M, production is expected to increase by 60 percent per annum over the next five years because of the new structure.

2. Create Cellular Systems

If any component used in the manufacture of a product is being pulled round and round the shop floor, and gathering dust several times a day, then the manufacturing systems are not cellular.

M & M's A-team found that at all its four factories, every component visited the same shop several times, travelled upto 1-5 km and frequently came to dead halt. According to the team, M & M was losing about 1000 man-hours a year per worker because of the time wasted in the transportation of components. This amounts to three hours a day. This would lower M & M's employee productivity.

M & M decided to discontinue function-based manufacturing under which factories were broken up into a number of shops, each of which specialised in a particular task. *For example,* in function-based manufacturing, a crank shaft would be going through a cumbersome machining process: from the central stores the raw component would travel to the cutting shop, to the lathe, to the milling, drilling and grinding shops and finally to the polishing and honing shops before being stored in an intermediate store prior to the final assembly.

In the cellular manufacturing system introduced by M & M, the plant has been broken into a number of cells. A cell is defined as the smallest building block of a factory. It consists of a natural group of machines and people to complete a task. The steps in the process of completing the task need not be sequential but follow a natural order. The cellular manufacturing system was invented by Toyota and is the key to the success of the Japanese automobile companies.

Since the parts processed by a cellular manufacturing system flow continuously from one operation to another in each cell - either one or a few at a time - the amount of time that elapses between the start of the first and last operations is approximately the same as the processing plus handling time for one piece. This is the reason for reduction of production time by 50 percent in cellular than in functionally organised factory.

So shop floors at M & M's Kandivili plant are being divided into 80 cells with each cell being responsible for completing one process. *For example*, the new jeep axles product unit is divided into 10 cells, which undertake all the functions needed to make them. At one end, the raw component enters and finished axles come out of the other end of the product unit.

Cell manufacturing promotes team work and thereby the workers are becoming more motivated. By March 1996, in the first year of its implementation, the company plans to reduce idle man-hours by half, reduce its inventory costs by Rs. 50 crores and boost employee productivity by 60 percent.

3. Deploy Flexible Processes

At M & M, it was found that production units were as rigid as rigormortis and that didn't come as a surprise. For, it manufactures seven basic models of utility vehicles which are classified by engine and transmission, at four different locations. While the Kandivli plant produces MDI 2500A, the direct injection diesel engines and the Peugeot XDP 4.90 four speed engines are produced at Igatipure plant, the commander 650 vehicle which uses the former engine and the Armada which needs the latter engine, are both assembled at Nashik.

While the commander-650 is also produced at Kandivli, so is the CL-340 short-chassis jeep. This interlocking grid of dependence also meant that if one factory ran into a glitter, the M & M machine would grind to a dead halt all across the country. Also the productivity levels at any one plant can not be pushed up unless the backward linkages were cranked up too.

The key to the future is a **flexible manufacturing system (FMS)**. Flexible manufacturing would allow M & M to use all their factories as complete production units. FMS allows M & M switch between manufacturing different products, or event different product lines without losing anytime while doing so.

FMS not only optimises resources but also boosts production. "The concept of sticking to the manufacture of only one kind of product is going out. Each manufacturing facility will have to start producing diverse and rich mix of products". In otherwords, cells at all the M & M's plants will learn to cope with all the vehicle configurations. The 'U' shaped shop layout in which each cell is laid out lends itself to easy switching between product lines since there is only a single-piece flow.

Critically, workers are being taught to tool, or put together subassemblies for various vehicles without loss of time (multiskilled workers). As a result, the axles unit at the Kandivli factory will soon roll out complete assemblies for the commander 650s and Armada with the same ease as the Nashik plant.

Flexible manufacturing will enable M & M to respond well to customers' requirements. Since the shop floor is broken into the smallest processes and each is managed by a team and the same team could start interacting with suppliers and customers to buy and produce what is required.

4. Try to Cut Cycle Times

Once, the time each component took to get processed and assembled - WIP infact - dragged on, at M & Ms factories averaging 20 to 24 days. In the process, costly component-like the shifter fork that is used in the transmission assembly lay idle for almost 65 percent of the time.

Similarly, a drive shaft languished in M & M's store for almost 20 percent of the time it was present in a plant compared to the 15 percent of the total time that was needed to perform operations on it. Hence it is necessary to tackle this is order to cut down time-consuming activities that do not add value and increase product cycle times.

To do this M & M set itself a **stretch target:** bring the high WIP time down to a maximum of four days once the rationalisation was fully under way. Going cellular is critical to the process of paring down WIP. For starters, M & M is abolishing the institution of intermediate stores. That instantly cuts some of the slack as time-wasting cartages from one shop floor to the other are eliminated.

All product units will also ensure that they only clear finished components which will then be shipped to the final assembly line. Cutting cycle times by almost a sixth, will result in huge profits - M & M estimates that it will save upto ₹ 2 crores a years by whipping WIP into shape. Even if there will be an increase in capital expenditure, it will be offset by increase in production and quick switches between products.

5. Customerise your Shopfloors

If a customer brings a manufacturing defect to the company's notice, and if no part of the production process will be ready to accept the responsibility for it, the problem bounces from one function to another and finally if the customer's grievance is put in the complaints file (the dust bin), then the company would lose the customer and soon the company wouldn't have any customer.

Whenever there was a problem with an M & M tractor or jeep, the system would uncoil slowly. The field services engineer would inform the service manager in the administrative office located near the shop floor. He would in turn, get in touch with the controller of operations who would then intimate the deputy general manager of production.

The latter would notify the department head, who would pass it on to the floor supervisor. The floor supervisor then shout at the machine operator who would reluctantly rectify the production fault. This process would take anything upto 2 weeks. By this, not only would the customers be unhappy, the same thing would happen with the suppliers too.

Recognising that the manufacturing can not remain insulated from the people who actually use its products, customer care is getting a new priority at M & M. Ever since the company has gone cellular, cross-functional teams on each shop floor are now responsible for interacting with customers. These teams are attached to each product unit and supply customer feed back every day.

Increasingly each product unit will also interact with suppliers and customers to get a first-hand feel of the market place that will not only help improve the quality of M & M's suppliers, but also it will make the company more responsive to customer demand. "The supply module and the customer interaction functions are going to play important roles in keeping the company's reaction - mechanism in place" says Anand Mahindra.

6. Let your Workers own the factory

Until recently, M & M's workforce consisted of 10,000 workers who didn't care how the wheel moved. There was no team spirit, no motivation, no quality consciousness and certainly no customer focus. Wage settlements were battle grounds between labour unions and management. If the management asked for a 10 percent increase in production, it had to be matched by a 10 percent increase in wages. M & M's management go into all these agreements without looking at what the existing machines and workmen would actually produce.

From the moment M & M began overhauling its systems, it tried to win the workers over. When the company directors and senior general managers went to England for an orientation course on manufacturing management and reengineering at various automobile and auto-component plants, they took with them union leaders like Devram Bosle, 53, the president of M & M's tractor division union and vice president of the Bhartiya Kamgar Sena, the Shiva sena's trade union wing.

Devram Bhosle returned a changed man. For him, the orientation was an eye-opener. He saw factories abroad actually practicing what was being told to him and his workers and producing effectively. The union leaders and the workers who participated in the orientation gave their peers presentation on effective manufacturing.

One concept that is lubricating operations on M & M's shop floors is **ownership**. Each worker understands that he owns the machine he operates and is responsible for its maintenance. (essence of the concept of total productive maintenance approach in total quality management). Moreover, hierarchy on the shop floor is crumbling, which is motivating. The cells function as teams, with the cell-leader at the top and the rest as co-workers.

Every cell which could have as many as 20 workers or as few as three, sets its own targets and reports to the module chief who, in turn will report to the product unit manager. This will reduce the number of hierarchical levels at the factory from the present eight to three in about a year's time: the product unit manager, supervisors and workers in the cells and modules. Soon, each cell will have its own office, which will consist of lockers for the workers, a conference table and an IBM. AS/400 terminal which will be a node to M & M's national network. Devasia says "If there is a problem in one machine, it affects everybody because the productivity of each worker and work station must be high. That is why ownership and employment are important".

To be sure, it is going to be a long and bumpy ride before M & M's new manufacturing systems drive home. Mahindra has set the company an ambitious mission: to become one of the largest global producers of tractors and a leader in the automotive business. "If M & M is successful in addressing technology upgradation and finance too, it could stand a chance of staking a claim in the global market place" says Raj Nair, 40, director, Business Consulting Group.

Like all revolution, this one too is beginning on the shop floor. For, only by involving its manufacturing into top gear today can M & M hope to emerge as a mean machine that will survive tomorrow.

(*Source:* Business Today)

CASE ANALYSIS

CASE 1. CHANGE MANAGEMENT AT CMC HOSPITAL

CMC Hospital has provided the residents of Canara district with high-quality health care services since 1945. It is a 150 bed, non-profit, intensive care hospital which provides practice privileges to about 120 doctors and renders a wide variety of health-care services. The hospital is committed to quality and was rewarded in 1995 by being named as one of the top 100 hospitals in India. Next year, the hospital moved to become one of the top 75 hospital in the country.

Inspite of past success, the CMC Hospital's top management, administration and medical staff are confronting a great deal of uncertainty and felt that the hospital must change to meet the challenges of today and the future. Parents, employees, insurance companies and state and central governments - all are demanding even better quality of services at reduced costs. The hospital and its leaders (managers) are involved in a fundamental shift in emphasis in the health-care industry - from a complete focus on care toward a balanced focus on care and business concerns. One major concern at CMC Hospital is that other hospitals in nearby larger cities can offer more attractive health-care packages and attract customers having better payment capacity away from CMC Hospital. This would leave CMC Hospital with poorer patients and those who are uninsured or under insured. Another concern is that an increasingly older population will require more time for diagnosis and treatment which might impede the hospital's ability to expand its emergency care.

The board, administration and medical staff have responded to the changing needs to CMC Hospital's constituencies and expressed its commitment to them in a variety of ways by *(i)* continuing to provide basic inpatient and outpatient health-care services, *(ii)* beginning to collaborate with other health-care providers, employees and consumers to provide access to a wide range of health-care products and services, *(iii)* striving to improve the health of the community at large and its patients and *(iv)* seeking to develop better methods of meeting consumer needs for quality and value in an integrated health-care delivery system. As an evidence to this commitment the hospital undertook a major renovation to accommodate new equipments to cater to the increasing needs of out-patient services including diagnostic, therapeutic, behavioural and surgical procedures.

Change is difficult and painful for most individuals and organisations and the problem is particularly severe in large health-care facilities. To be successful, CMC Hospital will have to overcome resistance to change and implement decisions that will best position it to meet the demands of the rapidly changing health-care environment and remain a leader in its industry.

QUESTIONS

1. What types of changes should CMC Hospital implement in order to respond to its environment and compete with other hospitals in the region?
2. List some of the recommendation for handling change submitted by the employee and administration of CMC Hospital.
3. How would you describe the type of organisational change being implemented at CMC Hospital?

CASE 2. BUSINESS PROCESS REENGINEERING AT ESCORTS

Escorts Construction Equipment Limited (ECEL) set up at Faridabad has around 500 employees of which 300 are members of labour unions of the company. ECEL belongs to Escorts group which has 12 plants employing around 15,000 people. Escorts Tractor Plant which employs around 200 employees is located in the same premises along with ECEL.

ECEL had a need to acquire and adopt new technologies which necessitated ECEL to take up business process and performance reengineering. Reengineering was defined as a process need for a quantum improvement in the level, methods and quality of the operations at ECEL. ECEL hired the services of a UK based consulting firm for reengineering its manufacturing processes. ECEL realised that changing the attitudes, work practices and making the employees accept change in role-set were the most difficult part of the entire process of BPRE. This difficulty was augmented by the fact that ECEL belongs to a big group with various plants located in the same locality and sharing almost same values, ethos, work culture and work practices.

The environment of ECEL consists of technology, customer base, government, information technology, media association - all in a state of flux and demanding changes. Hence there was a need for transition from a functional organisation to a process-oriented organisation. For this, the employees have to accept multi-skill mode of function including some menial jobs such as carrying materials, tools, filling oil, water etc.

Since the workers were not developed and business information was not being shared with them by managers, the workers had developed attitudes against the management, with perceptions that management has interests which are detrimental to interest of employees and workers must fight against the management for their rights. This kind of situation was discouraging for BPRE because worker's involvement is very crucial for its success. Hence this management had to deal with issues like trust, commitment, skill, attitude and values concerning employees. To do this, the following actions were taken.

(i) Introduction of extensive communication exercises. This included extensive sharing of ideas, information and facilities between management and employees.

(ii) Focusing on a set of commonly shared values through communication sessions and at individual levels.

(iii) Transparency in all the processes of implementation.

(iv) Mindset change programmes carried out for every employee.

(v) Multi skill approach training was provided for 8 to 45 days' durations.

(vi) Skill inventory analysis was carried out and training was provided to develop additional skills.

These processes motivated workmen to such an extent that they started demanding for multi skill training to be imparted to them.

QUESTIONS

1. Give reasons for ECEL to take up BPRE.
2. Discuss the issues that ECEL identified as those needed attention.
3. Describe the planning done by ECEL for introducing BPRE. What results did it achieve?

CASE 3. RESTRUCTURING MALNAD MANUFACTURING COMPANY

Malnad manufacturing company manufactures pneumatic control values. The firm has about 1500 employees and has successfully produced a line of control valves that are price competitive in the industry. However, problem arise whenever a new control valve has to be produced. Developments in electronics, metallurgy and flow control theory require the introduction of new products every year or two. The development of those new products have been associated with interdepartmental conflict and disagreement.

For instance, consider the case of a control valve code numbered CV 505 which is in process. In productionising this new valve, the following departments or groups are involved.

(i) **Research and development** departments or group which developed the basic design of the valve.

(ii) **Engineering department** which converted the design into a prototype control valve.

(iii) **Materials department** which must acquire parts for the prototype and make plans for procuring parts needed for the production runs.

(iv) **Production department** which has to manufacture and assemble the product and

(v) **Marketing department** which is responsible for sales.

Department heads believe that future work on the CV 505 valve should be done simultaneously instead of sequentially. Marketing wants to provide input to research and development so that the design will meet customer needs. Production insists that the design fit machine limitations and be cost efficient to manufacture. It also wants to speed up development of the final plans so that it can acquire tooling and be ready for volume production of standardised design of valve CV 505. Engineering, on the other hand wants to slow down development to ensure that specifications are correct and have been thoroughly tested.

All these problems with the CV 505 exist at present and department managers are frustrated and becoming uncommunicative. The research and development and engineering departments are keeping their developmental plans a closely guarded secret, causing frustration for other departments. Added to that, several departmental managers are new and are inexperienced in new-product development. Mr. Chandrakanth, the general manager likes to keep tight control over the organisation. Departmental managers are instructed to discuss with him before making major decisions. But with CV 505, the general manager has not been able to keep things running smoothly. The span of control for Mr. Chandrakanth is so large that he has no time to personally monitor the CV 505 development through the system.

On November 1, Chandrakanth received a memo from the marketing department head which read in part as below:

"The CV 505 must go to market immediately. This is very urgent. It is needed now because it provides the precision control which our competitor's products already have. Three of our sales people have reported that loyal customers are about to place order with competitors. We can keep this business if we have the CV 505 valve ready for production in 30 days".

QUESTIONS

1. Is there a proper balance between vertical and horizontal structure in Malnad manufacturing? Is it appropriate that department managers always run to the executive vice president for help rather than helping one another?
2. If you were Mr. Chandrakanth, how would you resolve this problem? What could you do to facilitate production of the CV 505 value over the next 30 days?
3. What structural changes would you recommend to prevent these problems in future new product developments? Would a smaller span of control help? A project manager with responsibilities for co-ordinating the CV 505? or a task force?

CASE 4. COMPETENCY DEVELOPMENT AT ROYAL DUTCH/SHELL

No one should expect a company as big as Royal Dutch/Shell (known simply as "shell" to many people) to make major changes quickly. With around one lakh employees and $ 130 billion in annual revenues, it is one of the largest companies in the world. It has more than 47,000 filling stations world wide serving more than one million customers daily. But Shell's big size could not shield it from competition being created by European hypermarketing, new competitors throughout the world and business customers that needed a truly global supplier. In France, sales declined by 50 percent in two years. If shell couldn't find a way to boost its sales, it would have to exit this market.

Eventhough it is quite difficult to predict how much time is enough for such a company to implement change, Steve Miller, managing director of Shell was of the opinion that change was happening too slowly. Two years after Shell began a change initiative to transform the company, he felt that not much effort has been put in this direction. Shell has reorganised and downsized. Right from top, managers at each level had attended workshops that explained the changes needed. Eventhough performance had improved a bit, morale was low at corporate head quarters. The company's leaders agreed that Shell had to move into the internet age, but they couldn't agree on how to implement that idea and hence the change effort slowed down.

Miller believed that empowered employees would help the company to find its way into the future. According to him, grass root level employees find their answers to their own problems better than others at higher levels. Miller wanted every front-line employee to understand the new vision for Shell. To get that message across, Miller set aside half his time to work with the employees, meeting them at the grass-root level in 25 countries.

One of the challenges facing shell was figuring out how to use its 47,000 retail outlets to boost sales of all the company's products. Miller organised a five day "retailing boost camp" to be attended by cross-functional teams (*e.g.*, a trucker, a dealer and a marketing employee). Those who attended the camp were expected is develop a new business plan. Later they returned to camp and received feed back from their peers. After another cycle of revising their plans and getting more feed back they went back to their work places to put their plans into action. After 2 months they returned to the camp for a follow-up session that focused on what had worked, what had failed and what they had learnt. Thus the grass-root employees participated in a "give-and-take" culture and this spread to the managers above them.

Most of the people involved at the grass-root level found the process to be "scary as hell". Top management had convinced them that change was essential to their survival, but they didn't have confidence in their ability to solve the problems. That scared them. Miller convinced them that creating change is a bottom-up task.

As people move up the managerial ladder, they get further away from the work that goes on the field. People at top get caught up in broad strategic issues, legal matters and stakeholder issues. But what really drives the business is the work that gets done down at the front-line.

QUESTIONS

1. What type of change was Shell undergoing? What triggered the company's realisation that change was needed?
2. In a company the size of Shell, implementing substantial change without a solid plan to guide the process would be difficult. Describe how a plan for a top-down approach to change might differ from a plan for grass roots change.
3. Steve Miller understood that "the whole point of the exercise is to improve performance" because Shell couldn't ignore profitability. If you were Miller, how would you measure the success of your change effort? Explain your rationale.

4. To what extent does Shell seem to be a learning organisation? What additional information do you need to make a full assessment of shell as a learning organisation?

(*Source :* Hellriegel, Jackson, Slocum, "Management" 9th Edition, Thomson-South-Western p 340 and 341)

CASE 5. RIGHT ORGANISATIONAL STRUCTURE FOR EXIDE TECHNOLOGIES HEADQUARTERS. USA

Exide technologies had a glorius past. They had supplied products that have been critical to many historical events such as:

(i) Supply of batteries in 1898 for US Navy's first submarine.

(ii) The first trans continental telephone and telegraph services in the US powered by Exide batteries in 1901.

(iii) Supplied equipment for power to establish a military base in Antartica in 1934.

(iv) Built the batteries for Nasa's Apollo space mission in 1969.

(v) Supplied tank and ordinance batteries for the US Army during Operation Desert Storm in 1991.

The question posing Exide Technologies top management is how to organise this company in the 21st century. Certainly designing the right organisational structure should be easier than designing new products. But it doesn't seem that way to the CEO of Exide Technologies. According to Exide's management consultants, the more global a company the more difficult it is to figure out who should have responsibility for what and who should report to whom. Exide has its presence in 89 countries and in that way it is a truly global company.

For example, under the "Ford 2000" plan, Ford tried to consolidate its functional departments, such as new car development, which had separate departments in Europe into one global department. Eventhough initially Ford had some savings, its market share declined from 13% to 8.8%. Likewise Procter and Gamble's "organisation 2005" plan was designed to take employees who had been organised by geographical markets into five global business units (GBU) such as "beauty care GBU" or the "food and beverage GBU".

After the changes, besides separating managers from subordinates, "organisation 2005" also created personal upheaval for managers, half of whom were assigned new jobs. 1000 managers and employees were transferred from various points across Europe to Geneva, Switzerland. Following the changes 25 percent of P & G marketing mangers left the company and market share and financial performance dropped significantly.

Unfortunately, with its geographical structure, Exide has found itself in situations similar to Ford and P & G. Financial losses increased and company share price dropped and company's debt load increased. Exide is organised geographically with "country managers" in charge of Exide operations in each country. This has led to competition as company managers try to steal business from each other. Also the geographical organisation encouraged country managers to build their own fiefdoms, adding offices and manufacturing plants whether needed or not.

Which organisational structure should exide use? Should it stay with geographical structure, but tinker with it to fix problem? What would be the advantages or disadvantages of that approach? or should it use a product structure – What P & G called "global business units" – to standardise what it does around the world? What would be the advantages of this approach? When will Exide know when it has found the right organisational structure?

QUESTIONS

1. If you were the CEO at exide technologies what would you go?

(Source : Chuck Williams, Management, International Student Edition, 3rd Edition, Thomson-South-Western p 386)

CASE 6. REORGANISING OTICON

Oticon, the well established high-tech company is the world's leading producer of hearing aids, employing over 3,500 people around the world. A new director was appointed to restructure the company, which has all the strengths and weaknesses of a traditional, hierarchical organisation, formal procedures, a conservative culture, employee loyalty and consensus - seeking behaviours.

After studying the company, the director observed that the company suffered from repeated losses and a massive exodus of employees. Oticon was suffering from some systemic problems. The company was structured around three major functional areas with distinct chains of command. Everyone know who to report to and career paths were well defined. The problem was that the three major functional areas had only limited interaction and cross-communication, making each other insular. That could be cause for decline of research and development activities. The top management had not only developed a reactive and status-quo approach to managing the company, but it also put great emphasis on signalling consensus to stakeholders. Differences of opinion and disagreement were regularly suppressed. What little communication occurred between functions was without open conflict. As a result of such management problems, the company was having difficulty establishing itself in the burgeoning "in-the-ear" design (more status guo). Overall, the company had become complacent.

Initially, the director tried to transform Oticon through rationalisation (paring the workforce and tightening production) and cost cutting. Those measures achieved costs savings of 20 percent in sales and administration, but after two years, he realised that more has to be done to break Oticon out of its management slump. The director wanted to be more radical. He wanted to transform Oticon from a mechanistic organisation with a formal structure to an organic organisation with decentralised roles, fluid job responsibilities, and most of all, horizontal communication. He thought that boundaryless organisation was the radical change Oticon needs to move it out of its status-quo culture.

The director just thought of some possible radical changes for the organisation.

(i) Increasing competitiveness by using human and technological resources more efficiently.

(ii) Moving to a project-based organisation where each employee is involved in a number of cross-organisational and cross-functional projects at the same time.

(iii) Letting each project function as a business unit, with its own resources, time schedule, success criteria and so forth.

(iv) Abandoning traditional managerial jobs and transferring authority to the project groups or individual employees.

(v) Creating an open office space, and giving all employees a cart instead of a fixed desk so that they can move around the office.

Then a doubt came across the mind of the director :

"Is Oticon ready for this?" An organisation that has insulated its employees from conflict may not be ready for such an open structure. If the management begins to encourage disagreement and conflict through more open communication, it might be like unleashing a monster that will take a lot of energy to tame. Moving fluidly with in a new project based organisation could sound the death-knell to the career path. People might feel aimless or wonder what their roles are in the organisations. Without clear direction, Oticon might sink deeper into a management morass. On second thought, may be all the company needs is to decentralise some authority and work on communication.

But will that help the company to increase productivity by 30 percent in three years? May be aggressive goals need aggressive actions.

QUESTIONS

1. What should be managements' priorities in reorganising Oticon, according to the director?
2. Does the director radically overhaul Oticon, or does he work within the functional organisational structure to change the company?
3. What should be the proposed organisational structure?

(*Source :* Chuck Williams, *Op.cit.*, p. 387)

CASE 7. WHAT THE CEO OF LEGO SHOULD DO?

The CEO of Lego, a toy manufacturing company is worried that the annual toy fair is right round the corner and news papers and magazines around the world are publishing their lists of the most successful toys of last year and their predictions of what will be hot next year. The CEO very well knows that none of his company's products will be on any of them. Founded nearly 70 years ago by the CEO's grand father, Leo has a long history in the toy industry, but it can't seem to keep up with today's kids' thirst for so called inter-active toys.

Technically, Legos are interactive, but nowadays that means battery-operated, software-driven, and "done-for-you" rather than "do-it-yourself". Today's children grew up in an entertainment saturated environment, and open-ended, self-guided play is fading into a nostalgic memory.

The Lego name was created in 1934 by a Danish toy maker who introduced the first plastic Lego brick in 1949. His son then designed an entire system of play around the bricks in the mid 1950's. Since these revolutionary moments, the only real innovation at Lego has been the introduction of theemed sets, like towns, farms and space stations, which didn't start until 1970's. Not even the formula for making the plastic bricks has changed since then!

The only thing brighter and more enduring than Lego's vividly coloured blocks is the company's core value of inspiring and nurturing creativity and play. An extension of this is Lego's refusal to produce any toy that resembles a modern day weapon. These admirable values however don't seem to be helping the company succeed. Lego hasn't had a toy on the list of the top 20 US sellers in the last seven years and this year doesn't look to be any different.

Lego is the seventh most powerful worldwide brand among families, behind giants such as Coca-Cola, and Disney; but Lego hasn't changed the way kids play; let alone the way they learn, for a long time.

QUESTIONS

1. Can Lego be that kind of leader again and if so how?
2. Will the CEO have to change his company values and management or just his products?
3. What are the risks of not changing?

(*Source* : Chuck Williams, *Op. cit.*, page 346)

CASE 8. BURGER KING LOOSENS UP

When Pilsbury Company bought Burger king corporation in 1967, Burger king was almost the same size as Mc Donald's. While both grew, Burger king grew more slowly. By the mid 1970s, it had fallen far behind Mc Donald's in terms of both numbers of restaurants and sales per restaurant. Burger king went through eight presidents, six chairmen and a score of advertising schemes in an effort to turn things around. By 1986, although it was solidly the number two hamburger chain, a clash of cultures between Burgers king and Pilsbury was evident.

Pilsbury was an older grocery products business; it had a "button down" conservative culture. Mangers wore dark suits, and earth tones dominated the decor. Burger king on the other hand, was more high flying and loose. Pink dominated the decor of its Florida offices. Further Burger king had become larger and more profitable than Pilsbury and so better able to compete for internal resources. No one was surprised, then when British Grand Metropolitan bought Pilsbury and hence, Burger king. By then Pilsbury's conservative culture had taken root at Burger king, however.

British Grand Metropolitan was once a major hotel operator but had become an international organisation dealing in food, liquor and retailing. Its International Distillers and Vintners is number-one in wine and spirits and its eye-care retailer, Pearle Vision Centers, is the largest in its field.

The conservative culture that had taken root at Burger king was strong. Working hours were rigid. A business dress code was strictly enforced. Executives occupied the top floor of the building with magnificent news from their offices. But in 1992, Hurricane Andrew literally blew it all apart. The building was destroyed. Lives were devastated. People came to work in any way they could. They had to come and go freely as transportation was not available. They had to have flexible hours so that they could meet with insurance agents or deal with numerous day-to-day crises resulting from the hurricane. The organisation changed radically but the work got done.

CEO Jim Adamson noted all this and decided it was better than the earlier culture before hurricane. So when the building was rebuilt, it was decorated in hamburger tone with a less-than-conventional decor, middle-level workers were given the best views and executive offices had no doors. Today everyone wears casual clothes and executives are more accessible.

In addition, Adamson developed a six-part strategic plan code-named Operation Phoenix to help Burger king recover from tis declining same-store sales. That plan is designed to improve operations, marketing, menus, facilities, value strategies and restaurant development. Further Burger king is expanding its international presence. It opened 170 international units during 1994 alone. It also restarted its "broiling versus frying" advertising campaign to more clearly differentiate its products from those of Mc Donald's. It also advertised stressing its "have it your way" service philosophy that was used successfully in the past.

QUESTIONS

1. What are the advantages and disadvantages of the changes Adamson is making at Burger King?
2. Who benefits from the changes at Burger king if they are successful? Who is hurt if the changes prove not to work or to be detrimental?
3. Do you think that the changes at Burger King will enable it to remain successful? Why or why not? What other changes might you suggest?

(*Source :* Ricky W. Griffin, *Management*, 5th Edition
AITBS Publishers and Distributors (Regd.), p. 377)

CASE 9. PROCTER AND GAMBLE TRAILS IN INNOVATION

Procter and Gamble Co (P & G) has been regarded as American's packaged consumer goods leader for many years. Nevertheless, even leaders can have problems. P & G's problems began showing up in the late 1980s. Eventhough it was spending nearly $ 1 billion annually on research and development, P & G was not getting to the market first with some of the latest products in certain lines. Despite P & G's introducing more than two hundred different product and packaging improvements between 1990 and 1993, it lagged behind on some major innovative product changes. For instance, late in 1993, Kimberly - Clark introduced a premium disposable diaper with Velcro fasteners and a cloth like outer cover and P & G was placed in the role of follower. As a result, P & G decided to undergo the most substantial reengineering the company had never had in its more than 150 years of existence.

By 1993, P & G announced a plan to close thirty plants and reduce employment by a total of about 30,000 jobs worldwide over a period of three to four years. In 1994, it announced that, in its North American operations, it would close four plants, eliminate production lines at six other plants and reduce its work force by nearly 2000. There were a significant numbers of layoffs eventhough some manpower reduction came from voluntary retirements and transfers.

Most observers did not expect P & G to get rid of laundry detergents, or for that matter any products that would cost its market share or shelf space in groceries. It was expected that P & G would continue to differentiate its brands and introduce new products, reduce package size, then strengthen secondary brands in regional markets they tend to sell best.

Indeed no clear pattern emerged from the plant closings. Plants that were closed produced dishwashing detergents and glycerin, soap and fatty acids, Falgus coffee and health and beauty care products. The closed production lines included health and beauty care products, fabric softeners, laundry and house-hold cleaning products. Given that P & G produces many of its products in different locations, the final impact of these closings on actual brand availability remained to be seen.

In addition to this massive restructuring, P & G adopted a value pricing strategy to lower the prices on its brands, hoping to keep customers. Indeed, the change in pricing was so abrupt that some grocers and distributors were upset and threatened to drop P & G's products.

QUESTIONS

1. Why P & G trails in innovation?
2. Why P & G decided to go for substantial reengineering of the company? What drastic measures P & G implemented in this regard?
3. What was the result of P & G's value pricing strategy?
4. What would you suggest to P & G to overcome its problems?

(*Source :* Ricky W. Griffin, *op. cit.*, p. 363)

CASE 10. READING BETWEEN THE LINES

Reader's Digest is a very popular, the world's number - one general interest magazine, translated into 19 languages for over 100 million readers world wide. The Reader's Digest Association, Inc. publishes Reader's Digest in addition to books, music, videos, TV movies, and special interest magazines. The company's products are marketed through well-targeted direct mailings and an extensive consumer data-base that is considered one of the world's best. The company had struggled through difficult times. In the mid 1990s, revenues and profits in key businesses were falling. Even Reader's Digest magazine had declining circulation and readership. Thomas O. Ryder, CEO had some serious charges to make.

The Reader's Digest Association was founded in 1922 by Lila and Dewitt Wallace. The company is committed to informing, enriching, entertaining and inspiring people of all ages and cultures. Over the years, the company established itself as a solid publisher, growing by moving into different areas both geographically and in terms of products. But along with growth in size, Reader's Digest Association developed a slow-moving, entrenched bureaucracy with a culture described as "like molasses". Its employees grew accustomed to a gentle way of doing business and enjoyed a work lifestyle that was paternalistic and cultured. For instance a $ 100 million art collection graced company headquarters at Pleasant ville, Newyork. Founder Dewitt Wallace was known to give rides on the corporate jet to employees who had never flown before. And at 4.30 Pm, sharp bells rang to signal the work day's end. It was a company clinging to the trappings of a bygon era.

As the company's performance continued to deteriorate, strategic and management changes were attempted. The company's board of directors changed four CEOs in as many years. These individuals tried and failed to reshape the company. Then Thomas O. Ryder was hired in 1998.

Coming from American Express Company, Ryder had a much more relaxed management style than the typical Reader's Digest Executive. He was open, accessible and sociable. However, he knew that the company had to make some serious changes and that these changes weren't going to be easy. A $ 350 million cost-cutting program led to 1000 people being laid off, the sale of the corporate jet and the elimination of senior executive perks such as country club memberships. Then the company sold its art collection. Many long time employees were up set by the sale, but Ryder believed that the art collection was an amenity that the company could no longer afford if it was going to be a nimble, web-savy publisher and direct marketer. Then Ryder tackled the company's way of working. Upon discovering, it took almost a year to develop mailing campaigns, he hired out-side firms to do some of the work. Some employees resisted tinkering with decades of standard procedure. According to Ryder, the cost-cutting strategies were signals that "everyone would have to change the way they worked".

To further instill a sense of moving forward, Ryder entered into several strategic alliances to expand the company's strong brand, including life insurance and credit cards.

Eventhough the changes seem to have made a difference in the company's financial performance, some long time employees say that Ryder's attempts to create a sense of energy and drive are no different from other previous failed efforts. They don't think the enthusiasm shown at top levels has filtered down to the lower levels. As Ryder's pedecessor said "when you have a company as successful as the digest was, the processes become embedded, and trying to change them is hard" Ryder counters by saying that his changes are different because he respects the Reader Digest's brand and the talents of its workforce which he says simply "lost its way".

QUESTIONS

1. Explain what external and internal forces created the need for Reader's Digest Association to change.
2. What conditions for facilitating cultural change existed in this company?
3. What problems did Ryder encounter in trying to change the company's culture?
4. Why did employees seem to be resisting change?

(*Source :* Stephen P. Robbins, Mary Coulter, *Management*, 7th Edition, Pearson Eduction Asia, p. 360 and 361)